The Objectives of the U.S. Information Agency

PRAEGER SPECIAL STUDIES IN
INTERNATIONAL POLITICS AND PUBLIC AFFAIRS

The Objectives of the U.S. Information Agency

CONTROVERSIES AND ANALYSIS

Ronald I. Rubin

Foreword by Edward W. Barrett

FREDERICK A. PRAEGER, Publishers
New York · Washington · London

The purpose of the Praeger Special Studies is to make specialized research monographs in U.S. and international economics and politics available to the academic, business, and government communities. For further information, write to the Special Projects Division, Frederick A. Praeger, Publishers, 111 Fourth Avenue, New York, N.Y. 10003.

FREDERICK A. PRAEGER, PUBLISHERS
111 Fourth Avenue, New York, N.Y. 10003, U.S.A.
77-79 Charlotte Street, London W.1, England

Published in the United States of America in 1968
by Frederick A. Praeger, Inc., Publishers

© 1966 by Ronald Ira Rubin

Library of Congress Catalog Card Number: 68-18927

Printed in the United States of America

TO MY MOTHER AND FATHER

FOREWORD

Some months ago Professor Ronald I. Rubin
showed me the draft of his book. I congratulated
him on it, made a few suggestions, and expressed
the enthusiastic hope that it would be published.
In his study of the U.S. Information Agency, he has
recorded the development of the Agency with great
care; he has intelligently appraised the many problems that face this nation in the field of international persuasion; and he has offered proposals
that deserve careful study and consideration.

The development of an honest and effective U.S.
information program abroad has involved a long and
arduous struggle--a struggle against obstructionists
and skeptics, and a struggle to find answers to a
wide array of complex problems, both philosophical
and operational.

The Objectives of the U.S. Information Agency:
Controversies and Analysis explores the problems
hindering the Agency's efforts to influence foreign
opinion. Within the Agency there is a need for intensive and expert training of information specialists, and a need for continuity. The parade of
Directors of the USIA (each having varying notions
of mission), the fluctuation of budgets depending
upon international tension and changing congressional opinion, and confusion over the goals of the
information program are long-standing weaknesses.

Within the Executive Branch, the Agency has
not always been consulted in crucial foreign policy
decisions. Its role in this regard has vacillated
according to the stature of the Director and the
attitudes of the Administration toward information
diplomacy.

Finally, the fragmentation of Congressional supervision over the information program has prevented it from effectively assessing the USIA's actual role. At least six major committees and an even larger number of subcommittees exercise control over the information area of foreign policy operations. The absence of a single committee in each legislative chamber--with members who are knowledgeable on international communications--lessens the contributions Congress could make in this area.

The evolution of a strong information program is only partially completed; the struggle must continue for a long while before we can approach the ideal. The faith that Americans bring to this effort will, in large measure, determine the outcome. This book is an important contribution to the progress that must be made. It deserves the attention of every government official, every congressman, and every student who is seriously interested in this important area of government activity.

Edward W. Barrett
Dean
Graduate School of Journalism
Columbia University

PREFACE

U.S. foreign policy is probably the most heatedly argued political issue in the world today. Precious little has appeared in print, however, about the United States Information Agency (USIA)-- the official American foreign information program. This work aims at meeting the shortage of material on the objectives of the USIA. Hopefully, the reader will come away with a deeper knowledge of the controversies over what the United States is, and should be, telling the world.

Some of the people who assisted with my re- search are acknowledged in the bibliography. In a less formal sense, many USIA staffers--past and present--contributed insights which are included here. Of course, this work in no way bears the official stamp of the Agency. My service as a Legislative Assistant during the 1965 Congressional session added to my understanding of the political process in which the USIA operates. My gratitude is extended to the many congressmen and their staffs for their views about the information pro- gram. I tried to remain faithful to their thinking in my article, "The Legislative-Executive Relations of the United States Information Agency," appearing in the spring, 1967, issue of Parliamentary Affairs (whose permission has been secured to reprint the information at the beginning of Chapter 2).

Professor Louis W. Koenig of the New York University Department of Politics patiently read an earlier draft of this study and provided construc- tive advice.

During my research at USIA headquarters in Washington in 1964, Mrs. Dorothy B. Stahl, Assist-

ant Librarian, USIA, and Miss Cecilia Johnson,
Archivist, were of valuable assistance. Mrs. Louise
Wolkis typed the manuscript with painstaking care--
as she has done often for me in the past.

    I alone am responsible for the ultimate opin-
ions and errors found here.

CONTENTS

LIST OF TABLES

ABBREVIATIONS

CIAA   - Coordinator of Inter-American Affairs

FAR   - Foreign Area Research Coordination Group

IIA   - International Information Administration

ICA   - International Cooperation Administration

MAAG   - Military Assistance Advisory Group

NASA   - National Aeronautics and Space Admin-
           istration

OCB   - Operations Coordinating Board

OIE   - Office of International Information and
           Educational Exchange

OSS   - Office of Strategic Services

OWI   - Office of War Information

PSB   - Psychological Strategy Board

The Objectives of the U.S. Information Agency

INTRODUCTION

THE PROBLEM

International politics, like all politics, has been described as a struggle for power. Whatever the ultimate aims of international politics, power is always the immediate aim.[1] Previous to the twentieth century, studies of international politics focused on the relations among sovereign nations. It is clear that international politics today embraces not only relations among nations, but also relations among peoples.[2] A nation in the 1960's seeking to attain world political power must court peoples as well as governments abroad. Indeed, the Preamble of the United Nations Charter, voicing much of mankind's hopes, takes the position that "We the peoples of the United Nations" (rather than the sovereign nations) will usher in the good society.

While campaigns of international persuasion were not unknown in earlier times, two developments culminating in the twentieth century served to elevate the information instrument into one of the major tools of statecraft.[3]

First, the development of mass communications has made possible the dissemination of political information to great masses of people in countries that have experienced only a small amount of modernization. For the first time in history, leaders of one nation communicate directly with the peoples of another nation. Second, the twentieth century has seen the expansion of the potential or actual power base of society.[4] This phenomenon has been especially true of democratic states with the

1

bestowal of the franchise and other rights of
citizenship upon an increasingly larger segment of
the population. Even the most totalitarian of the
modern dictatorships, such as the Soviet Union, can
be distinguished from its authoritarian predecessor
by the fact that the former is seemingly compelled
to solicit the active support of its subjects,
whereas the latter could survive through simple
passive acquiescence.[5] Thus, the new-found power
of the masses, and the ability of a foreign nation
to speak directly to these masses have succeeded in
making the information instrument of statecraft a
formidable one.

     Despite the foregoing considerations for the
importance of an international information program,
there is reason to argue that there exists much
domestic criticism of the United States Information
Agency--the unit disseminating American information
overseas. Acknowledging this situation, Thomas C.
Sorenson, a past Deputy Director of the Agency for
Policy and Plans, observed that "much of what exists
on the USIA is inaccurate, misleading and incom-
plete."[6] Although there is a paucity of published
material on the USIA, both scholarly and popular, a
sampling of what has appeared on the Agency in the
press and periodicals indicates dissatisfaction
with its performance and misunderstanding of its
purpose. Press references are instructive in introducing this study's theses regarding the information program. In reporting the appointment of
Edward R. Murrow as Director of the Agency, James
Reston noted :

     Considering the fix it's in [the USIA],
     this is quite a job, for no country
     ever had a better story to tell or
     failed so lamentably to tell it as
     well as the United States in the six-
     teen years since the war.[7]

     Publications representing both liberalism and
conservatism have often expressed disappointment
with the Agency's record. The liberal magazine The
Nation editorialized, in 1957:

Just what is the USIA? An information
agency, a propaganda means, a booking
agency, a psychological warfare brigade,
a means of subsidizing "our friends" in
foreign lands, an overseas subsidiary of
the Advertising Council.[8]

Again, in 1961, The Nation observed:

The USIA has not been a light amid
the encircling gloom; at times it has
been a pretty sick medium in America's
effort to make herself understood abroad.
This is not only because a country as
rich and powerful as the United States
almost automatically evokes dislike...
A more plausible theory is that Agency
policies have so often been misstated,
that resentment abroad was not unnatural.[9]

The conservative National Review likewise has
been critical of the information program. Prakash
C. Jain, said to be a "prominent Indian anti-Communist," asked in 1962, "What Are Our Propagandists
Up To?"

Apart from projecting a good image
of America is it or is it not one of
USIA's jobs to inform people about
Communism? I ask this question because I see a strange discrepancy in
what this organization says in Washington and what it does in New Delhi. When
it asks for larger allocations from the
American Congress it emphasizes its
activities against Communism but, at
least in India, its chief preoccupation
seems to be how to avoid even mentioning
countries like Soviet Russia and Red
China.[10]

In applying their professional training to
the USIA, public relations and advertising specialists are often unable to ascertain the present
purpose of the information program. Bert Goss and
William A. Durbin, executives of Hill and Knowlton,

one of the nation's largest public relations firms,
noted:

> The basic problem is not only that
> people don't know what USIA is, but they
> don't understand the role of the infor-
> mation program in the cold war.[11]

We will not attempt, at this point, to assess
the validity of the aforesaid judgments. The purpose of citing these diverse sources was to indicate
the existing dissatisfaction with the USIA. Assuming the need of some sort of overseas information
program--a premise unchallenged by most national
political figures and communications experts--this
study will aim at analyzing the controversies over
the role of the USIA in advancing the U.S. national
interest. The intention of this examination is not
only to trace historically the goals of the American
information program. More important, its purpose is
to question whether the Agency's conception of its
mission, its internal organization, its place in the
foreign policy establishment and its relations with
the Congress are best suited to the program's goals.

Considering the exigencies of international
competition, it is remarkable the extent to which
social scientists in all areas, particularly
students of government, have neglected systematic
treatment of USIA objectives. With regard to foreign
policy instruments, the Department of State continues
as a source of traditional attention. Even the relatively recent foreign aid program has received more
detailed study than the USIA.

Substantive issues concerning the Agency's work
appear in scattered congressional hearings. However,
except as an incidental part of the annual hearings
of the Committees on Appropriations, the policies
and procedures for formulating and executing information objectives have been permitted to develop
without benefit of close and systematic attention.
When Congress participates in determining information objectives, it does so incidentally, relying
on the budgetary hearings as policy-reaching sessions.

Since 1953, the USIA has been the subject of a
few independent studies authorized by the Chief
Executive. Here, too, the results were marked by
insignificant legislative attention to the reports'
recommendations. Presidents have issued various
statements and memorandums in an effort at clarifying the role of the Agency. These attempts have
also failed to specify with finality the objectives
of the USIA and the program's place in the American
scheme of foreign operations. For instance,
President Kennedy issued a "Memorandum for the
Director" of the Agency on January 25, 1963. It
set forth in general terms the mission of the
Agency including such goals as influencing public
attitudes in other nations and advising the
President and other agencies concerned with foreign
affairs on the implications of foreign opinion for
American policies. However, the Memorandum did not
resolve such long-standing problems as whether the
program would function more effectively through an
objective, dispassionate presentation or through
serving as a vehicle for day-to-day commentary on
American political involvements--considerations
that will be treated below.

The U.S. Advisory Commission on Information
submits annual reports to Congress evaluating the
Agency's performance. The Commission was established under the U.S. Information and Educational
Exchange Act of the 80th Congress (Public Law 402).
The Commission consists of five private citizens
appointed by the President and confirmed by the
Senate for three-year overlapping terms. According
to the authorizing legislation, the Commission represents the public interest. Informally, the Commission has served as one of the main supporters of
the USIA when both the purpose and content of the
information program were under attack in Congress.
In its favor, it is worth emphasizing that Commission Reports have also been critical of alleged
operational shortcomings of the USIA. Legislative
critics of the Agency occasionally seize on these
indictments in support of their own cases against
the information program. With respect to recommendations extending beyond the strictly internal pro-

graming of the USIA, the Commission has been far
less successful. Its proposals for improved interdepartmental coordination, higher stature for the
Agency and its Director in the foreign policy
establishment, and for increased information appropriations are traditionally overlooked in USIA
budgetary hearings.

Accordingly, it is difficult to assign specific responsibilities to either the Agency, Congress
or the Executive Branch for the controversies over
the objectives of the information program. Historically, the USIA has been guided by a de facto
(rather than de jure) prohibition against domestic
distribution of its material. This wall may start
to crumble, however, due to the recommendation of
the U.S. Advisory Commission in its Twenty-Second
Report (1967) that the Agency "make available"
material to American audiences. The Commission
proposed that distribution should not be initiated
by the Agency, but should be permitted in response
to requests.

Congress is particularly watchful that the
Agency avoid "propagandizing" the American public.
Since legislative budgetary hearings concerning the
USIA are characterized by a lack of systematic inquiry, it is principally through chance that Congress uncovers confused information objectives.
Thus, responsibility for unnoticed failures must be
charged to weaknesses in the Agency's strategy itself.

Or it may be maintained that the uncertainty
and frustrations of the USIA are symptomatic of the
larger problems involved in coordinating American
foreign affairs operations. Has the United States
adapted its diplomatic machinery to meeting the demands of the "New Diplomacy"? Are the Agency's
problems merely variations of those facing not only
the designated instruments of foreign policy--such
as the Department of State and the Agency for International Development--but also of the many agencies
and departments of the Executive Branch which are
increasingly engaging in overseas undertakings?

It is also arguable that the Agency's problems
in this regard are attributable to its treatment--
or mistreatment--in Congress. The unwillingness of
Congress to allocate funds requested by the Executive Branch for the USIA may be said to result in
the Agency's impotence in the face of well-financed
Communist information programs. Moreover, the
tendency of Congress to examine USIA programs
through rigorous cost scrutiny may be cited as
evidence for the Agency's reluctance to engage in
experimental projects or those extending beyond a
single fiscal year.

Finally, it is possible to contend that shortcomings in the information program stem from an historical combination of all the foregoing factors--
that they result from uncertain strategy within the
Agency, disjointed coordination arrangements in the
Executive Branch, and entrenched suspicion in the
Congress. The present difficulties of the Agency
regarding objectives may be said to be a carry-over
from the days preceding its inception in 1953. The
American experience with an official information
program in World War II and the postwar years revealed indecision as to its role in American
foreign affairs and its organization for influencing foreign opinion. To what extent is the existing information program marked by the "dead weight"
of predecessor programs?

This study will not attempt to assign any
specific share of responsibility to the aforesaid
considerations. It will maintain that there is
merit in each of the arguments cited for weaknesses
in the Agency's mission. While each of these
factors is tied up with the others, this study will
attempt to isolate them individually insofar as this
does not detract from our basic theses.

The relatively few previous studies of the
Agency have not approached the program from the
perspective of information objectives. Rather they
have concerned themselves with less substantive
aspects of the Agency's activity. Ben Posner,
Assistant Director of the USIA for Administration,

deals with the issue of "Major Budgetary and Programming Problems of the United States Information
Agency in its Operation of Overseas Missions."[12]
Ton Peter DeVos' study, "A Field Study in the Effectiveness of the United States Information Service
in the Netherlands," is necessarily confined to the
Agency's record in one country.[13] Members of the
USIA, such as Stephens, Dizard, and Goodfriend,
have published works which are more in the nature
of personalized, narrative accounts than scholarly
treatments of the information program.[14] None of
the foregoing works, however, is strictly concerned with the controversies over the organizational relationships, locations, and objectives of
the official American information program.

   This work will assess these controversies insofar as they are fundamental to the Agency's policies and operations. In a democracy such as the
United States, where policy information is decen-
tralized and policy suggestions may arise within
government or outside it (in contrast to the case
of the Soviet Union), the information program must
organize its own policy formation so as to be in
touch with the real sources of policy initiatives.
Posner's study of internal administration within
the USIA argues for a detailed independent account
concerning substantive issues of the information
program. Most of the following questions have been
examined at one time or another, he acknowledged,
by the Legislative Branch. Hitherto they have been
largely neglected by students of government. Among
these questions are: Does the USIA duplicate the
function of making foreign policy, which should be
the exclusive prerogative of the Department of
State? Is it properly located, organizationally,
within the federal government? Does it have sufficient influence on major U.S. Government policies?
Should its output be objective so as to establish a
reputation for credibility, or should it be frankly
propagandistic, as are the Communist information
programs? To what extent should it rely on private
organizations to achieve its objectives? Should
the Agency concentrate on long-range conditioning
of foreign audiences, or should it attempt a "hard

sell" designed to influence foreign reactions to
current problems?

This study will demonstrate the controversies
within the Agency, the Executive Branch, and Congress regarding the foregoing questions. In order
to most forcefully develop the information instrument of American foreign relations, it must be
first acknowledged that there exists much disagree-
ment--most of it unsystematically presented in
random legislative treatments--over the USIA's contemporary direction. This condition is not attributable to any one Agency chief, nor can it be
traced to any one year. It has been integral to
the Agency from its controversial birth through the
present where it operates in some 250 posts in
approximately 110 countries.

The result of the controversies concerning the
roles of the USIA in advancing the national interest
is that the information program lacks well-defined
goals as well as means to accomplish these goals.
Rather than relying upon detailed plans for serving
U.S. security, the USIA is forced to measure its
success on the quantity of its programs. In a talk
before the Foreign Relations Council of Chicago,
for example, Henry Loomis, former Director of the
Agency's broadcasting services, sought to explain
the Voice of America's effectiveness on the basis
of facts and figures. He noted that the Voice
broadcasted in thirty-nine languages and that it
planned to double its Spanish-language broadcasting
in Latin America. He expressed pride in the fact
that the Voice could count a daily audience of
twenty million. He argued that the Voice, combined
with the British Broadcasting Company, reached more
listeners than Moscow and Peking.

But when it came to defining the mission
and goals of VOA, he faltered. Finally,
he shrugged, tossed his hands upward
and said: "It is a mission too complex
to explain in the time I have. We
provide the news and we try to tell the
world what the United States is

thinking and doing."[15]

Any national information program in the 1960's
should serve national interests and should be related to grand strategy. To produce maximum effectiveness, the program should be kept constantly
coordinated with all major elements of national
action: political, military, and economic; long-run
and short-run. The objectives of the United States
in international affairs may include war or peace.
Consequently, an information service must be sufficiently flexible to build peace or to wage war, depending upon strategic national requirements.

This study will argue in the following chapters
that the USIA suffers from a lack of strategic doctrine and cogent objectives. The USIA has been
prevented from implementing the various goals established for it by the Executive Branch and Congress
due to internal as well as external factors. Among
these considerations are the following:

1. The inability of the Agency to clarify its
basic operating assumptions. These include a determination as to whether it is to function as an
information or propaganda instrument, as the terms
are understood by communications students. In
addition, the USIA has failed to develop a systematic policy as concerns the population groups whose
favor should be most pursued in promoting American
objectives. A sharpening of the Agency's operating
objectives is essential to the success of the
American information effort.

2. The failure to clearly define the role of
the USIA in the Executive Branch in reaching
foreign policy decisions. The presence of various
government agencies in the ideological area has
raised delicate issues regarding interdepartmental
communication and resource coordination. The implementation of the American information program
has been handicapped by uncertain lines of operational authority. While the two recent Administrations have stressed USIA participation in policy
decisions, their innovations have been inadequate

to the needs of the "New Diplomacy." As a result
of such neglect of USIA, national strategic objectives have suffered.

    3. A paucity of understanding in the Congress
as to the nature of the American information program. This shortcoming has led to a situation
whereby the USIA is continually investigated, and
reproached over:

    A. Budgetary requests and expenditures
    B. Internal organization and administration
    C. Operating strategy

The fact that at least six major committees and an
even larger number of subcommittees exercise supervision over the ideological program (exclusive of
the USIA) has prevented Congress from judging
the Agency from the theoretical standpoint it merits.
Programs of the USIA are evaluated on an individual
and annual basis. Congressional questions concerning these programs often reveal an inability to
draw a distinction between specific incidents and
the over-all strategy of the USIA.

LIMITATIONS OF THE STUDY

    Many of the USIA's critics fail to appreciate
the hardships imposed on it by the democratic nature
of American society. Communist information programs do not experience competition, and, perhaps,
contradictions from private undertakings. The
American democratic system is cognizant of the desirability of private enterprise and of open debate
and discussion. Free speech, limited government,
separation of powers--all of these are responsible
for a multitude of divergent voices from America.
Thus, any scholarly treatment of the USIA must acknowledge at the outset distinct limitations in its
effort to separate the impact of the official information program from the various unofficial ones.

    The voluminous output of the Agency renders
any large-scale evaluation of its content beyond

the range of topics included in this work. The
study of communication is sufficiently complicated
if we confine it to the domestic scene. When we
turn our attention to international political
communication where the "who" is a complicated persuasion apparatus in one culture, the "whom" is an
amorphous audience in another culture, and the purposes and circumstances are bound up with all the
intricacies of international relations, then it is
clear that we are not yet qualified to undertake a
definitive study of the content of the information
program.

Accordingly, this study is limited to illumi-
nating the controversies regarding the objectives of
the USIA according to the Congress, the Executive
and the Agency itself. It is the author's intention that the subsequent inquiry may contribute to
advancing the national understanding of total strategy which Lasswell had in mind when he wrote fifteen
years ago:

> By continuing to build a non-Soviet
> network of specialists in international
> communications research it is possible
> to contribute to the formation of a
> common frame of world attention. This
> frame of attention will clarify the iden-
> tity of genuine allies and enemies in
> actual and potential alignments that
> arise in the process of building a
> united body politic for free world.
> It is to be hoped that it leads to the
> eventual resumption of an unchallenge-
> able march toward narrowing the gap be-
> tween our ultimate goal values of human
> dignity and the everyday performance of
> world institutions.[16]

RESEARCH MATERIALS USED

The following study is based mainly on official documents. Currently, there exist few unofficial works dealing with the USIA. It is be-

lieved that there are none dealing with the aspect
of the information program that this book attempts
to treat.   Among the official materials used are:
congressional hearings, reports and studies relating to the information program and, more broadly,
to foreign policy operations; Agency issuances,
studies and reports such as the Annual Review of
Operations--all of which are unclassified; the
Reports of the U.S. Advisory Commission on Information; and Executive studies concerning the information program.

        In addition, the public addresses by Agency
Directors and staff were examined in the preparation of this study.   Also consulted were the few
books and articles by Agency staff and academicians
concerning the USIA.   Press and periodical comment
were of slight import in this project.

        Although there are no quoted references below
to interviews with USIA officials, the latter technique proved to be one of the most worthwhile.   The
comments of other officials of the federal government and nongovernmental individuals familiar with
this topic were also highly valuable.

        The remainder of this study is organized as
follows :

        Chapter 1 presents the main problems within
the Agency in determining information objectives.
It also introduces subsequent discussion on the
USIA's position in the foreign policy establishment
as well as the main considerations governing the
Congress' attitude towards the Agency.

        Chapter 2 examines the problems encountered by
U.S. information programs preceding the establishment of the USIA.   It aims to show the continuity
of the handicaps plaguing all such information
enterprises.

        Chapter 3 concerns the organizational struc-
ture of the Agency and presents methods for coordinating its activities with other agencies of the
Executive Branch engaging in foreign policy opera-

tions. It deals with the internal and external
organizational arrangements insofar as they affect
information objectives.

Chapter 4 evaluates the Agency's relationship
with the congressional Appropriations Committees.
It describes the means through which these committees determine the information budget and what
they consider to be the goals of the USIA.

Chapter 5 sets forth the conclusions of the
study and suggestions for treating the aforesaid
problems.

NOTES TO INTRODUCTION

1. Hans J. Morgenthau, Politics Among Nations
(3d ed.; New York: Alfred A. Knopf, 1964), p. 27.

2. Quincy Wright, The Study of International
Relations (New York: Appleton-Century-Crofts, 1953),
p. 2. See Harold G. Nicolson, Diplomacy (3d ed.;
New York: Oxford University Press, 1963), in this
connection, for a description of the evolution of
diplomacy.

3. The words "information" and "propaganda"
will be defined below in Chapter 2.

4. See Gabriel A. Almond and James S. Coleman,
The Politics of the Developing Areas (Princeton,
N.J.: Princeton University Press, 1960), for a comparative description of political systems in
developing areas.

5. Alex Inkeles, Public Opinion in Soviet
Russia (2d ed.; Cambridge, Mass.: Harvard University
Press, 1958).

6. Letter from Thomas C. Sorenson, Deputy
Director for Policy and Plans, USIA, April 13, 1964.

7. The New York Times, January 1, 1961.

8.   The Nation, CLXXXIV, No. 18 (May 4, 1957),
381-82.

9.   Ibid., CXCII, No. 6 (February 11, 1961),
110.

10.   The National Review, XIII, No. 16 (October
23, 1962), 307.

11.   Bert Goss and William A. Durbin, "How
Effective Is the United States Overseas Information
Program," Challenge, XI, No. 2 (November, 1962), 18.

12.   Ben Posner, "Major Budgetary and Programming Problems of the United States Information
Agency in its Operations of Overseas Missions" (unpublished Ph.D. dissertation, American University,
Washington, D.C., 1962).

13.   Ton Peter DeVos, "A Field Study in the
Effectiveness of the United States Information
Service in the Netherlands" (unpublished Ph.D.
dissertation, University of Oklahoma, 1962).

14.   Oren M. Stephens, Facts to a Candid World
(Stanford, Calif.: Stanford University Press, 1955);
Wilson P. Dizard, The Strategy of Truth (Washington,
D.C.: Public Affairs Press, 1961); Arthur Good-
friend, The Twisted Image (New York: St. Martin's
Press, 1963).

15.   Arthur E. Meyerhoff, The Strategy of Persuasion (New York: Coward-McCann, 1965), p. 162.

16.   Harold D. Lasswell, "Psychological Policy
Research and Total Strategy," Public Opinion Quarterly, XVI, No. 4 (Winter, 1952-53), pp. 491-500.

CHAPTER **1** THE OBJECTIVES OF THE
AMERICAN FOREIGN
INFORMATION PROGRAM

FOREIGN POLICY OBJECTIVES AND
INFORMATION OBJECTIVES

The USIA illustrates the changing role of contemporary diplomacy. The idea of a serious foreign
information program is perhaps the most striking
feature of what has been termed the "New Diplomacy."
In discussing this innovation, the Committee on
Foreign Affairs Personnel noted:

> Traditional diplomacy was designed almost
> exclusively to govern relationships be-
> tween representatives of heads of states.
> Today, much foreign activity involves
> the representation of whole peoples
> before whole peoples of other societies.
> This relationship between peoples is
> most conspicuous in connection with in-
> formation programs, cultural programs,
> educational exchanges, trade fairs, and
> like enterprises.[1]

Previously, the man in the street distrusted
anything bearing a foreign identification. He
wished that the United States be an observer rather
than a participant in world affairs.[2] Increasingly,
however, national policy-makers have acknowledged
that if the United States is to advance its national
objectives in the world it must assume a vigorous
role in international politics. The nature of the
new role of the United States in international affairs was summed up by President Kennedy in a letter
of transmittal accompanying a bill for the establishment of a National Academy of Foreign Affairs. He
observed:

16

> Today we live in a new world--a world
> marked by the continuing threat of com-
> munism, by the emergence of new nations
> seeking political independence and eco-
> nomic growth, and by the obligations we
> have assumed to help free peoples main-
> tain their freedom. To meet the challenges
> of this new world, we have enormously ex-
> panded and diversified our overseas com-
> mitments, operations and activities. 3

The Cold War of the 1950's and 1960's has been
depicted as a power struggle between the Communist
world and the West. In a more basic sense, however,
it is a conflict between two political ideologies.
In such a conflict, the outcome may depend not so
much on armed might as on the capacity of each side
to gain the sympathy of the uncommitted nations of
the world. The USIA must compete with the extensive-
ly financed Communist propaganda program. The two
major Western confrontations with Communism in the
USIA's career, the 1956 Suez Canal crisis and the
1962 Cuban Missile crisis, indicate that both sides
are reluctant to employ nuclear might in political
disputes. In such a state of stalemate the ideological factor in diplomacy is formidable. The
weapons of combat become words rather than bombs.

Accordingly, Edward R. Murrow, in addressing an
association of educators, warned:

> We are in combat--but a combat of a
> different order. That the sound of shot
> and powder is only rarely in our ears
> does not make it less a struggle. If
> anything, it increases the mortality of
> danger. Everyone knows when to resist
> when attacked. But our decisions today
> are not easy ones like resistance inva-
> sion. There is threat abroad but its
> danger is more indirect, and for that
> reason more insidious. 4

To be sure, the past fifteen years have seen a
growing awareness by the American public of the

nature of the world political contest. Defense expenditures consuming some one-half of the federal
budget, military conscription, and commitments to
regional and international organizations have all
served to eliminate notions of a "Fortress America."
Since its establishment, the Agency may not have
witnessed an overwhelming national appreciation of
its contribution to the new role of the United States
in international politics. However, the Agency's
supporters need no longer fear a climate of opinion
regarding world affairs similar to the one discussed
in the Report of the President's Committee on International Information (Jackson Committee). The recommendations of this landmark study led to the creation of an independent foreign information program.
In the Committee's view, the American people did not
understand that the nation lived in an age, not an
instant, of peril. As one of its press releases
states:

> A greater effort is needed to inform our
> citizens of the dangers that confront them,
> the power of the enemy, the difficulty of
> reducing that power, and the probable
> duration of the conflict.[5]

In the years following the appearance of the
Jackson Report, the Executive Branch has accorded
the information program increasing recognition.
While some students have complained that the USIA
merits even wider influence in the foreign policy
establishment, the information program has grown
appreciably in stature from its humble role in World
War II. In his account of the war information program, Thomson noted that the information specialist
was usually not invited to contribute to policy
decisions from his special resources.

> He often was not told of important
> developments long enough in advance
> for him even to carry out the mechan-
> ical operations of propaganda of "news,"
> efficiently and expeditiously. It was
> hardly a surprise to the propagandist
> that he should have had no opportunity

> whatsoever to help central leaders
> estimate the effects on world opinion
> of the atomic bomb.[6]

The circumstances of the information role have changed to the extent that Edward R. Murrow, in testifying to the Senate Foreign Relations Committee could boast that:

> Who would have thought 15 years ago that
> the psychological element would be so
> important a component in modern diplomacy,
> or that the psychological element must
> in turn have regard for so many other
> disciplines and demands in the modern
> world.[7]

Thus, the information program has come to be recognized as one of the chief instruments of American foreign policy. It is classified together with the military, economic, and diplomatic instruments in accounts of American foreign policy resources. Of these four means available to the United States for influencing world events, the information role has been the least understood. Consequently, the power and utility of the USIA have been often overlooked.[8] As a result the objectives of the USIA, as distinct from the many other nonmilitary and noneconomic programs directed at foreign audiences, remain poorly defined. To some degree, this situation can be blamed, as a subcommittee of the Foreign Affairs Committee found, on the over-all "sluggish" reaction of the Executive Branch "to the increased public involvement in foreign affairs."[9]

More directly, uncertainty over information objectives not only marks the Agency's operations in the late 1960's, but before the creation of an independent USIA in 1953, information goals were also poorly defined and inconsistently applied (see Chapter 2). In the post-World War II era, information objectives oscillated between a strident preoccupation with Communism, on the one hand, and the casual dissemination of material about American life, on the other. The principles behind the "Campaign

of Truth" (a propaganda offensive against Communism)
were at odds, for example, with those of the Smith-
Mundt Act (stressing a "full and fair" picture of
the U.S. to the world).[10]

Many explanations are advanced for the unsettled
nature of USIA objectives in the late 1960's. One
source of difficulty stems from the presence of a
number of federal agencies and departments each with
its own goals, in foreign information and cultural
operations. According to the 1964 study of the
House Committee on Foreign Affairs, "The U.S. Ideological Effort," the USIA is only one of some two
dozen governmental agencies and departments conducting a wide variety of campaigns aimed at foreign
audiences. The USIA wages the U.S. ideological offensive with the following other governmental units:
the Departments of State and Defense, the Agency for
International Development, and the Peace Corps. The
range of agencies and departments engaged in appealing to foreign audiences is so broad as to include
the Atomic Energy Commission, the TVA and even the
Post Office Department.

Differences among geographic and functional
areas also inhibit a precise definition of USIA objectives. Since information objectives must mirror
basic American policy objectives, a statement of
aims applicable to one area is rarely applicable to
another--unless the level of generality is so high
as to render it nearly meaningless.

Furthermore, there is the belief that certain
objectives should be kept secret. For the USIA to
disclose its country-by-country objectives is
thought to nullify the desired effects. Complete
frankness on this score, it is believed, would encourage forces hostile to the implementation of
these objectives to take countermeasures. As a
result, USIA Country Plans--establishing Agency objectives for the country--are classified documents.

The operational factor is the final one working against a clear-cut definition of Agency objectives. Statements of objectives by USIA offi-

cials at congressional hearings, for instance, often have little direct relationship to the activities of Agency staff in the field. While this study argues that many flaws exist in congressional treatment of the USIA, to its credit the Appropriations committees have uncovered notorious discrepancies between goals set forth by Washington officials and the activities of USIA employees down the line.

In view of these considerations, it is impossible to set forth a fully satisfactory statement of the official foreign information program. Despite such limitations, Davison finds seven approximate objectives of the USIA.[11] They are:

1. Promoting the free flow of ideas. The policy of the information program has been to abolish all barriers standing in the way of international freedom of the press and communication in general. Behind the goal of fostering a free flow of ideas are several deep-seated assumptions:

> . . . . that those who come to know American society will appreciate that it is, by and large, rational and moral, that peoples will be more likely to live in peace and cooperate fruitfully if they are able to communicate freely; and that our own enlightened self-interest will be advanced by encouraging international communication. These assumptions are difficult to prove, but they have been basic to the conduct of our official information and cultural programs, and many private ones.[12]

2. Providing a correct picture of the United States and the American policies. The definition of "correctness," of course, is open to various interpretations. Closely related to this objective is the role of the USIA in disseminating information on the seamier sides of United States life. President Kennedy, in a statement of the Agency's mission (January 25, 1963), observed that the USIA

should "identify the United States as a strong, democratic, dynamic nation."[13]

3. Countering Communist propaganda and showing
the true nature of Communist totalitarianism. The
stress on this point has varied depending on the intensity of the Cold War, but it has always been
present. Attacks on Communism reached a peak in the
early 1950's. This goal receded somewhat regarding
industrialized areas of the world, but it continued
to apply to the developing nations. Significantly,
in his redefinition of the Agency's mission, President Kennedy did not mention Communism by name. He
instructed the USIA to "unmask and counter hostile
attempts to distort or frustrate the policies of the
United States."[14]

4. Supporting current U.S. foreign policies,
not merely by explaining them but by persuading
people of their merit and providing information that
will assist in their implementation. This feature
of information objectives has also been modified in
relation to the changing international situation.
In the early 1950's using the "hard sell," the information program sought to promote cooperation
among the free nations while convincing the Soviet
and satellite peoples that the United States was
friendly toward them, but that their governments
were war governments. Thus, the information program
aimed at making the "captive peoples" realize that
they were still considered by the United States as
being part of the free world. The 1963 Presidential
pronouncement altered this viewpoint. The Agency
was asked to "emphasize the ways in which United
States policies harmonize with those of other peoples
and governments."[15]

5. Promoting good will and mutual understanding between the United States and other countries.
Many activities of the USIA are undertaken by personnel in the field without any specific objective
in mind beyond that of being helpful. This outlook
was incorporated into the Smith-Mundt Act (U.S.
Public Information and Educational Exchange Act--
Public Law 402 1948),   one of the basic measures

upon which the activities of the USIA are rooted.
The objectives of the information program, it stated,
were:

> . . . to promote a better understanding
> of the United States in other countries,
> and to increase mutual understanding be-
> tween the people of the United States
> and the peoples of other countries.[16]

6. Serving as a public relations service for
the United States. According to President Kennedy,
this function included:

> . . . advising the President, his repre-
> sentatives abroad, and the various depart-
> ments and agencies on the implications of
> foreign opinion for present and contem-
> plated United States Policies, programs
> and for official statements. [17]

Public relations also refers to the Agency's efforts
to disseminate material that will calm ruffled feelings when certain American policies or individual
statements arouse resentment abroad.

7. Advancing education, the arts, and the sciences. This is usually carried out in the context
of specific policies, but it is sometimes recognized
as a legitimate function in itself--similar to the
objective of promoting good will and understanding.
Exchanges of scholars in the arts and sciences ultimately help not only the countries immediately involved, but the entire world.

The techniques of communication used by the
USIA in support of the foregoing objectives vary.
They include personal contact, radio, libraries,
book publication and distribution, press, motion
pictures, television, exhibits, English-language
instruction, and cultural exchanges. According to
the Agency, these techniques are used selectively
from country to country under Country Plans (see
Chapter 3) devised to help achieve United States
objectives.

How successful is the USIA in implementing information objectives? In the Introduction, it was
argued that evaluation of the USIA's programs is not
a simple process for reasons relating to America's
democratic process and the voluminous output of the
Agency. Moreover, the USIA--as with all international political communication programs--faces certain
research problems in measuring the effectiveness of
the message communicated. Especially with regard to
congressional budgetary hearings (see Chapter 4),
this issue represents a source of misunderstanding
and frustration. Congress is reluctant to allocate
funds to the Agency on the "gamble" that its projects will influence overseas opinion. USIA Directors candidly acknowledge the limitations of information machinery in this connection. Arthur Larson,
a former Director, observed:

> We all know also that measuring what
> takes place inside people's heads by
> way of changes in attitudes, and the
> real reason for the change, is impos-
> sible to either side of the Curtain.
> One can only piece together the best
> clues available and try to form some
> judgments.[18]

Among the obstacles facing the researcher in
measuring the impact of the USIA are the following:
The researcher is faced with the fact that the communicator frequently has only a vague knowledge of
what he is trying to achieve. The communicator
often pursues many goals with many audiences simultaneously. The communication itself cannot be neat-
ly structured in order to facilitate the researcher's
job of evaluation. The foreign audience is often
inaccessible for direct observation and measurement.
Clear-cut, simple criteria of effectiveness are
wanting.[19]

Notwithstanding difficulties standing in the
way of evaluating the success of the information
program, the USIA makes estimates as to the number
of people it reaches. For instance, between January
and June, 1966, the USIA broadcasted 845 hours

weekly in 38 languages to a world -wide audience of 25 million daily. It exhibited motion pictures to 350 million people in 120 countries. USIA television programs and series appeared on 2,082 TV stations in 94 countries. Its 233 libraries were visited by over 12 million people. It distributed more than 1,300,000 copies per month of 24 magazines in 29 languages in 90 countries.[20]

The judgment of the U.S. Advisory Commission on Information must also be taken into account in weighing the effectiveness of the Agency in implementing these objectives. The Advisory Commission was set up by Public Law 402 (1948). It consists of five members appointed by the President with the approval of the Senate. It submits annual reports to Congress on the effectiveness of the information program. In its Twenty-First Report to Congress (February, 1966), the Advisory Commission credited the information program with playing an "important role" regarding the following events:

1. European developments in which politically viable countries withstood the threat of Soviet domination and in which the devastation of the war years was followed by a remarkable economic recovery.

2. The rehabilitation of conquered countries, e.g., Japan, Germany, and Italy.

3. The Korean War.

4. The emergence and development of African states.

5. The Alliance for Progress in Latin America.

6. Unmasking Communist lies and setting the record straight on Communist distortions of the intentions, policies,and life of the American people.

7. Helping wherever possible to create atmospheres more favorably disposed to the acceptance of U.S. foreign policy.[21]

Beyond these general means for evaluating the
effectiveness of the USIA's implementation of objectives are the studies of the Agency's Office of
Policy and Research. The purposes of this unit of
the Agency's operations are to study the opinions
and attitudes of the audiences the USIA seeks to
reach; to determine the best means for communicating
with selected audiences; and to evaluate the effectiveness of USIA programs. Despite such broad goals,
the USIA spent only about $2 million in 1966 for
communication research. Moreover, about 20 per cent
of the 1966 research budget went toward maintaining
a reference library in Washington.[22]

Most USIA audience studies are actually con-
tracted for by private research organizations.
While the findings of these studies are classified,
their themes are disclosed. Thus, research studies
during fiscal year 1965 included the following: a
project on the Voice of America (the USIA radio network) audience in Burma with the purpose of providing "indications of the size, composition, and
geographic distribution of listeners to the Burmese
language broadcasts of the VOA"; an analysis of
student activities in Nigeria "to determine attitudes and aspirations of university students"; and
a study of reaction to an Agency cartoon booklet in
Chile.[23]

Moreover, the USIA coordinates its research
with some twenty other governmental agencies through
the Foreign Area Research Coordination Group (FAR).
This group was instituted early in 1964 to supplement informal interagency contacts as a means of
research coordination. As of 1966, the Agency participated in the following subcommittees of FAR:
China Subcommittee, Latin American Subcommittee,
African Committee, International Education Subcommittee, and Behavioral Sciences Subcommittee.[24]

Clearly, the limited funds allocated to the
Agency's research activities only begin to enable it
to explore the opinion of mankind. Long-range planning cannot be formulated in a vacuum or one of mere
speculation. The U.S. Advisory Commission on Infor-

mation has repeatedly called for more research and
better use of research by the USIA. In its 1966
Report to Congress, the Commission complained

> Although the process of international
> political communication is complex,
> there appears to be little desire to
> utilize the facts that research has
> made available. The use of research
> has been seriously neglected in USIA
> to the detriment of the program.[25]

Despite the hardships of the USIA in determining and evaluating information objectives, the basic
goals of American foreign policy in this period have
remained fairly consistent. These goals are designed
to promote the national interest and security by
encouraging a peaceful world community of free and
independent nations whose governments are responsive
to the wishes of their people. They aim at thwart-
ing Communist intentions for world domination.
Thus, the United States seeks to encourage what
President Kennedy described as "a peaceful world
community of free and independent states, free to
choose their own future and their own systems so
long as it does not threaten the freedom of others."[26]

President Johnson said of national objectives:

> There is in our heart the larger and
> nobler hope of strengthening the family
> of the free, quite apart from our duty
> to disappoint the evil designs of the
> enemies of freedom.
>
> We wish to build a world in which
> the weak can walk without fear and in
> which even the smallest nation can
> work out its own destiny without the
> danger of violence and aggression.[27]

In a similar vein was Director Edward R.
Murrow's statement at a congressional hearing when
asked to supply a "broad definition for U.S. ideology." He explained:

> We are trying to convey to the rest of
> the world the kind of people we are, the
> kind of government we have, the hypothesis
> upon which this country was founded, the
> achievements we have made, the aspira-
> tions we share in common with other coun-
> tries in the free world.
>
> We are attempting to refute the lies pro-
> duced by the Communist world . . . We
> reflect disagreement when it exists in
> this country, divergence of opinion.[28]

Together with the remaining three instruments
of foreign policy, the USIA suffers whenever there
is an absence of generally understood strategic
doctrine, such as that described above. Indeed a
failure to clarify American foreign objectives is
perhaps more keenly felt in the information realm
than the other foreign policy instruments. Inasmuch
as the information program must operate on a more
subtle plane than the other available instruments,
it must evidence a surer understanding of national
objectives than they. Henry A. Kissinger, a student
of the strategic challenges posed by nuclear weapons, observed:

> In the absence of a generally under-
> stood doctrine, we will of necessity act
> haphazardly; conflicting proposals will
> compete with each other without an effec-
> tive basis for their resolution. Each
> problem as it arises will seem novel,
> and energies will be absorbed in ana-
> lysing its nature rather than in seek-
> ing solutions. Policies will result
> from counter-moves to the initiatives
> of the other power; our course will
> become increasingly defensive.[29]

It is difficult to ascertain precisely to what
extent the American information program is harmed
by incidents indicating an absence of strategic
doctrine. Moreover, one cannot easily determine
whether to place the responsibility for the gains
or successes of the information program on the national policy-makers or the information specialists

themselves. Yet it is known that the potential effectiveness of a government information program has been
sustained by every postwar American study. In this
area, the Hickenlooper Committee concluded in its investigation of the Overseas Information Program that:

> Recognition of the importance of the
> information program is general and is
> characteristic of those witnesses who
> were highly critical of certain aspects
> of the program. The committee is unani-
> mous in endorsing the continuance and
> the strengthening of this program.[30]

Similarly, the Drogheda Committee which investigated the British overseas information program
reported in its conclusions that:

> First. The Overseas Information Ser-
> vices play an important and indeed
> essential role in support of our
> Foreign Commonwealth and Colonial
> policies.
>
> Second. This work should be done
> well, continuously and on an adequate
> scale.
>
> Third. If all these requirements
> are to be met more money must be spent
> on the Overseas Information Services.
>
> Fourth: Changes are required in the
> pattern of the work in order to bring
> it into line with our political,
> strategic and commercial needs.[31]

In a theoretical sense, therefore, the USIA
represents a formidable instrument of American
foreign objectives. Inasmuch as foreign policy
stems from dynamic processes, adjustment of information to foreign policy is a continuous function.
Information policy cannot concentrate on any particular policy goal as immutable. Even the most
firmly set long-run goals, such as the realization
of a just and durable lasting peace, admit of way
stations that appear very much like war.

The information policy specialist must choose
from various policy initiatives in transmitting his
message abroad. In the operating field, the speeches
and deeds of key congressmen, of the President, and
key government officials as well as key private citizens constitute the bases of the USIA program.

The history of the information program in Congress, originating with the Office of War Information, suggests that there is little difference of
congressional opinion that overseas information
should implement foreign policy. There appear sharp
differences, however, as to whether the activities
of the USIA lead up to that end. As Chapter 4 will
argue, the Agency's legislative relations have been
marked by attacks on its personnel, methods and program operations. Congress has been especially watchful that the Agency avoid influencing domestic
opinion.

The President, as chief diplomat, bears primary
responsibility for the conduct of foreign relations.
He is the major spokesman overseas to governments or
to peoples. The role of the USIA, as well as the
other units of the foreign policy establishment, is
shaped largely by the degree to which the President
delegates responsibilities to them. The relations
of the Overseas Information Program to the Chief
Executive must be adjusted in the light of his attitudes toward his role as a world spokesman. On the
strength of his World War II experiences, Thomson
warns that an information service cannot take a
strong line in foreign persuasion which may be belied by the President in his dealings with the U.S.
public.[32]

Finally, the USIA's relations with the Executive departments must assure the Agency of close
coordination in decision-making as well as operational matters. The Agency's coordination arrangement with the Department of State should enable the
information program to secure necessary political
intelligence. As this study will demonstrate, the
past reluctance of central policy-makers to concern
themselves with information matters has forced the

USIA to interpret foreign events often through its
limited resources.

BRITISH AND SOVIET PERSUASION PROGRAMS

Because his study is concerned with the controversy over USIA objectives, it would prove instructive to examine the aims of other national information programs. The objectives of the Soviet and
British programs will be discussed here inasmuch as
they both reveal definite, conscious purposes.

Britain, like the United States, and unlike the
Soviet Union, did not recognize the value of overseas information programs in the conduct of peacetime foreign affairs until the late 1930's. The
British overseas information program is based on a
more modest budget than that of the USIA. It is mainly concerned with presenting abroad a picture of the
"British way of life." On the need for a foreign
information service, a British White Paper published
in 1957 noted:

> As a nation Great Britain has a great
> deal to offer in the shaping of world
> society. We have brought to a fine art
> the working of democratic institutions.
> We have high standards of justice,
> tolerance and truth. We have great
> resources of scientific knowledge and
> inventiveness. We possess industrial
> skill of the highest order. We are
> the center of a unique Commonwealth
> of free nations. Our colonial record
> is one of enlightenment and progress.
> We see ourselves as a people proud of
> the past but living in the present and
> confident in the future . . .
>
> . . . The primary emphasis should be
> placed on retaining the goodwill and
> understanding of our friends and on
> winning the respect of uncommitted
> countries . . . . While the sympathy of

> the influential few must always be sought,
> it is no less important, in many areas,
> to seek to enlist the goodwill of the
> general population.[33]

British international information is the concern of a number of ministries, government departments, and two independent public corporations.
These are the Foreign Office, the Commonwealth Relations Office, the Colonial Office, the Economic
Information Unit (Treasury) and the Board of Trade,
the Central Office of Information, the British
Broadcasting Corporation, and the British Council.

The Foreign Office has primary responsibility
for foreign publicity and information. The Information Service Department of the Foreign Office is
responsible for the British information agencies
overseas, the Cultural Relations Department for the
British Council and UNESCO activities, and the News
Department for the foreign and domestic press in the
United Kingdom. There exists no autonomous foreign
information unit such as the USIA in the British
arrangement.

Information policy is determined within the
overseas departments by consultation between information and policy-making divisions. The day-to-day
flow of material in all media is provided by the
Central Office of Information, in close consultation
with the overseas departments. These departments
also seek to obtain sympathetic treatment of official policy through independent channels such as
the British and overseas press, radio and television
services. In part, this is secured by ensuring that
correspondents in London are as fully briefed as
possible,and in part through informal contact and
consultation.[34]

It would appear that with the activity of such
a varied group of official agencies in the information field, problems of coordinating objectives
would arise. To be sure, the British effort in this
connection is no less plagued by a confusing framework of authority than is the American one. Thus,

upon examining the organization of British overseas
information services the Drogheda Committee noted:

> For anybody who approaches the Infor-
> mation Services from outside the first
> impression is likely to be one of bewil-
> derment at the complexity of the organi-
> zation and its lack of any central
> direction. One seeks in vain for any
> individual or Department in a position
> to lay down an overall policy for our
> propaganda overseas or able to decide
> in what manner the resources available
> for propaganda can be deployed to best
> advantage. In fact, there is nothing
> which constitutes a "High Command" for
> overseas propaganda.[35]

Nevertheless, the Drogheda Committee found the reasoning behind this separation of authority to be
essentially sound. Its recommendations in this area
called for closer contact between the Central Office
of Information and the field departments.

As for the actual responsibilities of information officers overseas, they would seem to be similar, in the main, to their counterparts in the USIA.
These responsibilities in the British setup include
advising the Heads of Missions on all questions of
public relations, answering day-to-day press inquiries, assisting visiting British journalists and
making the most effective local use of publicity
material provided by the Central Office of Information. It is expected that British information
personnel build up close working relationships with
local editors.

The most prominent difference between the
British and American overseas objectives relates to
the concern of the former in promoting British commerce. This point has been stressed in several
British studies. The Drogheda Committee stated:

> The aim of the Information Services
> must always be to achieve in the long

      run some definite political or com-
      mercial result. Overseas propaganda
      which meets a demand without producing
      some ultimate political or commercial
      benefit for this country represents
      so much public money wasted.[36]

Another White Paper noted: "Furthermore, we shall strengthen our economic position only if our efforts include vigorous salesmanship overseas."[37]

By contrast, the USIA is not charged with the responsibility of advancing American commerce abroad. In this connection it is noteworthy that the Office of Private Cooperation of the USIA is engaged in enlisting the support of American business firms abroad in advancing information objectives. It is estimated that in 1964 some 450 corporations were cooperating in this project and that it reached 7,000 to 8,000 of the 35,000 American businessmen overseas. (The Office of Private Cooperation was abolished in 1967, although its activities were distributed among other USIA units. The Agency continues to enlist private efforts in its program.)

In describing this program, the Director of the Office of Private Cooperation observed that:

      American business abroad should take
      the leadership in establishing forward-
      looking company policies, not policies
      which look forward fearfully to expro-
      priation but eagerly to a partnership
      in economic and social development . . .
      It should make the company a good
      participating citizen in its community,
      as many firms already have. It must,
      in short, identify the company's in-
      terest with the interests of the host
      country and community.[38]

There is no evidence that the British information services are as exhaustively engaged as is the USIA in using business firms to advance national objectives.

A final point deserving attention in this com-

parison of British and American information objectives relates to the segment of the population to
which each nation's program is directed. As will be
argued below, the American position has been an uncertain one in this connection. There is disagreement as to whether the USIA should concentrate primarily on the "opinion-leaders" of the population or
the "masses."

The British program, however, is directed chiefly to the influential few in the nations in which it
operates. The Drogheda Committee noted:

> There is, however, a limit below which
> the work will be ineffective. Informa-
> tion Services must be sufficiently com-
> prehensive to reach a cross-section
> of the most important people in the
> country to which they are directed.
> They must have quality and continuity.[39]

There is reason to believe that in recent years the
British have been seeking to enlist the support of
as broad a group of the population as possible.[40]
Yet the nature of the British information program
precludes it from striving for the popularity among
the masses which characterizes the Soviet program,
for example. Foreign illiterates would hardly be
fitting subjects for an information campaign seeking
understanding of British institutions and the fostering of commercial ties. Furthermore, the comparatively limited appropriations for the British program
force it to be more selective in its audience appeal.

The objectives of Soviet propaganda can best be
understood in the context of Soviet political ambi-
tion to undermine the social order of capitalism and
to reconstruct society on "Marxist-Leninist" foundations. Organized propaganda is more complex in
the Soviet Union than in the United States or Great
Britain.[41] Many of Communism's battles are fought
with ideological weapons, and among these propaganda
is the most important.

In order to appreciate the nature of the Soviet

propagand program one must recognize, as E. H. Carr
put it, that:

> . . . Never since the medieval church
> evolved a complete set of rules for
> human conduct and thought and harnessed
> to it the temporal power of the emperor,
> has so bold an attempt been made to
> establish a comprehensive and coherent
> body of doctrine concerning the whole
> of man's social, economic, political
> activities and providing the ideolog-
> ical basis for a system of government.[42]

The vigorous propaganda of Communism with its
air of certitude regarding values has often proved
persuasive to disillusioned, alienated and unsophisticated audiences. Frederick C. Barghoorn, a student of Soviet propaganda, has argued that Soviet
propaganda has succeeded in intensifying and
channelling in directions desirable to the Kremlin
such attitudes as fear of war, anticolonialism, and
anti-Western nationalism. It has pushed many individuals far enough along the road to conversion to
win at least their benevolent neutrality toward
Soviet political ambitions.[43]

The propaganda weaknesses of a democracy such
as the United States in competing with Soviet propaganda are readily apparent. The USIA must mirror
the diversity in American political life. The USIA
cannot practice the deception in which a totalitarian propaganda machine freely engages. The USIA
cannot prevent private information media from
circulating reports harmful to the national interest.
Instead, the USIA must make a virtue of national
pluralism in publicizing the American message overseas. In this connection, Edward R. Murrow explained:

> The message we convey to them is not a
> simple one.
>
> Ours is a land of the multiple ideology.
>
> Democracy is not simple but complex.
> We allow, even encourage dissent.

> Variety is our hallmark. We have made
> it a national credo not to have one
> belief, one rationale, one guide, one
> dogma. We have made a veritable dogma
> of having no dogma.[44]

In contrast to Western usage, Soviet writers,
nurtured in a tradition of political messianism,
have tended to use the term "propaganda" in a highly
positive sense, as though it were the equivalent of
education. As part of the ceaseless Soviet effort
to capture attention abroad, propaganda objectives
are taken into account in major economic, military,
and scientific decisions. The propaganda campaign
in the launching of Sputnik I and Sputnik II in 1957
is a striking example of the pains that the Soviet
Union took to impress upon the world that it deserved political pre-eminence.[45] Although there is
doubt as to whether the USIA should concentrate its
efforts on the leaders or masses of foreign populations, Soviet propaganda is most effective when it
is addressed to the masses.

As regards the organization of the Soviet propaganda program, Barghoorn breaks it down into three
main categories. The essence of the system is
located in the central mechanism of the Communist
Party of the Soviet Union (CPSU), which, through its
Department of Propaganda and Agitation, directs both
domestic and foreign propaganda. The second major
category of organizations consists of various
"front" or peripheral organizations as the World
Federation of Trade Unions (WFTU), the World Peace
Council (WPC), the International Association of
Democratic Lawyers (IAIL), and others. The third
group is composed of regional organizations that
Communists seek to control. Such an organization
is the Afro-Asian People's Solidarity Organization,
which grew out of the 1955 Bandung Conference.[46]

In attempting to assess the impact of Soviet
propaganda in recent years, one must consider the
candidness of Moscow in worrying over its effectiveness. In June, 1963, the Moscow radio announced
that the USIA "provokes sleepless nights in social-
ist countries." Komsomolskaya Pravda wrote indig-

nantly on March 21, 1963, that "USIA is a truly
tremendous monster of the cold war, which has no
equal in other capitalist countries."[47]

A further indication of Soviet concern with
American intentions of clarifying its information
objectives in the Cold War relates to Soviet comments
on the hearings conducted by the Subcommittee on
International Organizations and Movements of the
Committee on Foreign Affairs. The purpose of these
hearings was to strengthen the American ideological
offensive abroad. In an issue of New Times, a Soviet
magazine published in English, an "Open Letter"
appeared containing the following warning to the
Committee. It said:

> And just as ideological struggle is
> inevitable in the world we live in,
> so is your defeat in that struggle . . .
> Try as you will, you cannot win the
> battle for men's minds. All your
> efforts are doomed to failure. You
> can complicate, you can retard, the
> triumph of communism but you cannot
> prevent it. Just as you cannot
> prevent the coming of spring.[48]

Despite the energetic Soviet propaganda campaign, especially its design to lead a world-wide
peace offensive, there is reason to believe that
the USIA possesses one overriding factor in its
favor. This advantage relates to the open nature
of American society. It is likely that to all but
the least sophisticated intellectuals the conspira-
torial, totalitarian structure of Soviet society is
by now a proven truism. The mounting protests in
the Soviet Union, as well as in other Communist
nations, to permit greater intellectual freedom
detracts from whatever claims the Soviet Union
advances for representing the democratic "wave of
the future."

Furthermore, the USIA need not attach any importance to so broad a theoretical doctrine as
Marxist-Leninism in its overseas strategy. The

Soviets still use the obsolescent descriptions of
capitalism as it functioned in the 1840's to cast
aspersions on the welfare state society of Western
Europe or the United States in the late 1960's. By
contrast, the USIA has a wider choice of means to
present its arguments abroad. The American sense
of mission is not grounded in the right theoretical
statements of an author or two. Indeed the diversity
of American society may be the nation's most appealing quality to a world caught up in the many nonmilitary revolutions of the twentieth century.

USIA: INFORMATION OR PROPAGANDA?

The activities involved in the American information program have been variously titled and described. A basic thesis of this study is that the
USIA campaign has suffered due to an absence of
widely accepted information objectives. Fundamental
to the issues relating to a national information
program is that of information technique itself.
What type of material should the USIA emphasize in
its operations? How intensely should it press a
certain point or dramatize a political problem?
Should the USIA distribute information merely for
the sake of adding to objective understanding of
the United States or should it do so with the intention of prompting a specific response?

Essentially, the issue involved in the foregoing questions is whether the USIA should serve as
an information or propaganda agency.[49] In the American experience the term "propaganda" has acquired
a derogatory meaning. Propaganda has traditionally
been looked upon as a dirty business necessitated
only by such foreign threats as the Nazis in World
War II and, more recently, the Communist powers.[50]
The American people have believed in the inherent
power of truth and its ability to make its way without active efforts to support it. The United States
was forced to undertake a concerted information program following World War II in response to the
falsified internal and external propaganda disseminated by the Communists.

At this point it is appropriate to define what
is meant by "information," "propaganda," and other
terms related to the effort of national persuasion.
There are nearly as many definitions of these terms
as there are writers on the subject. According to
Lester Markel, whose training is that of a journal-
ist rather than a political scientist or psycholo-
gist, the distinction is that:

> Information is the communication of
> facts and opinions in an effort to
> enlighten.

> Propaganda is the communication of
> facts (or non-facts) and opinions in
> an effort to influence.[51]

In the judgment of Smith, Lasswell, and Casey, propaganda is considered to be "language aimed at large
masses" for the purpose of influencing "mass attitudes of controversial issues."[52]

The notion of "deliberate attempt" at persuasion is introduced by Terence H. Qualter in his
definition of propaganda:

> . . . the deliberate attempt by some
> individual or group to form, control,
> or alter the attitudes of other groups
> by the use of instruments of communi-
> cation, with the intention that in
> any given situation the reaction of
> those so influenced will be that
> desired by the propagandist.[53]

Much of the literature dealing with the definition of information and propaganda is concerned
with hairline distinctions between "education" and
propaganda, or whether or not propaganda is "false,"
"good," or "neutral." Yet there are certain quali-
ties in the terms "information and "propaganda" to
which many scholars subscribe. Among these is that
persuasion campaigns must involve a mass audience.
Secondly, both information and propaganda attempt
to influence behavior in some relatively specific manner.[54] This study will argue that the

program of the USIA suffers from confusion with regard to both doctrines. Despite the success of
recent Agency Directors in giving definition to the
information program, there remains confusion both as
to the extent to which it should concern the masses,
and pursue a "hard-sell" campaign to accomplish
American objectives abroad.[55]

Officially, American operations in this area
have been termed "information." That label has
appeared in almost every title that the national
information campaign has borne. Thus, Public Law
402 (the Smith-Mundt Act), one of the basic laws
on which the activities of the Agency are based,
states that the intention of Congress is to promote
a better understanding of the United States in other
countries through:

> . . . an information service to
> disseminate abroad information about
> the United States, its people, and
> policies promulgated by the Congress,
> the President, the Secretary of State
> and other responsible officials of
> Government having to do with matters
> affecting foreign affairs.[56]

Even in the formative stage of the American information program, one detects a reluctance by
educators and cultural officials to be associated
with it. They argued that it would prove disadvan-
tageous for their own projects to be associated
with the national information campaign. This group
of educators was led by Ben M. Cherrington, who had
served as the first Chief of the Department of
State's Division of Cultural Relations from 1938 to
1940, and George F. Zook, of the American Council on
Education.

While these educators fully recognized the
necessity of the information program in a time of
acute international tension, they drew a definite
line between information and cultural activities.
In their view information was closely involved in
politics while cultural activities should be "non-

political." It was further contended that information, no matter how accurate and fair in its content always will be interpreted by citizens of other
countries as propaganda of the American Government.[57]

In spite of governmental efforts to remove the
disagreeable taint of propaganda from the information program, the attitude cited above has been
representative of the American understanding of the
USIA. The Agency has not been entrusted with the
bulk of the American foreign cultural program. Instead, authority in this area rests mainly with the
Department of State.

The attitude of the USIA regarding book subsidies may have strengthened the State Department's
notions in this connection. In order to assure the
publication of books advocating USIA foreign policy
goals, the Agency has subsidized certain works.
The Agency kept secret the titles of books and man-
uscripts it subsidized. The list for fiscal year
1965 was forty-three subsidations costing $90,258.
In the wake of much public protest about this subsidy program--only a few months before the heated
debate over CIA secret grants--USIA Director
Leonard H. Marks revealed the end of secret subsidies.[58]

The role of the USIA in the cultural program is
merely one illustration of the way the Agency suffers due to the profusion of schemes in the foreign
ideological offensive. From the time of its establishment through the present the USIA has been
handicapped by the absence of strategic themes as
the bedrock of its program. In part, this may explain the presence of other governmental units in
the ideological area overseas.

The Jackson Committee in 1953 observed that the
lack of coordination and planning in the postwar
information programs resulted in the haphazard pro-
jection of too many and too diffuse information
themes. The report even went so far as to charge
that no single set of ideas has been registered

abroad through effective repetition.[59] A decade following the report's publication, Edward R. Murrow expressed a similar opinion as to the need to sharpen
USIA themes before a House subcommittee investigating
the American ideological offensive. After describing
Agency achievements in its ten-year existence, Murrow
cited the importance of improving the quality and
pertinence of USIA media output as the first in a
list of future requirements.[60]

To be sure, the Agency's technique in expressing
American objectives has become increasingly sophisticated in recent years, even if its themes lack
clarity. Whether it be considered as operating in
the field of information or propaganda, the USIA no
longer attempts to combat Communism in the strident
tones which characterized its first campaigns.
Much of this progress might be attributed to the
changing international climate itself. It would be
unusual for a USIA Director in the mid-1960's to refer to the East European nations as did Theodore
Streibert in 1954:

> To the enslaved peoples of the satellites,
> our news and commentaries from the outside
> world can also continue to bring evidence
> of our interest in their freedom and hope
> for their ultimate liberation.[61]

Nevertheless, there still exists in the Congress
a lack of accepted doctrine as to whether the USIA
should serve as an objective information agency or
an overt propagandistic organ. The hearing concerning the nomination of Edward R. Murrow as Director
of the Agency is indicative of the widespread disagreement over what is, perhaps, the most fundamental objective of the American information effort.

> Senator Hickenlooper: Mr. Murrow, what
> do you consider the primary overall ob-
> jective of the job as Director of the
> United States Information Service? In
> other words, is it a propaganda agency,
> is it an objective reporting agency, or
> just what do you consider the major area
> of the operation?

Mr. Murrow: I regard it as primarily
an objective reporting agency. I feel
that part of its obligation is to destroy
and expose the lies that are constantly
circulated about us . . .

Senator Hickenlooper: In the presentation of the image of the United States
and our ideals and in connection with
an objective presentation of those, do
you believe that we should indulge in
self-examination as well as in the
presentation of what we believe to be
our strong points and our most appealing points to those people and nations
who are seeking for the truth?

Mr. Murrow: If, by self-examination
you mean should we reflect in our broadcasts and in our literature significant
controversy on matters of importance in
the country, I feel that within limits
we should . . .

What I mean by reflecting controversy
was when it occurs on matters of national importance we should reflect the controversy with restraint.[62]

The significance of the above exchange cannot
be overemphasized. Some eight years following the
establishment of the formation program, there
apparently existed such widespread confusion relating to USIA objectives that a senator was motivated to pose these elemental questions. In
subsequent discussion, Senator Hickenlooper indicated he would prefer the USIA to offer an "objective presentation" of American strong points, as
well as an "honest discussion" when the occasion
arises of "criticizable" aspects of American life.[63]
This view hardly resolves the issue as to whether
the USIA should operate as an information or propaganda agency.

It remained for Senator Capehart to express the
belief that the USIA would best serve American interests through functioning as a propaganda agency.

He questioned the thesis that the USIA should offer
a straightforward account of American life regardless of the possible harm in such a position. He
likened the task of the USIA to that of a sales
manager in a commercial firm.

> Senator Capehart: But my point is that
> my understanding of your position and
> that of the Agency is that it is to sell
> the United States to the world, just as
> a sales manager's job is to sell a Buick
> or a Cadillac or a radio or television
> set.
>
> Now I never knew of a salesman who was
> successful, or a company that was very
> successful, that ran in advertisements
> and sales stories the weakness of their
> product and the weakness of their com-
> pany. I never knew one like that which
> was successful. But isn't this position
> you are going into the same, in reality,
> as selling a physical thing? You are
> selling ideas, are you not?[64]

The above position as illustrated by Senator
Capehart's statement, is concerned with the propaganda aspect of the USIA program to the extent that
too "objective" a description of American problems
might ultimately prove harmful to the national interest. It urges the Agency to follow a policy which
avoids publicizing the less attractive features of
the United States. This is an argument expressed
frequently in Congressional examinations of the information program.[65] The disclaimers of USIA officials in this regard have been unsuccessful in
raising Congressional confidence in the Agency.
Clearly, Congress is skeptical of USIA material reflecting negatively on the United States.

A further source of contention relating to the
issues of information versus propaganda is the
criticism that the Agency has failed to stress a
sufficiently positive approach in advancing American objectives. The USIA has been accused in Congress of being too diffuse, general, and routine in

its program. To some extent, the USIA has followed
a more direct and affirmative path following the
appointment of Murrow to the directorship. Yet the
argument continues in Congress for a program of
greater selectivity and intensity. The suggestion
that the USIA be more systematic in its objectives
has also elicited much support from advertising and
publishing figures. In effect, advocates of this
theory desire that an information service fill the
role of a propaganda service.

Illustrative of the attitude that the USIA
should lean more in the direction of aggressive
persuasion rather than impartially disseminated information is the following comment of Senator John
J. McClellan, Chairman of the Senate subcommittee
dealing with USIA appropriations, to Director
Murrow :

> Senator McClellan: It seems to me, and
> I think there are others who share this
> view, that somehow the Western countries,
> including our country, in our efforts to
> counteract Communism, we are on the de-
> fensive all the time. We are always
> reacting or trying to dispel some prop-
> aganda that is put out against us. I
> think this agency should display more
> initiative toward putting itself in the
> position of making an attack on Communism,
> rather than continually defending our-
> selves against the charges that are
> made against the Western World . . . [66]

The approach desired by such advocates of a
more dynamic persuasion effort differs considerably
from that which would have the Agency purvey
straight information. A propagandist selects the
story he wishes to relate. He is primarily concerned with the effect of the account on his audience. He knows how to use repetition imaginatively.
He is aware of the emotional appeals that will
excite his audience.

Support for the foregoing tactics is found in

the writings of some American experienced in such
communications fields as advertising, public relations and editing.   Trained as these men are in
"selling" a particular product, they take issue
with a low-keyed approach to information strategy.
These critics attribute the "to-know-us-is-to-love-
us" attitude as being a misguided basis for a foreign information program.   While acknowledging the
intensification of objectives that took direction
during Murrow's directorship, Joyce, for one, urged
a further movement in that direction.[67]

Among the measures advanced to strengthen the
persuasion effort is the creation of a Freedom Commission that would, in turn, establish a Freedom
Academy.   The purpose of the proposed institution
would be the training of propagandists and others
engaged in communications "warfare."   The first
priority of the Freedom Academy would be given to
a massive research program on all aspects of nonmilitary warfare, including political, ideological,
psychological, and economic activities.   The Academy then would train not only government personnel
formally employed in the information program, but
foreign students and private citizens as well.[68]

While there is reason to argue that a more intensive training program might produce more skilled
USIA personnel, one should not conclude that this
step would seriously affect the issues discussed
here.   An intensive training effort would improve
the techniques available to the USIA.   However, it
would not appreciably resolve the widespread confusion as to whether the USIA should stress
straightforward dissemination of information or
pursue fewer themes with more subjectivity than
exists at present.   It remains for the Agency as
well as the Congress to determine the future objectives of this area of the information program.

THE ELITE AND THE MASSES
AS INFORMATION TARGETS

Of the many disputes relating to the objectives
of the USIA, none is more fundamental than that

which concerns the level of the population to which
the information program should be directed. An examination of the annual budgetary hearings for the
Agency in Congress reveals conflicting judgments on
the part of congressmen and, surprisingly enough,
Agency officials themselves,in this connection.
However much the USIA has sharpened program effectiveness in recent years, it has neglected to clarify, once and for all, whether it is chiefly concerned with gaining the sympathy of the elite or the
masses; whether the masses must be taken as a target
or the target. The British program, as described
above, stresses the friendship of the influential
few. The Soviet Union places its hope on mass support. The USIA, however, still has not made up its
mind whether it is best to concentrate on one or
the other of the two groups--or both simultaneously.

A determination of the foregoing issue is basic,
for instance, to nearly every observation of legislators during hearings of both Appropriations Committees. These include references to the location
of USIA posts, the quality of the overseas cultural
effort, the content of Agency publications,and the
broadcasts of the Voice of America. The question
of whether it is more profitable for American foreign objectives to court the masses or the classes
is therefore most crucial to a study of USIA objectives.

To be sure, a similar problem arises in the
communications process within the American political system itself. This relates to the role of
the press in reporting foreign policy news. Presently, most American newspapers have sacrificed
intensive coverage in this area on the theory that
these events do not hold the interest of the typical reader. Bernard Cohen maintained that the
press should exert a conscious effort to present
foreign affairs information for a relatively small
policy and opinion elite and a somewhat larger at-
tentive public. In effect, Cohen argued that an informed political leadership cannot afford a press
dominated by interests of mass circulation. Notwithstanding his conclusion, however, American inter-

nal communications media still reflect a predilec-
tion for mass rather than elite appeal. [69]

The USIA has been far less certain of its operating objectives, by comparison. The Agency's indecision in this area can be traced to disagreements
among communications experts themselves. R. H.
Bruce Lockhart, who headed the British information
program during World War II,observed:

> One of my first efforts was to eliminate
> an undesirable eagerness on the part of
> our experts to indulge in wordy warfare
> with the German Propaganda Ministry.
> However entertaining and occasionally
> useful it may be to score off the enemy,
> propaganda is not and should not be a
> duel of dialectics between the political
> warriors of the rival propaganda organi-
> zations. It should be addressed to the
> masses.[70]

Hans Speier, who also participated in operations
countering German propaganda in World War II, concluded that information programs should aim for the
support of the elites in the countries concerned.
He argued:

> Since in modern societies the mass of
> the population cannot overthrow, or
> actively influence the politics of,
> despotic regimes without armed domestic
> or foreign support and without organized
> leadership, the population at large is
> no rewarding target of conversion prop-
> aganda from abroad. Any notion to the
> contrary may be called the democratic
> fallacy of democratic propagandists who
> disregard the differences in political
> structure between the regimes under
> which they and their audiences live.[71]

Speier bases his case on the view that despotically
controlled masses lack the military wherewithal to
overthrow their political leaders. A change in the

control apparatus might take place from forces within the society, he conceded, but hardly on account
of attempts at converting those who are controlled.[72]

While it would appear that the USIA would not
willingly sacrifice the attention of either the
elite or the masses in its information program, it
is forced to come to a decision as to which group
it should cultivate as a result of budgetary considerations. Edward R. Murrow would frequently re-
mark that the entire sum appropriated to the USIA
for its annual expenses amounted to less than the
cost of equipping a single Polaris submarine. No
doubt, the USIA would prefer resources adequate for
reaching the world's masses. However, Congress has
not seen fit to increase substantially the Agency's
budget.[73]   (See Tables 1 and 2.) The USIA must
therefore seek to gain the most public relations
value of every dollar appropriated by the Congress.[74]
As will be shown below, it feels it can best do
this by working with the elite.

A further consideration limiting the magnitude
of the USIA program among the masses relates to
the nature of American democracy itself. A democrat
does not find in freedom a cure-all for every other
ill besetting society. He differs from a Communist
who contends that Marxist-Leninism offers the hope
of an untroubled future. The USIA cannot argue as
simply as the Communist propaganda machine in defense of political freedom. In mirroring the American message abroad, the USIA must remain faithful
to the truism that it is no less difficult to maintain freedom than to win it in the first place.
Such reasoning has been integral to the Agency's
opposition to dramatic schemes for a Freedom Academy,
such as described in the preceding section, which
ostensibly would produce graduates with "miracle
messages" for American objectives abroad and the
cause of freedom in nondemocratic countries.
Edward W. Barrett, one of the original leaders of
the American information program, cautioned that
freedom is not a first-rank objective of fanatical
mass movements.

TABLE I

USIA APPROPRIATIONS HISTORY 1954-65

The table below summarizes the amounts appropriated for the Agency's principal programs from 1954. The table indicates, for the Salaries and Expenses, Radio Construction, and Informational Media Guarantee Fund appropriations, the amounts that have been appropriated each year since the Agency was established on August 1, 1953; and the amounts requested for fiscal year 1965. Funds appropriated prior to 1964 on a supplemental basis are included in the amount shown for the appropriate fiscal year.

Summary of S&E, Radio, Construction, and IMG Appropriations and Estimates
(Fiscal Years 1954-65)

Fiscal Year	Salaries and Expenses	Radio Construction	IMG Program	Total Regular Appropriations
1954	$ 84,217,000	$ --	$ --	$ 84,217,000
1955	77,299,000	--	--	77,299,000
1956	87,336,630	--	--	87,336,630
1957	113,000,000	--	--	113,000,000
1958	96,517,000	1,100,000	--	97,617,000
1959	101,673,800	14,750,000	2,500,000	118,923,800
1960	101,557,300	9,000,000	2,750,000	113,307,300
1961	105,330,300	8,740,000	3,691,680	117,761,980
1962	111,500,000	10,750,000	1,500,000	123,750,000
1963	123,145,000	16,150,000	1,000,000	140,295,000
1964	134,000,000	12,070,000	750,000	146,820,000
1965 (Estimate)	143,800,000	15,116,000	1,000,000	159,916,000

TABLE 2

CHRONOLOGY OF APPROPRIATION ACTS

The Acts cited below have provided the Agency with
funds for the fiscal years indicated. Other appropriations have been made available from time to
time on a supplemental basis to meet specific additional needs.

Appropriation Acts	Fiscal Year
P.L. 207, 83d Congress, approved August 7, 1953 (67 Stat. 418)	1954
P.L. 471, 83d Congress, approved July 2, 1954 (68 Stat. 314)	1955
P.L. 133, 84th Congress, approved July 7, 1955 (69 Stat. 264)	1956
P.L. 603, 84th Congress, approved July 20, 1956 (70 Stat. 299)	1957
P.L. 85-49, 85th Congress, approved July 11, 1957 (71 Stat. 55)	1958
P.L. 85-474, 85th Congress, approved June 30, 1958 (72 Stat. 244)	1959
P.L. 86-84, 86th Congress, approved July 13, 1959 (73 Stat. 182)	1960
P.L. 86-678, 86th Congress, approved August 31, 1960	1961
P.L. 87-264, 87th Congress, approved September 21, 1961	1962
P.L. 87-843, 87th Congress, approved October 18, 1962	1963
P.L. 88-245, 88th Congress, approved December 30, 1963	1964

In political fields, what attracts
fanatical men often repels reasoning
men. Most such movements can get out
of hand. Moreover, the things in which
Americans believe and for which they
will fight are the antithesis of simple
dogma and unreasoning conformity.
Basically, the free nations are strug-
gling for an absence of rigid doctrine,
restraints, and regimentation.[75]

Similarly, Carl T. Rowan, in one of his first
speeches as Director of the USIA, said:

. . . we cannot promise shortcuts or
quick solutions. None exist. There is
no way to plenty but by labor, to learning but by study, to dignity but by
nurturing respect. And there is no way
to peace but by the slow, deliberate,
step-by-careful-step that harnesses
the passions of conflict.[76]

The fact that the USIA faces financial and ideological limitations to however zealous a campaign
it might wish to wage for the support of the world's
masses is therefore apparent. On the strength of
congressional testimony, however--even the most
recent--it would appear that the USIA has failed to
clarify its goals in this area. This study will
cite several representative statements illustrating
that "the masses or the classes" still remains an un-
resolved issue in the USIA program objectives.

Congressman Rooney: Do you not agree
it is a waste of time and money for us
to direct broadcasts at the hard-core
Communists who never had it so good,
like the principal of the public school,
who wore a full-length mink coat, has
a fine apartment, never had it so good
in her life, and other Communist people
of this type, or should they be directed
toward the farmer out on the farms who
comprises 90 per cent of the population
in Poland?

Mr. Murrow: I would agree with you
that the broadcasts aimed at the first
category are not likely to be very
effective.

Congressman Rooney went on to cite a statement of
Mr. Murrow's assistant that seemed to indicate the
contrary. It stated:

Our Voice of America broadcasts are
purposely designed to appeal to the
intellectual elite and cadres of party
officials. These are the people in
a position to make changes if they
desire in Polish society . . .

According to Congressman Rooney such broadcasts
constitute:

. . . utter waste of the taxpayer's money. We are never going to win the cold
war if that is the sort of thing we
are doing. Our broadcasts should be
directed to the bulk of a population.[77]

In a hearing before the same subcommittee a
year earlier, Mr. Murrow upheld the viewpoint that
favored an appeal to the masses over the elites.
He noted that the Agency's objective is to encourage
its officers to travel among the rank and file of
the population. He said:

I have the feeling, sir, that the
paper reporting can be further reduced. I am not sure. Our objective is to permit our officers
abroad to wear out more shoe leather
in the performance of their duties
rather than wear out typewriter
ribbons in writing lengthy reports.[78]

It is noteworthy that Ray Mackland, then
Director of the USIA's Press and Publications Service, offered a different version of the Agency's

mission in his appearance before the subcommittee.
Mr. Mackland testified only a few days following
his superior, Mr. Murrow.

> Mr. Bow: Your objective is what?
> What are you attempting to reach?
> What do you think you are attempt-
> ing to accomplish?
>
> Mr. Mackland: I think we are trying
> to reach two groups, the leaders and
> the masses. I personally feel we
> have to have a product that appeals
> to both.[79]

Despite this statement of the USIA's target
group, Congressman Rooney expressed a sentiment
favoring the masses, similar to the one noted above.

> Mr. Rooney: . . . Theodore Mann, 8
> Barrow Street, New York; article:
> "The Financial Aspects of the Off-
> Broadway Theatre," $100. Is this
> one of the things that might appeal
> to the masses?
>
> Mr. Mackland: I think it would not
> appeal to the masses.
>
> Mr. Rooney: I wonder why we would
> spend a hundred dollars for a story
> on that subject. Can anyone here
> figure that one out?
>
> Mr. Cannon (Deputy Director--
> Editorial): There is a great deal
> of interest in this subject in some
> groups overseas and in some publica-
> tions that would want this sort of
> thing.
>
> Mr. Rooney: How did this sort of
> thing turn up in the battle to win
> the minds of men.[80]

One final illustration demonstrating the confusion within the USIA in this regard relates to
testimony given by J. Leonard Reinsch, who at the
time was Chairman of the U.S. Advisory Commission
on Information. Mr. Reinsch supported a policy
stressing the elite over the masses.

>Mr. Derwinski: . . . When we are
>sending these broadcasts do we aim
>them at the intelligentsia, which is
>a small proportion of the public,
>hoping that some of this rubs off
>on the masses, or do we aim the pro-
>grams with mass appeal with the
>assumption that the intelligentsia
>will understand plain and unornamented
>reporting. Which is the basic policy?

>Mr. Reinsch: The present policy is
>to aim this news at the intelligentsia,
>the thought leaders, the leaders of
>the various communities.[81]

One cannot attribute this inability of the USIA
to determine conclusively whether it is best to aim
at the leaders or the masses, solely to confusion
within the ranks of Washington policy-makers.
Under the Agency's latest project to reach specific
audiences, the Country Plan, the USIA field office
finally decides which groups in a particular country
are most worth pursuing. The Country Plan is first
formulated in the field, then commented on in
Washington, and finally approved in the field.[82]

Accordingly, the public affairs officers in each
country contribute heavily to the ultimate USIA
country objectives. There are two schools of
thought involved in formulating information objectives among the field officers themselves: expo-
nents of targeting and those who think essentially
in terms of mass programs. With regard to the
latter attitude there is a strong tendency for the
operator, in his zeal to spread a message in which
he believes and his understandable eagerness to
prove the worth of his medium, to consider it essen-

tial to reach as many people as possible. This
notion is often supported by the operator's conviction that he is working in a mass medium: All possible opportunities should therefore be taken to
reach large numbers of people,and any available
audience should not be ignored.

The desire of some USIA officers to reach as
many people as possible no doubt relates to the
nature of an information program sponsored by a
democracy. Such a program, they believe, assumes
an appeal to the people beyond the decision makers
in the government. This outlook may reach back to
the political premise that government rests upon
the consent of the governed, and that even in authoritarian countries there is a concern on the part
of the rulers with the demands of the people.

In a series of interviews with USIA officers in
the field, Bogart noted the various arguments they
would offer to express preferences for a program
appealing to the masses rather than the elite. A
typical observation, he noted, would be that which
sees making foreigners knowledgeable of the
United States--regardless of their social rank--as
an end in itself. In many vital areas of the
Agency's operations Bogart reported a fair degree of
consensus among operators. Included in these views
was the general belief that interpersonal contact
is a more effective means of changing opinion than
any mass medium. Agency officers also reasoned that
writing a single program for a mass audience was an
easier assignment than drawing up different ones
for specialized or elite audiences.

Critics of the mass approach cited arguments
similar to those noted earlier in this study. In
defense of their position they pointed to the limited
USIA budget as preventing an effective program designed for the masses. With a small budget, they
maintained it was necessary for the USIA to be more
selective and accurate in its target campaigns.
Moreover, some officers held that public opinion has
a slight influence on state policy,particularly in
areas of great poverty and illiteracy. One officer

said: "Any given area, country, or city can be
divided into five per cent operators, ten per cent
stooges, and eighty-five per cent slobs."[83]

In addition to communications specialists such
as Bogart, the issue of the elite versus the masses
has also been a lively source of controversy among
USIA officers themselves. It is not unusual for a
disillusioned USIA officer to return home and publish an indictment of the alleged American tendency
to favor the elite over the masses. The scholar
must allow for exaggeration in such accounts by
veterans of the information program. One criticism
of the USIA in this connection worthy of attention
is Arthur Goodfriend's The Twisted Image. It is a
diagnosis of alleged USIA setbacks in India, where
he served as a Public Affairs Officer. Despite this
published attack on the Agency's operating strategy,
he has been retained as a key "troubleshooters."
We can therefore assume that there exists some
measure of accuracy in his work.

Goodfriend addressed himself to the issue of
city-centered, elite-oriented USIA activity. In
his judgment, some of his USIA colleagues felt
bound by the protocol rules governing State Department officials. In preoccupying itself with a
tiny Indian minority, Goodfriend contended that the
USIA overlooked the degree to which the Indian
masses were exercising their franchise. Meanwhile,
the Communists would take advantage of these uncon-
tested opportunities for gaining mass approval.
Furthermore, USIS publications contained items of
self-conscious Americana, supposedly appealing to
Indian elites. Communist publications, in comparison, were characterized by an earthy, people-to-
people approach.

I wondered how often the errors would
have to be repeated before the lessons
sank in. USIA aimed at the pinnacle of
India's population; communism burrowed
at the base driving toward farmers,
workers, minor government officials,
and educated malcontents. While we

> dealt with those presently in power,
> communism aimed at the successors to
> the present regime. USIS cultivated
> presidents of major universities.
> Communists infiltrated the faculties.
> USIS sought out the owners and editors
> of principal newspapers; Communists
> operated at the levels of subeditors,
> leader writers, reporters, printers . . .[84]

In all of this, Goodfriend is simply documenting the consequences in the field stemming from the uncertain strategy of the USIA. The foregoing excerpts of congressional hearings revealed the indefinite outlook of the Agency's chief officials concerning the population element(s) most worth pursuing. Why should a field officer have a more precise understanding of Agency strategy than its foremost policy-makers?

There may be much to be said in the Agency's disfavor on this score. Yet we must consider another aspect relating to the confusion over USIA population strategy. Essentially, the Agency's restricted resources preclude it from waging a campaign, in any degree of intensity, for courting the masses. This factor, perhaps more than any other, makes argument as to the masses or the classes largely academic. So long as Congress denies the American information program less funds than General Motors spends to advertise automobiles and Proctor and Gamble to sell soap, it is of slight value to debate whether the USIA should stress the elite or the masses in its strategy.

The Agency is therefore forced to defend its approach, which has essentially favored elites, however much it may find merit in arguments urging a wider dissemination of USIA effort. Agency supporters question the rationale that judges effectiveness by quantitative rather than qualitative standards. They take issue with the view that determines the success of the information program by the magnitude of its efforts instead of the results actually achieved. There exist no stock

formulas as to the circumstances under which it
would be profitable to direct an information program
at the elite or the masses, they maintain.

With the growing sophistication of the USIA
effort, USIA defenders explain, the strategy of
the American information program must be adapted to
the internal situation in each different country.
Thus, the country Public Affairs Offices (CPAO)
determines the level of the information objectives.
He bases his estimate on his understanding of the
problems and political goals of the country where
he is assigned. At times, it may prove most profitable concentrating the USIA program on a few individuals in such a country. Under different circumstances, it would be best to widen the Agency
program to include the entire population.

In a developing country where one man rules,
the Public Affairs Officer may argue that that one
man represents the sole worthwhile target. In another, he may find the support of one or several
factions sufficient to his purposes. In a progressive democracy, where one man counts as much as another, he may think it beneficial to sway large
numbers.[85] Besides, in discussions of this type,
there always exists the rejoinder that of the three
billion people on earth, two billion of them are
functionally illiterate or so unsophisticated as to
be unapproachable in ways available to the USIA.

The importance in pointing up the confusion
surrounding this issue, however, is that it illustrates the imprecision of the over-all American information program. The United States is engaged
in an information effort, whose outcome may well
determine the future of freedom, while its Congress
and even its information disseminators disagree as
to whom this program should be directed. The
Administration has the responsibility for control-
ling information policy. Instead it has left the
USIA to the mercy of Congress. Despite its minute
analysis of Agency appropriations, Congress has
failed to contribute to the sharpening of USIA objectives. Meanwhile, the Agency left on its own

and having a miniscule budget, must in a catch-can operation devise a program which simultaneously appeals to the elites and masses of the countries concerned. Given the newness of the American information effort, its fluctuating status in the federal hierarchy, its limited funds, its lack of a specific constituency to argue its case before the public and Congress, it might be demanding too much that the Agency more clearly determine whose support abroad is most essential and how to obtain such support. One sympathizes with the predicament of the USIA-- its inadequate budget on one hand, and its responsibility for the opinion of mankind, on the other. Yet the conclusion remains that the Agency has failed to define its population and program strategy with the precision demanded by the exigencies of the Cold War.

COORDINATING INFORMATION OBJECTIVES

Some two dozen governmental agencies and departments are now conducting a wide variety of campaigns aimed at foreign audiences. The USIA is only one such agency engaged in these activities. The interest of all these agencies in ideological objectives stemmed from the realization that a nuclear standoff exists between the two principal antagonists of the Cold War. These agencies are concerned with contributing to the area of foreign policy that may prove decisive in determining the course of the world political struggle.

According to a study prepared by the Subcommittee of International Organizations and Movements of the Committee on Foreign Affairs, the USIA must wage the American ideological offensive together with the following governmental units: the Department of State, Agency for International Development, Peace Corps, and the Department of Defense. Other departments involved in this effort include Health, Education and Welfare, Commerce, Agriculture, Treasury, Interior, and the Post Office; also the National Science Foundation, the National Aeronautics and Space Administration (NASA), and the Atomic Ener-

gy Commission. Other independent agencies include
the Veterans Administration, Federal Communications
Commission, Housing and Home Finance Agency, Civil
Service Commission, Federal Aviation Agency, and
the Tennessee Valley Authority. [86]

To be sure, the USIA serves as the principal
instrument in relating the American story abroad. A
major problem in administering the many-sided governmental effort at international persuasion is that
of coordination. For one, there must be some means
of enabling these governmental agencies and departments to advance their viewpoints at the policy-
making level. Secondly, there must be a method for
assuring that the decisions concerning the ideological and psychological aspects of foreign policy
are enforced with both internal and external con-
sistency. This study will argue that the USIA program suffers on both accounts due to inadequate
coordinating arrangements in the federal government.
As a result, the USIA has only limited authority in
the information area of foreign policy, and its
strategic objectives lack flexibility and clarity.

An examination of the many agencies with which
the USIA must consult in preparing its strategy
indicates the problems inherent in an area overpop-
ulated by governmental programs. In order to advance the USIA viewpoint in the formulation of
general national objectives, the Director of the
Agency has been brought into meetings of the National Security Council. At the outset of the Kennedy
Administration, it was announced that the USIA
Director would attend such meetings regularly.
Prior to this policy directive, many scholars associated with the communications field argued for
bringing the Director into such a policy-making
group. [87] Nevertheless, there is some doubt as to
what extent the Director's presence on the NSC has
heightened the USIA's authority in the decision-
reaching process. [88]

The Director gives policy guidance to the
President, should his advice be requested. He also
represents the USIA at the Secretary of State's

staff meetings and at Cabinet meetings when matters
of Agency interest are discussed. The Director be-
longs to the Senior Interdepartmental Group (SIG),
formed in 1966, and composed of representatives of
the foreign policy establishment. The aim of SIG
is to coordinate interdepartmental issues of foreign
affairs.

The USIA takes guidance from the Department of
State in reaching daily operating policy. A daily
liaison exists between the USIA's Office of Policy
and Research and the Public Affairs Office of the
State Department. In addition, the Assistant
Directors of the Agency for the geographic regions
are members of the Interdepartmental Regional Groups
(IRG) and maintain direct liaison with their counterpart geographic bureaus in the State Department.

Furthermore, the USIA must cooperate with the
following agencies in setting operating objectives.
It works with the Department of Defense, particularly the Office of Assistant Secretary of Defense for
Public Affairs. USIA advises on foreign psychological aspects of public statements and actions in
the defense field, and works directly with the
various services in Washington and Commands abroad
to increase psychological support for U.S. policies.
This relationship has especially marked the USIA's
operations in Vietnam. [89]

In cultural affairs, an Agency adviser participates in the staff meetings of the Assistant Secretary of State for Educational Affairs. This is
a formal and continuous source of communication between the USIA and the State Department's Bureau
of Educational and Cultural Affairs. A USIA science adviser maintains contact with the President's
science adviser and the Scientific Office of the
State Department, with NASA, the National Science
Foundation, and the National Academy of Sciences.

In order to obtain guidance on youth matters, a
USIA youth affairs adviser maintains contact with
all agencies conducting youth programs. A national
security affairs adviser concerned with nuclear
energy and disarmament serves as the channel for

information from agencies involved in such activity.
These include the AEC and the Arms Control and Disarmament Agency. A women's affairs adviser is concerned with the programs of agencies administering
programs of special interest to women.

The USIA must also collaborate with the Department of Commerce in arranging American participation
in trade fairs and exhibitions. The Office of International Trade Promotion in the Commerce Department is the operating unit with which the USIA sets
up objectives for participation in trade fairs
abroad and for the trade mission program.

The USIA maintains its own liaison with the
Agency for International Development, even though
the latter agency is technically a part of the
State Department. The interests of the two agencies overlap on such matters as the creation of
media production capabilities for foreign governments, the production of textbooks for teaching
English, and the promotion of American studies.

The above account gives some indication of the
difficulty the Agency confronts in reaching clear
and flexible information objectives. The USIA, to
be sure, is not the only federal agency whose policies suffer from a multitude of coordinating responsibilities. The entire foreign policy establishment has experienced administrative problems
growing out of the "New Diplomacy." The hearings
conducted by the Senate Subcommittee on National
Security Staffing and Operations of the Committee
on Government Operations have explored this problem with particular emphasis on the Presidency and
the Department of State.

A salient observation of these studies, relative
to discussion here, is that the needs of the President and the needs of the departments are not identical. There exists no one agency in the sphere of
national security affairs, Professor Richard Neustadt,
of the Department of Government at Harvard University,
emphasized, designed exclusively for advising the
President, such as the Bureau of the Budget in domestic matters. While the State Department is

the nearest counterpart to the Bureau of the Budget
in foreign affairs, it has not yet filled the role
with regard to advising the President. Professor
Neustadt observed:

> So far as I can judge, the State De-
> partment has not yet found the means
> to take the preferred role and play
> it vigorously across the board of
> national security affairs.90

It was further established in these hearings
that the effectiveness of the Department of State
in discharging policy is limited by present arrangements for other federal agencies to engage in
foreign affairs. As an illustration, Ambassador
Kennan's comments in this regard are helpful. He
wrote the Committee that he was seriously handicapped in shaping policy toward the country where
he was assigned due to ineffective coordinating
arrangements with other agencies.

> With these latter, in particular, I
> felt the lack of any effective liaison.
> They included, I suppose, people in the
> Immigration Service, and in the FBI.
> I was never sure that they understood,
> or shared, or respected the policy
> determinations of the Department of
> State with relation to Yugoslavia.91

This study will offer below some suggestions
for instituting more effective coordination procedures regarding foreign policy, especially as it
concerns information objectives. We can note at
this point, however, that if the relatively established Department of State, headed by the chief
Cabinet official, faces such problems in coordination and communications, how much more so does
the fifteen-year-old USIA, which even lacks
Cabinet status.

In any event, the USIA must rely heavily on
the informal aspects of administration in coordinating its strategic program. Institutional ar-

rangements are deliberately kept to a minimum. The
danger to the USIA under these circumstances is
that the Agency must make the most of its own resources, lacking the cooperation, at times, of such
more traditional policy-making units as the
Departments of Defense or State. This condition is
especially critical for the USIA in instances of
international crises. In the excitement of these
crises,the USIA has found itself relying upon
private press reports rather than government intelligence for information. The following excerpt from
a Congressional hearing into the conduct of the
American ideological offensive is relevant:

> Mr. Gross: Were you or were you not
> closely identified with the preparations
> for the Bay of Pigs invasion.
>
> Mr. Sorenson (Deputy Director for Policy
> and Plans of USIA): We were not, sir.
>
> Mr. Gross: You had no one assigned to
> the invasion preparations in Florida
> and elsewhere? You had no one there?
>
> Mr. Wilson (Deputy Director of USIA):
> No, sir. We did not.
>
> Mr. Gross: Didn't you have the rug
> pulled out from under you on your
> broadcasts with respect to the success
> of the Bay of Pigs invasion?
>
> Mr. Wilson: We had a pretty rough
> time in our broadcasts at the time of
> the Bay of Pigs; yes sir.
>
> Mr. Gross: This is what I thought.
> Where did you get your information?
> Did it come from the military or
> from the State Department, or where?
> Where were you getting your information
> in that case?
>
> Mr. Wilson: Well . . .

Mr. Gross: Were you in the USIA at
the time, Mr. Wilson?

Mr. Wilson: Yes, sir. This was in
the spring of 1961 and I was at the
USIA. We were getting our information,
at least in the early hours from the
wire services.
    I might say that, being very candid,
we had a very tough row to hoe at
that time, obviously.[92]

Despite this incident, USIA officials contended
that they had experienced increasingly fewer problems in coordinating information strategy with the
agencies cited at the outset of this section. In
view of the numerous agencies operating in the
foreign arena at present--there has been no significant agency mortality since the Bay of Pigs--this
position of the USIA appears shortsighted. Indeed,
as will be shown below, a major international
incident since the Bay of Pigs occurrence demonstrated that the USIA remains somewhat neglected
in policy-making councils.

    Nevertheless, it was President Kennedy's inten-
tion to strengthen the role of the USIA in foreign
affairs decisions, however much the coordination
problem persisted. The statement of mission for the
USIA that he issued on January 25, 1963, would
seemingly go a long way in enhancing Agency influence in vital decisions. In it, he noted that one
of the two chief purposes of the Agency is advising
the President, his representatives abroad, and the
various departments and agencies on the implications
of foreign opinion for both present and contemplated
U.S. policies. This advisory function was to be
carried out at various levels in Washington, and
within the Country Team at American diplomatic
missions abroad. While the Director of the Agency
was to take the initiative in offering counsel, the
various departments were asked to seek such counsel
when considering programs that may substantially
affect or be affected by foreign opinion.93

Even with this statement designed to give the USIA greater influence with its competition in the foreign policy establishment, it would appear that the Agency was still not always consulted on issues relating to foreign opinion. One such instance concerned a controversial press release by the CIA dealing with economic conditions in the Soviet Union. The public release by the CIA of a statement alleging a worsening economic situation in the Soviet Union marked a dramatic departure from the CIA's traditional role as an intelligence rather than policy-making unit.

According to testimony before the Subcommittee on International Organizations and Movements, the CIA issued this statement without any previous consultation with the USIA as to its effect on foreign opinion. The circumstances of this event led the Chairman of the Subcommittee to include:

> Mr. Fascell: More importantly, Mr. Anderson, I think the question is very obvious that a major international political decision had been made and USIA had no voice in the making of the decision.
>
> Mr. Wilson: I did not have a voice at my level; no, sir. I do not know. Perhaps there was discussion at a lower level, but I do not know about it.
>
> Mr. Anderson (Assistant Deputy Director, Policy and Plans, USIA): There was discussion but nothing conclusive . . .
>
> Mr. Fascell: If there was an agreement to leak and USIA had part of that agreement, then I can understand where the input of USIA on policy is. On the other hand, if USIA had no part to reach an agreement on the leak, then I would say USIA was out in the cold as far as affecting international policy is concerned.94

As a result of its findings relating to the role
of government agencies in ideological operations,
this same Subcommittee observed in its Report to the
House that the nonmilitary and noneconomic programs
directed at foreign audiences have yet to be orches-
trated into an effective instrument of American
foreign policy. "Basically, what seems to be lacking," it continued, "is a recognition that all programs in this category belong to the 'third dimension' of foreign policy." A number of programs
operating in this dimension suffered from fuzziness
of concept. "Their purposes and the roles which
they are supposed to play in the execution of
United States foreign policy have not been clearly
defined."[95]

The difficulties facing the USIA in coordinating
the American information program are further compounded by the existence of private organizations
disseminating messages abroad. To be sure, the
Agency welcomes private efforts in the information
program. It, therefore, established the Office of
Private Cooperation to encourage private groups to
supplement the Agency's work and to assist it in
the accomplishment of its objectives abroad. (This
unit of the USIA was abandoned in 1967. Its activities were parceled out among the Agency's media
divisions. Such an administrative reorganization,
however, does not detract from the USIA's efforts
in spurring private groups to assist in its activities.)

Despite the salutary effect of private efforts
in this connection, the USIA must allow for inevitable problems of program coordination and policy
harmony. The case of Radio Free Europe is instructive in weighing the benefits and drawbacks of a
large-scale private program. RFE was established
by a group of private citizens in December, 1949,
for the purpose of conducting a propaganda campaign
against six Communist-dominated satellites in
Central and Eastern Europe. Radio Free Europe is
not an American voice, but it is the American
management of five European exile voices. The
essential responsibility of RFE is described in the

organization's official <u>Policy Handbook</u> as follows:

> As a non-governmental station
> responsible to the millions of
> American citizens who support it,
> RFE cannot take a line contrary to
> United States Government policy or
> to the beliefs of the people of the
> United States and American institutions.
> It holds itself free, however, to ex-
> press independent views concerning
> the omission of the U.S. government
> to act in respect to the countries
> to which its broadcasts are addressed,
> as well as views concerning the timing
> of acts and pronouncements.96

According to Holt, the advantage of a private
organization such as RFE is that it has greater
latitude in what can be said as well as the techniques used to carry the messages. By contrast, a
government agency must respect the diplomatic
recognition of the target countries to which official broadcasts are aimed. In reaching its objectives a private information agency is not subject
to possible political pressure as is the USIA
through the medium of annual appropriations.
Finally, a private agency does not suffer from
being stamped as a governmental propaganda unit.
In that way, RFE may possibly develop greater credibility for what it disseminates.97

The central problem presented by the operation
of RFE for the stategic objectives of USIA is that
the former unit may be mistakenly identified abroad
as the official American information organization.
The responsibility of RFE in the anti-Soviet riots
in Poland and Hungary in 1956 illustrates the
difficulties arising from the existence of a nonofficial instrument of American foreign policy.
Holt defended RFE in these two incidents. He attributed the responsibility of RFE not to any
institutional lines of control, but to the self-
imposed discipline of the individuals who hold
positions of authority. RFE employees, he argued,

possess a "built-in" awareness that they are operating an instrument that could have a grave impact on the position of the United States in Eastern Europe.

Indeed, Holt maintained that the performance of RFE is superior to that of the official American information instrument, the USIA. He noted:

> It is the considered opinion of this
> writer that the policy analysts at
> RFE have not been unaware of events
> and changes behind the Iron Curtain
> (as some of its critics maintain)
> but that they have been more aware
> of developments, more skilled and
> sophisticated in their analysis and
> more diligent in the development of
> strategies than those responsible
> for the official policy of the United
> States government.[98]

Accordingly, Holt's argument for the efficacy of RFE is based substantially on alleged failures of the USIA to formulate clear-cut policy objectives. While there is validity in Holt's case for a private information organization, it should be noted, in fairness to the USIA, that government information personnel have not been as incompetent as the above quotation may indicate. Given the Agency's limited budget and its problems in coordinating objectives with other government departments, the USIA's record is hardly as pathetic as Holt made it out to be.

To some extent, however, private broadcasting organizations justify their existence on the failure of the government to clearly define the role of its official information service in American foreign objectives.[99] Radio Free Europe may not be a competitor of the USIA, as are other government bodies, but it is a reminder that some extremely influential and knowledgeable Americans believe that the Agency has failed, in some measure, the people of Eastern Europe.

The main coordination obstacles in the way of
the USIA's becoming an optimum instrument of American foreign objectives still remain those within
rather than without the government. So long as
there exist the problems described in this section
regarding program coordination, American information objectives are bound to suffer. The American
information effort can only echo the confusion of
the foreign policy establishment.

CONGRESS AND INFORMATION OBJECTIVES

The discussion above relating to the controversial objectives of the American information program
has given some indication of the role of Congress
in this area. The relationship between Congress
and the USIA will be treated at length in a subsequent chapter. Our purpose here is to evaluate
the causes of Congress' misunderstanding of the
information program.

The USIA has been one of the most heavily investigated agencies of the federal government. The
newness and intangibility of the information program, its departure from the traditional forms of
statecraft, and the difficulty of determining what
goes on in the minds of men are all factors contributing to Congressional concern. Furthermore,
the absence of a particular constituency to champion the Agency's case enables it to become a ready
target for legislators seeking publicity.

To its credit, Congress in its annual review of
Agency appropriations has often uncovered instances
of ineffective planning, careless administration,
and shortsighted objectives. In spite of its
detailed investigations, however, Congress still
seems to lack an understanding of the purposes of
an information program and the magnitude of the
effort necessary to compete effectively in the
Cold War. In sharp contrast to the treatment
accorded military programs, Congressional discussion of the USIA is usually concerned with reducing costs. Legislators are reluctant to approve

budgets unless immediate and visible results can be
guaranteed. Experimental military programs com-
mitting billions of dollars are readily authorized.
A modest increase of a few million for the USIA, as
recent Agency Directors wearily pointed out, is subject to minute critical examination conducted in an
atmosphere of skepticism and even antagonism.

The headline-making attacks on the USIA during
its formative years were usually launched by congressmen intending to drive home issues that were
more basic than information techniques or goals.
Such points, for instance, related to coexistence
with Communism or the direction of American society.
In the main, congressional criticism of the Agency
represents a conscientious effort for improvement.
The record is clear, however, as the Nineteenth
Report of the U.S. Advisory Commission notes, that
none of the thirteen directors of the U.S. foreign
information program has succeeded in communicating
to the Congress an adequate understanding of this
program. [100]

How does the USIA communicate with Congress?
In addition to Congressional hearings and informal
contacts, the chief institutional contact is the
USIA Office of Congressional Liaison. The USIA
is one of the few federal agencies lacking an in-
dependent office for Congressional relations. The
Agency's Office of Congressional Liaison is attached
to the Office of the General Counsel. In the
USIA's organizational arrangement, the General
Counsel is also known as the Congressional Liaison.

The General Counsel's Office assists in draft-
ing proposed legislation, orders, contracts and
Executive Orders. The Office is also responsible
for developing and executing basic USIA policies
in obtaining and licensing the intangible rights
associated with USIA program material.

The Congressional relations function has been
part of the General Counsel's Office since the
founding of the USIA in 1953. As of December, 1967,
seven different attorneys have served as the USIA's

General Counsel. The names of the General Counsels
and their dates of service follow.

TABLE 3

DATES OF SERVICE OF USIA GENERAL COUNSELS

Name	Dates
Raymond R. Dickey	December, 1953-January,1955
Olive L. Duval, II	January, 1955-January,1959
Harry T. Carter	January, 1959-August, 1960
Thomas G. Roderick,Jr.	September,1960-February,1961
Donald J. Irwin	February, 1961-November,1961
Stanley Plesent	December, 1961-November,1965
Richard M. Schmidt,Jr.	December, 1965-Present

Significantly, four of the General Counsels
served for periods of two years or less. Inasmuch
as the USIA's delicate activities require close
communications between the Agency and the Congress,
the high rate of turnover may have been to the USIA's
detriment. The inadequate understanding Congress
has of the information program stems, in part, from
the frequent comings and goings of the Agency's chief
Congressional relations officer.

The size of the USIA General Counsel's staff is
small in comparison with that of the Department of
State.[101] The 1966 Agency budget called for the
General Counsel's Office to be staffed by 21 people.
Of this figure--excepting the General Counsel--
only 4 staff members engaged in legislative re-
lations--2 officers, an administrative assistant
and a secretary. The 2 legislative relations
officers were veterans to their jobs, as of
January, 1966. One had served in this position for
3 years, and the other 6 years. Both held public
relations posts on Capitol Hill before joining the
USIA.[102] The legislative relations officers did
not first serve abroad at USIA installations

before coming to the General Counsel's Office. In
this regard, the USIA differs from the Department of
State--the latter assigning career officers to the
Congressional Relations staff usually following
overseas experience.

The General Counsel confers with any Agency
official to secure information desired by Congress.
According to Stanley Plesent, hardly a week went by
during his four years as General Counsel that he
did not personally meet with the USIA Director.
Moreover, the General Counsel is one of some twenty-
five Agency staff members who would attend the
Director's weekly meetings at 10:30 on Monday morn-
ings.

The General Counsel also provides the White
House staff for Congressional relations with a detailed report every Monday afternoon on USIA activities with Congress for the previous week and USIA
projections of the current week. The USIA, like all
other federal agencies and departments, has experienced increased centralized control of its Congressional relations activities during the Kennedy and
Johnson Administrations.

All mail addressed to the USIA from Congress is
automatically channeled to the Congressional Liaison
Section Office unless the mail is marked "personal"
or bears a postage stamp (as opposed to franking).
In these two cases, the mail is routed directly
from the USIA mail room to the addressee.

The policy of the Congressional Liaison is to
reply to all Congressional mail within three days.
If the liaison staff lacks adequate information for
answering a piece of Congressional mail, the letter
is sent to the relevant USIA section for detailed
reply. In the routing process, Congressional mail
is accompanied by a one-page "Correspondence Action
Slip," carrying stylistic instructions for the USIA
staff. After the letter is answered by either the
USIA media or regional bureau, it is returned to
the Congressional Liaison Office for review before
being mailed to the Capitol.

What information does Congress seek from the
Congressional Liaison Office? It is difficult to
reach specific estimates concerning this question,
insofar as the USIA neither keeps topical, numerical,
nor partisan political statistics on Congressional
inquiries. Liaison officials maintain that the cost
of tabulating Congressional inquiries along the
aforesaid lines would be prohibitive. However, the
Agency has a file on each congressman's correspondence, as well as cross-files for subjects most frequently appearing in Congressional letters (the USIA
film of President Kennedy, for example).

While there is no precise information in the
Agency records concerning these queries it is possible to record some typical topics of Congressional
concern on the basis of a one-and-one-half day
sample taken during the first week of September, 1965.
The sampling is based on mail and phone calls.

> Information on possible domestic showing
> of JFK film (Approx. 25).
> Transmitting suggestion that television
> be used in conflict in Vietnam (Approx. 7).
> Request for information for constituent
> back from Army service on establishing
> library for Ethiopian village (Approx. 1).
> Request for courtesy tour cards through
> Voice of America studios (Approx. 7).
> General employment referrals (Approx. 5).
> Inquiry on contract for mowing grass on
> 6,000 acre VOA transmitter sites at
> Greenville, North Carolina (Approx. 4).
> Status on job application of constituent
> fluent in Russian (Approx. 1).
> Transmitting inquiry on Government spend-
> ing for film on President Johnson
> (Approx. 15).[103]

Congressional inquiries may be answered by the
USIA through correspondence, or in person by one of
the two USIA officers assigned to Congressional
Liaison. Essentially, one officer deals with written replies to the Capitol and also turns out a
one- or two-page summary of material in the past day's

Congressional Record of concern to the Agency. The
summary is distributed to the Agency offices in
Washington. The other officer spends most of his
time on the Hill, meeting with congressmen and their
staffs.

Underscoring the attitude of the USIA liaison
staff toward Congress is the notion that Congress,
rather than the Agency, should take the initiative
in their relations. One officer noted: "These
people [Congressmen] are busy enough without us.
They don't want us coming up from downtown and telling them what to do."104 In addition to the reluctance of the USIA to impose on the limited time of
congressmen, another factor may be the suspicion with
which legislators invariably regard a "propaganda"
agency. Both considerations result in a Congressional Liaison operation devoted mainly to putting out
brushfires from within Congress, rather than an operation designed to solicit advice from the legislators
and to keep them informed on subtle shifts in information policy.

An evaluation of the relationship between the
USIA and Congress must take into account the Agency's
most formidable critic, Congressman John J. Rooney,
Chairman of the Committee on Appropriations' Subcommittee on Department of State, Justice, and Commerce, the Judiciary, and Related Agencies. Congressman Rooney, of the 14th District of Brooklyn, New
York, considers himself a friend of the American information program. Nevertheless, USIA officials
have found his minute program analyses disconcerting.
Goodfriend describes Congressman Rooney as follows:

> Brilliant, remorseless, indefatigable,
> he left witnesses in little doubt about
> how cheaply he valued their words, how
> dearly he counted the dollars they ex-
> pended. Like a sidewinder missile, he
> swooped toward his target whenever a
> witness showed signs of warmth around
> the collar. Time and again he shattered
> a nervous officer with a burst of irony,
> making a shamble of his months of earnest
> effort.105

Congressman Rooney's approach to foreign policy
has been a subject of much controversy outside the
Agency as well.

The two chief criteria by which Congressman
Rooney measures the effectiveness of the USIA are
the economy of its operations and the cogency of
its programs. He advocates an information program
which would result in visible support of American
policies abroad. His repeated exposures of the
USIA's failure to develop clear-cut strategies, as
well as instances of diffuse, packaged programs,
were undoubtedly responsible for the sharpening of
objectives that were accelerated under the directorship of Edward R. Murrow. Congressman Rooney's
opposition to an information program with an inordi-
nate concentration on the elite rather than the
masses, as discussed earlier in this study, has also
been taken into account by Agency officials in planning future campaigns.

The chief shortcoming of Congressman Rooney's
conception of an information program, insofar as it
concerns strategic objectives, is its tendency
toward simplification and "practicality." Wishing
the USIA to produce obvious information successes,
he waxes suspicious over any undertaking showing
the least subtlety. As the level of political education in the less-developed nations progresses,
the task of a foreign information program becomes
increasingly delicate. The USIA cannot rely on
well-worn arguments and clichés in competing with
Communist propaganda in such circumstances. Congressman Rooney, it would appear, discounts the advantages
of these untried approaches in comparison with the
traditional hard-sell method of information dissemination. The following exchange illustrates the
difference between the two viewpoints:

Mr. Rooney: Let me understand this
one correctly: You bought 25 copies
to give away free of charge entitled
"Modern Brazilian Poetry" to give to

prominent Brazilian poets. How does
this make an impact on the minds of
men and the people of Brazil, to send
them their own poetry and give them
away to poets whom one would expect
would be thoroughly acquainted with
poetry in Brazil.

Mr. Weing: Sir, this was an English
translation of their poetry and the
intention of the book was to show an
interest in Brazilian culture, that
the people of North America have an
interest in their culture. There is
a very strong feeling among Latin
American intellectuals, I am told,
that the North American does not pay
very much attention to their literary
works, and since they have a rather
strong literary tradition, they tend
to resent this.106

To be sure, there may have been much merit to
Congressman Rooney's outlook as it related to the
international climate during the early years of the
information program in the 1950's. However, the recent world situation has been one of sensitive
maneuvering for foreign political support. As the
mounting appeal of Communism in Latin America indicates, the United States cannot take for granted
the attachment of even its closest neighbors. Under
these conditions, the USIA is justified in utilizing
indirect means, such as described above, for ac-
complishing American information objectives abroad.

Carl T. Rowan, in one of his first speeches as
Agency Director, criticized the notion that there
exist nostrums for spreading the American message
abroad. Acknowledging the complexity of international society, Rowan took issue with men who become
impatient simplifiers of political issues.

I have pressed hard to explain that
the easiest way to destroy USIA, to
render it totally ineffective, would

be to have it feed the world nothing but
superlatives about America and the American way of life. And I have been hard-
pressed to make the "simplifiers" understand that USIA can and has worked minor
miracles in the propaganda field, but it
can never do the undoable or hide the
unhideable.[107]

As long as Congressman Rooney measures the effectiveness of the USIA by one yardstick and Agency officials
measure it by another, the confusion in Congress regarding information objectives will never be resolved.

Congressman Rooney's other criterion for determining the effectiveness of the information program is
the cost approach. Despite the growing sums expended
by the Communist nations for foreign propaganda, the
House remains adamant in opposing substantial increases for the Agency's budget. At times, friends
of the Agency have been forced to conduct fights on
the floor of Congress on its behalf. Perhaps the
chief setback stemming from the fear of Congressman
Rooney's financial scrutiny is that program objectives are predicated primarily on budgetary and
appropriations considerations. There is need for a
more objective and sustained effort to formulate
programs first, provide a thorough justification for
them, and then calculate the fiscal resources necessary to implement these programs.[108]

This issue was raised in a different context by
Congressman Fraser in the House hearings on the
United States ideological offensive. In questioning
Agency Deputy Director Wilson on program effective-
ness, Congressman Fraser noted that the problem in
this regard is that:

The problem is so many people think in
terms of the way it was done last year.
They think in terms of the limitations
within which they must become accustomed
to living. Who is it that produces the
breakthrough that says, "What we don't
need is one guy down there. We need a

hundred," something like that.109

This study argues that much of the responsibility
for stultifying the Agency's development of such
bold programs is, in large measure, that of the
House Appropriations Subcommittee.110

Congressman Rooney's most recurring objection
in USIA budgetary hearings concerns what he terms
"giveaways." "When I say 'giveaway,' I mean your
presentations of free subscriptions at the expense
of the American taxpayer."111 Included among such
giveaways, according to Congressman Rooney, are
presentations abroad of subscriptions to American
newspapers and magazines, as well as dictionaries,
encyclopedias, and other reference works. It is
not unusual for him to inquire as to a list of the
names and addresses of people receiving these subscriptions. He also breaks down such lists for
comparative costs for domestic and international
subscriptions. The transcript of the Subcommittee's
hearings as regards this aspect of strategic objectives would appear to the unfamiliar reader to re-
semble, at times, a courtroom comedy.

> Mr. Rooney: I am going to perhaps
> appear naive, but I should like to
> inquire what is Humpty Dumpty's
> magazine at page 12 of this list.
> 36 subscriptions of Humpty Dumpty's
> magazine. It sounds like a kid's
> book; is it?
>   I am serious. I am seeking
> information.
>
> Mr. Evans: It is a child's magazine,
> Mr. Chairman. My young daughter sub-
> scribes to it.
>
> Mr. Rooney: Is Jack and Jill a kid's
> magazine, too?
>
> Mr. May: Yes, sir.112

On a more serious plane, Congressman Rooney's

Subcommittee examines in detail the allocation of
personnel positions in the USIA. Such investigation,
to Congressman Rooney's credit, often turns up instances of negligent administrative management.
What concerns us here, however, is the tenor of the
way the Subcommittee expresses itself in this regard. In its Report to the House on 1958 Agency
hearings, for instance, the Subcommittee notes:

> The examination by the Committee of
> the justifications presented in con-
> nection with the 1958 fiscal year
> budget presented a most amazing and
> unprecedented situation in that,
> despite the fact that Congress had
> made sizable reductions in the 1957
> fiscal year budgets for salaries
> and expenses in the Department of
> State and the United States Infor-
> mation Agency, they proceeded to
> establish in 1957 over 950 positions
> more than they had requested in
> their 1957 budget presentations.
> These agencies come along and request
> funds to "annualize" these positions
> in fiscal year 1958, which is merely
> a means of obtaining funds to continue
> these positions on the public payroll.[113]

The result of this approach by the House Appropriations Subcommittee is that in its picayune
appraisal it has failed to contribute to long-term
planning of information strategy. It does not require any great depth of intellect to quarrel over
free foreign subscriptions to American publications.
Nor is much insight needed into foreign policy objectives to bare inefficient aspects of USIA administration, as has the Subcommittee commendably performed in this area.

That Congress misunderstands the nature of the
American information program becomes more apparent
upon examining the hearings of committees that deal
with the Agency on a less regular and intensive basis
than the Appropriations Committees. It is ques-

tionable to what extent American objectives have
suffered due to Congress' reluctance to grant larger
appropriations. The only certainty in this regard
is that in magnitude the American program is far
below that of the Communist nations. Inasmuch as a
budget is integral to policy formulation, we can
contend that the method with which Congress has
treated the USIA has not seriously enhanced information objectives. Indeed, Congress' budgetary
outlook may have set back these objectives. While
it has laboriously examined the parts of the information program, it appears that Congress has lost
sight of the whole. The confusion over information
strategy discussed at the outset of this study continues despite much Congressional attention to
budgetary detail. Meanwhile, the subtle scheme, the
daring innovation, the long-term program, should
they be proposed by the USIA, remain as unwelcome
as ever.

NOTES TO CHAPTER 1

1. Report of the Committee on Foreign Affairs
Personnel: Personnel for the New Diplomacy
(Washington, D.C.: Carnegie Endowment for Interna-
tional Peace, 1962), p. 3.

2. Only five years preceding the establishment
of the USIA, a historian, in a study of the attitudes
of the average American, said: "The Man in the
Street is a rugged individualist who has learned to
hoe his own row without foreign support, who has
developed an inherent distrust of foreigners, who
has no deep-seated interest in foreign trade, and
who, with true Yankee thrift, does not like to
squander his money fighting what he conceives to be
'other people's wars.'" Thomas A. Bailey, The Man in
the Street (New York: The Macmillan Co., 1948),
p. 245.

3. U.S. Congress, House Committee on Foreign
Affairs, National Academy of Foreign Affairs:
Executive Communication, 88th Cong. 1st sess., 1963,
p. v.

4. U.S. Information Agency, Remarks by Edward
R. Murrow, Director, before the Educational Press
Association, at the National Educational Association,
(Washington, D.C.), May 17, 1962, p. 5.

5. James C. Hagerty, Press Secretary to the
President, The White House, July 8, 1953, p. 5.

6. Charles A. H. Thomson, Overseas Information
Service of the United States Government (Washington,
D.C.: The Brookings Institution, 1948), pp. 364-65.

7. U.S. Congress, Senate Committee on Foreign
Relations, Training of Foreign Affairs Personnel,
88th Cong., 1st sess., 1963, p. 107.

8. Some students of the communications process
argue that the USIA is potentially the most "powerful" instrument of American foreign policy. However, this study will not attempt to make comparative judgments as to the power of each instrument.
See, in this regard, Ithiel de Sola Pool, "Information Goals," Foreign Service Journal, XL, No. 7
(July, 1963),   21.

9. U.S. Congress, House Subcommittee of the
Committee on Foreign Affairs, Report No. 5: "Modern
Communications and Foreign Policy," Hearings:
Winning the Cold War: The U.S. Ideological Offen-
sive, 90th Cong., 1st sess., 1967, p. 5R.

10. The official history of the U.S. informa-
tion program has yet to be written. For descrip-
tions of the fluctuation of information objectives
during the history of the USIA, see Wilson P.
Dizard, The Strategy of Truth (Washington, D.C.:
Public Affairs Press, 1961), and W. Phillips Davison,
International Political Communication (New York:
Frederick A. Praeger, 1965).

11. Davison, op. cit., pp. 277-82.

12. Ibid., p. 278.

13. U.S. Information Agency, The Agency in

Brief (Washington, D.C.: USIA, 1966), p. 4.

14. Ibid.

15. Ibid.

16. U.S. Congress, Joint Committee on Foreign
Relations and Committee on Foreign Affairs, Legislation on Foreign Relations with Explanatory Notes,
88th Cong., 2d sess., 1964, p. 204.

17. The Agency in Brief (1966), U.S. Information
Agency, op. cit., p. 4.

18. Arthur Larson, "The USIA: How Effective
Is It?" Vital Speeches of the Day, XXIII, No. 16
(June 1, 1957), 492.

19. W. Phillips Davison and Alexander L. George,
"An Outline for the Study of International Political
Communications," Public Opinion Quarterly, XVI, No.
4 (Winter, 1952-53), 506.

20. United States Information Agency, 25th
Review of Operations, January-June 1966 (Washington,
D.C.: USIA, 1966), p. 1.

21. U.S. Advisory Commission on Information,
Twenty-First Report (February, 1966), p. 12.

22. U.S. Congress, House Subcommittee on Department of State, Justice, Commerce, the Judiciary,
and Related Agencies of the Committee on Appropriations, Hearings, 89th Cong., 2d sess., 1966, p. 667.

23. Ibid., pp. 671-78, for examples of USIA
research projects.

24. U.S. Congress, House Subcommittee of the
Committee on Foreign Affairs, Report No. 4:
"Behavioral Sciences and the National Security,"
Hearings: Winning the Cold War: The U.S. Ideolog-
ical Offensive, 89th Cong., 2d sess., 1966, pp. 157-
83, for description of the USIA research program.

25. U.S. Advisory Commission on Information, Twenty-First Report, p. 24.

26. U.S. Congress, House Subcommittee of the Committee on Foreign Affairs, Report No. 2, 88th Cong., 2d sess., 1964, p. 3.

27. Ibid.

28. U.S. Congress, House Subcommitee of the Committee on Foreign Affairs, Hearings: Winning the Cold War: The U.S. Ideological Offensive, 88th Cong., 1st sess., 1963, p. 12. Hereafter cited as House, Hearings.

29. Henry A. Kissinger, Nuclear Weapons and Foreign Policy (New York: Harper & Bros., 1957), p. 405.

30. U.S. Congress, Senate Committee on Foreign Relations, Interim Report: Overseas Information Programs of the United States, 83d Cong., 1st sess., 1953, p. 33.

31. Great Britain, Summary of the Report of the Independent Commission of inquiry into the Overseas Information Services (Drogheda Report), Cmd. 9138 (London: Her Majesty's Stationery Office, 1954), p. 3. Hereafter cited as Drogheda Report.

32. Thomson, op. cit., p. 326.

33. Great Britain, Overseas Information Services, Cmd. 225 (London: Her Majesty's Stationery Office, 1957), p. 3.

34. British Information Services, British Government Information Services, R. 5256 (London, 1961), p. 5.

35. Drogheda Report, p. 11.

36. Ibid., p. 6. The scope of USIA objectives has broadened substantially since the mid-1950's, when the Committee on Foreign Relations' study noted

that the "objectives of British information are similar to those of the United States." Overseas Information Programs of the United States, p. 97.

37. Overseas Information Services, Cmd. 225, p. 3.

38. Address of Sanford S. Marlowe, October 28, 1963, to the International Communications Council, Princeton, N.J., p. 8.

39. Drogheda Report, p. 7. The observation of a USIA officer in this connection is instructive. The basic aims of British information were, he noted,

> to create an impression of overwhelming objectivity, to achieve total credibility, and when it really counted, to capitalize on this credibility by slipping in something serving the British cause. The audience comprised 'respected leaders of opinion' who were supplied with relevant facts leaving them to draw the right conclusions and then publicize them. The message was often deliberately aimed over the audience's head. Whether or not it was understood, didn't matter.

Goodfriend, op. cit., p. 45.

40. As for the relative effectiveness of both the Voice of America and the British Broadcasting Corporation, one study of refugees from the 1956 Hungarian uprising indicated that there is no appreciable difference. While 67 per cent of the respondents said they listened to the BBC, and 82 per cent to the VOA, 91 per cent thought that BBC broadcasts were generally reliable and 85 per cent VOA broadcasts were generally reliable. Quoted in L. John Martin, International Propaganda: Its Legal and Diplomatic Control (Minneapolis, Minn.: University of Minnesota Press, 1957), p. 40.

41. This study will take the position that the Soviet foreign ideological program is "propaganda," whereas the American one fits the description of "information." See "USIA: Information or Propaganda?" above, p. 39.

42. E. H. Carr, The Soviet Impact on the Western World (New York: The Macmillan Co., 1954), p. 84.

43. Frederick C. Barghoorn, Soviet Foreign Propaganda (Princeton, N.J.: Princeton University Press, 1964), pp. 300-301.

44. Quoted in an article by Tad Szulc, The New York Times, September 8, 1963.

45. See Murray Dyer, The Weapon on the Wall (Baltimore, Md.: The Johns Hopkins Press, 1959), p. 3, for an account of this incident.

46. Barghoorn, op. cit., pp. 244-45.

47. Szulc, op. cit.

48. Quoted in House Subcommittee of the Committee on Foreign Affairs, Report No. 2 p. 2.

49. Inasmuch as the USIA has been called an information rather than propaganda service in official legislations dealing with it, this study will refer to it as such.

50. The dread of the weighted word is so great that there is actually a law regulating it. In 1913, the Department of Agriculture decided to employ a public relations man. The outcry in Congress was horrendous. The legislators were angered that an Executive department was actually proposing to set up machinery that, by operating on voters, might bring pressure to bear on them. An act of Congress was passed--which is still in effect today--making unlawful the use of federal funds "for the compensation of any publicity expert unless specificially appropriated for that purpose." United States Code (1913), title 5, sec. 54.

51. Lester Markel, Public Opinion and Foreign Policy (New York: Harper & Bros., 1949), p. 16.

52. B. L. Smith, Harold D. Lasswell, and R. D. Casey, Propaganda, Communication, and Public Opinion (Princeton, N.J.: Princeton University Press, 1946), p. 1.

53.   Terence H. Qualter, Propaganda and Psychological Warfare (New York: Random House, 1962),
p. 26.   This volume is one of the best brief accounts
available on the subject.

54.   Robert T. Holt and Robert W. van de Velde,
Strategic Psychological Operations and American
Foreign Policy (Chicago, Ill.:   University of Chicago
Press, 1960), pp. 26-27.

55.   Fundamental to this issue is the matter of
research into communications effectiveness.   This
topic will be treated in a subsequent chapter.   For
a theoretical description of information technique,
see Stephens, op. cit.

56.   Legislation on Foreign Relations with
Explanatory Notes, p. 208.

57.   Cited in Charles A. H. Thomson and Walter
H. C. Laves, Cultural Relations and U.S. Foreign
Policy (Bloomington, Ind.:   Indiana University Press,
1963).   On U.S. educational and cultural programs
conducted abroad, see Philip H. Coombs, The Fourth
Dimension of Foreign Policy (New York: Harper &
Row, 1964), and Charles Frankel, The Neglected Aspect of Foreign Affairs (Washington, D.C.:   Brookings Institution, 1966).

58.   The New York Times, September 28, 1966.

59.   President's Committee on International
Information, (Jackson Committee), p. 3.

60.   House, Hearings, p. 5.

61.   Theodore Streibert, "Remarks at Opening
of Voice of America Studio," Department of State
Bulletin, XVI, No. 808 (December 20, 1954), 963-65.
In this regard see the USIA's First Review of
Operations (1954) for an indication of the bombastic
picture displays used against Communism.

62.   U.S. Congress, Senate Committee on Foreign
Relations, Hearings, 87th Cong., 1st sess., 1961,
p. 13.

63. Ibid., p. 16.

64. Ibid., pp. 26-27.

65. Another illustration of this attitude:

  Mrs. Bolton: You say you give all the
  news, yes, even when it hurts, yes; but
  what of the overemphasis that is placed
  on some phases of news, which are facts;
  is it necessary to overemphasize some
  of the things that occur?
    Mr. Murrow: Mrs. Bolton, I do not
  believe that we do overemphasize the
  things that hurt. We report them for
  credibility. We report them because
  if we do not do so others will, and
  distort or exaggerate them in the
  process. House, Hearings, p. 15.

66. U.S. Congress, Senate Subcommittee on Departments of State, Justice, Commerce, the Judiciary,
and Related Agencies of the Committee on Appropriations, Hearings, 87th Cong., 1st sess., 1961, pp.
666-67.

67. Walter Joyce, The Propaganda Gap (New York:
Harper & Row, 1963), p. 48.

68. The training facilities and objectives of
the USIA will be evaluated in a further chapter.
See U.S. Congress, Senate Subcommittee of the Committee on the Judiciary, Hearings: Freedom Commission
and Freedom Academy, 86th Cong., 1st sess., 1959,
for the many different approaches to the organizing
of such an institution.

69. Bernard C. Cohen, The Press and Foreign
Policy (Princeton, N.J.: Princeton University
Press, 1963). For a related account in the area of
international organization, see Ronald I. Rubin,
"The UN Correspondent," Western Political Quarterly,
XVII, No. 4 (December, 1964), 615-31.

70. R. H. Bruce Lockhart, Comes the Reckoning
(London: Putnam, 1947), p. 154.

71. Hans Speier, "Psychological Warfare Reconsidered," in Daniel Lerner (ed.), Propaganda in War and Crisis (New York: George W. Stewart, 1951), p. 473.

72. Ibid., p. 474.

73. For discussion of this point, see Ben Posner, "Major Budgetary and Programming Problems of the United States Information Agency in its Operations of Overseas Missions" (unpublished Ph.D. dissertation, American University, Washington, D.C., 1962).

74. An Agency official related the following incident concerning its budgetary problems. A touring congressman, he said, once posed the following hypothetical question: "What would you do if we gave you only $20 in program money for the entire year?" The officer replied: "I'd take the Minister of Education out, give him the best lunch $20 would buy, and try to persuade him to install courses in American civilization in all the universities." John P. McKnight, "Target: The Masses or the Classes," Foreign Service Journal, XLI, No. 4 (April, 1964), 24.

75. Edward W. Barrett, Truth is Our Weapon (New York: Funk & Wagnalls Co., 1953), p. 263.

76. U.S. Information Agency, Address by Carl T. Rowan, Director-designate, before Printing Week Convention (Minneapolis, Minn.), February 21, 1964, p. 2.

77. U.S. Congress, House Subcommittee of the Committee on Appropriations, Hearings, 88th Cong., 1st sess., 1963, pp. 12-13.

78. Ibid., 87th Cong., 2d sess., 1962, p. 43. USIA officials have often used an analogy involving "shoe leather" when appearing before Congress for some curious reason. For instance,

Mrs. Bolton: How much do your people

abroad get out among the people of the
countries which they serve.

Mr. Wilson: It is our injunction, Mrs.
Bolton, that they should get out just as
much as they possibly can and wear out
shoe leather instead of desk leather.
House, Hearings, p. 790.

79. U.S. Congress, House Subcommittee of the
Committee on Appropriations, Hearings, 87th Cong.,
2d sess., 1962, p. 317.

80. Ibid., p. 323.

81. House, Hearings, p. 63.

82. The concept of the Country Plan will be
treated at greater length in Chapter 3.

83. Leo Bogart, "A Study of the Operating
Assumptions of the U.S. Information Agency," Public
Opinion Quarterly, XIX, No. 4 (Winter, 1955-56),
376.

84. Goodfriend, op. cit., p. 106.

85. McKnight, op. cit., p. 23.

86. U.S. Congress, House Subcommittee of the
Committee on Foreign Affairs, Committee Print: The
U.S. Ideological Effort: Government Agencies and
Programs, 88th Cong., 1st sess., 1964.

87. This was, perhaps, the principal theme
of Holt's Strategic Psychological Operations and
American Foreign Policy, op. cit. It maintained
that the Director of the USIA should be brought
into the Cabinet as well.

88. Edward R. Murrow, by strength of his
personality and prestige, carried much more influence
in Washington policy decisions than probably all of
his predecessors. Yet as of early 1963, after being
at his post for two years, Murrow is said to have
cited only one significant instance in which his

views had a bearing on policy decisions. This instance related to the American resumption of nuclear testing. Joyce, op. cit., p. 130.

89. For a thorough analysis of the USIA role
in Vietnam (based chiefly on secondary sources), see
John Hohenberg, Between Two Worlds: Policy, Press,
and Public Opinion in Asian-American Relations
(New York: Frederick A. Praeger, 1967), chap. vi.

90. U.S. Congress, Senate Subcommittee on
National Security Staffing and of the Committee on
Government Operations, Hearings: Administration of
National Security, 88th Cong., 1st and 2d sess. Of
particular value to the present discussion are
Basic Issues (1963), and The Secretary of State
(1964).

91. Ibid., p. 359.

92. House, Hearings, p. 784.

93. "Memorandum by the President to the
Director, U.S, Information Agency, Describing the
Mission of the Agency," in Legislation on Foreign
Relations with Explanatory Notes, op. cit., p. 222.

94. House, Hearings, pp. 786-87.

95. U.S. Congress, House Subcommittee of the
Committee on Foreign Affairs, Report No. 2, 88th Cong.,
2d sess., 1964, p. 9.

96. Cited in Robert R. Holt, Radio Free
Europe (Minneapolis,: University of Minnesota Press,
1958), p. 18.

97. Ibid., p. 200.

98. Ibid., p. 211.

99. As concerns the advantage of an intensive
private persuasion effort, this essay shares the
conclusion of the Brookings study on foreign policy
formulation that: ". . . the possible gains are
likely to be more apparent than real." H. Field

Haviland (ed.), <u>The Formulation and Administration</u>
<u>of United States Foreign Policy</u>, (Washington, D.C.:
The Brookings Institution, 1960), p. 77.

100. U.S. Advisory Commission on Information,
<u>Nineteenth Report</u> (January, 1964), p. 5.

101. See James A. Robinson, <u>Congress and Foreign</u>
<u>Policy-Making</u>, Revised Edition (Homewood, Ill.:
The Dorsey Press, 1967), chap. v, for a description
of the liaison arrangement of the Department of State.

102. Ronald I. Rubin, "The Legislative-Executive
Relations of the United States Information Agency,"
<u>Parliamentary Affairs</u>, XX, No. 2, (Spring, 1967), 160.

103. <u>Ibid</u>., p. 161.

104. <u>Ibid</u>.

105. Goodfriend, <u>op. cit</u>., p. 6.

106. U.S. Congress, House Subcommittee of the
Committee on Appropriations, <u>Hearings</u>, 88th Cong.,
1st sess., 1963, p. 431.

107. U.S. Information Agency, <u>Remarks by Carl</u>
<u>T. Rowan</u>, Director, at the International Radio and
Television Society, New York City, March 11, 1964,
p. 3.

108. U.S. Advisory Commission on Information,
<u>Eighteenth Report</u>, (January, 1963), p. 23.

109. House, <u>Hearings</u>, p. 791.

110. This is not to say that the Senate Committee
on Appropriations possesses an impeccable record
with regard to understanding and promoting the information program. USIA officials must contend with
basic challenges to their operating strategy in this
body, such as Senator Ellender's advocacy of binational information centers replacing the present overseas
units. This point will be discussed at greater
length in a succeeding chapter dealing with the way
in which the Agency program has been evaluated by

Congress.

111. U.S. Congress, House Subcommittee of the Committee on Appropriations, Hearings, 88th Cong., 1st sess., 1963, p. 429.

112. Ibid., p. 439.

113. U.S. Congress, House Subcommittee of the Committee on Appropriations, Report No. 351, 85th Cong., 1st sess., 1957, p. 2.

CHAPTER **2** THE EVOLUTION OF
INFORMATION OBJECTIVES

THE PREWAR INFORMATION PROGRAM

The preceding chapter argued that the development of the USIA as an effective instrument of
American foreign relations has been handicapped by
both theoretical and operational shortcomings. A
main thesis of this study is that these weaknesses
are not new to the USIA, but have characterized its
predecessor organizations. The unsettled nature of
contemporary information objectives is an outgrowth
of the confusion regarding the program in previous
years. The purpose of this chapter is to set forth
in historical perspective the continuing obstacles
to clarifying information objectives. An examination
of the flaws in earlier information programs is in-
dispensable for appreciating the present problems
of the USIA.

The first official American information service
was the Committee on Public Information or the Creel
Committee, after its Chairman, George Creel. It was
authorized by President Wilson in 1917 for the purpose of intensifying domestic support for the war as
well as conducting propaganda operations. The record
of the Creel Committee is not particularly relevant
to the present discussion because it merely represented a two-year effort that was abolished with the
cessation of hostilities. Unlike the case of the
World War II Office of War Information (OWI), no permanent specialized government agency, such as the
Department of State, was left to continue the work of
representing the United States abroad. Yet even in
Creel's evaluation of his organization's limited campaign, one observes a confidence in the potency of

"truth" that would characterize subsequent American
attitudes toward the information program.

> Our effort was educational and in-
> formative throughout, for we had such
> confidence in our case as to feel that
> no other argument was needed than the
> simple, straightforward presentation
> of facts.[1]

The United States was the last major power to
develop an official program disseminating information
and culture abroad. The climate of isolationism between the world wars fortified the traditional national resolve to avoid engaging in these activities. Books carrying titles such as The Propaganda
Menace underscored the prevailing suspicion of
persuasion efforts of all sorts.[2] The decision to
sponsor an information program was motivated by the
growth of education and communications facilities
overseas. The threat to freedom posed by both
Nazism and Communism also demanded that the United
States make its presence felt abroad in the field
of international persuasion.

The United States embarked on this program in
1938 by creating a Division of Cultural Relations
in the Department of State and the appointment of
an Interdepartmental Committee on Cooperation with
the American Republics,which joined together thirteen government agencies. Even at the outset,
there appeared divergent notions as to objectives.
Basically, the disagreement concerned whether cultural and related undertakings should supplement
national foreign policies or whether they were
meritorious in their own right,lacking any ulterior
attachment to political schemes. Regarding cultural activities, the debate centered on whether
they should be in the form of "propaganda" or education. The sides were drawn, accordingly, before
the outbreak of World War II,in what represents
today the most classic point of disagreement over
the objectives of USIA--information or propaganda.
This issue has persisted for nearly three decades
following America's engagement in these activities.

In this debate, one view regarded the cultural
program as a means for promoting the Good Neighbor
Policy in Latin America. Under Secretary of State
Sumner Welles observed that the purpose of the Interdepartmental Committee was: ". . . to develop and
strengthen inter-American political solidarity, and
the economic and social well being of the Americas."[3]

Contrasting with this outlook was the position
of the Department's Division of Cultural Relations.
Its officers held that the cultural program must not
represent a shifting propaganda campaign. Instead,
the program should be a long-term one emphasizing
purely educational values. Exchanges should be
carried on for their own worth rather than for ulterior strategic designs. "Any implication of a tie-
in between cultural interchange and foreign policy
invalidates the effort of cultural activities."[4]

Notwithstanding these differences, the campaign launched by both the Department of State and
the Interdepartmental Committee grew increasingly
inadequate as the danger of war approached. In
August, 1940, the Office of the Coordinator of Inter-
American Affairs (CIAA) was set up,with Nelson A.
Rockefeller appointed Coordinator. His initial
authority went beyond foreign information or cultural
programs. He was to coordinate the activities of all
federal agencies and private undertakings,such as
business firms and charitable foundations,into an
integrated blueprint of inter-American activities.
The Coordinator was empowered to direct activities
of established agencies,as well as to devise programs
of his own.

In its overseas information program, CIAA was
handicapped through the coordination arrangements
with the Department of State. It took two years
for the CIAA to learn officially that below the
Presidency,control over political policy rested primarily with the Department. This decision was expressed in a letter from President Roosevelt to Mr.
Rockefeller. In order to achieve desirable central-
ization of responsibility for the conduct of foreign
relations, the President advised that the Coordinator:

> . . . take appropriate steps to institute
> arrangements for assuring that in all
> instances projects initiated by your
> Office shall be discussed fully with,
> and approved by, the Department of
> State, and a full meeting of minds
> obtained before action is undertaken
> or commitments made.[5]

Once the terms had been thus defined, both
agencies built up close coordination on policy and
operating levels. CIAA established a series of
liaisons much like those presently existing between
the USIA and the Department. High policy matters
were cleared with the Secretary or Under Secretary
at least once a week. For a time, regular weekly
meetings were held between officials of the CIAA
concerned with information operations and the staff
of the Department's Office of Public Information.
CIAA enjoyed Department support for its budget requests and efforts to maintain organizational independence.[6]

These arrangements, however, failed to be
uniformly harmonious or satisfactory for CIAA. In
this respect, CIAA shared the difficulties of the
Office of War Information (OWI), as will be argued
below. Although CIAA depended upon the Department
for fast-breaking specialized information about
Latin America, the Department was frequently slow
in fulfilling its requests. In Rockefeller's
judgment:

> . . . the Department is not giving the
> necessary policy direction to the
> other agencies of the Government
> with the result that it is impossi-
> ble for them to take the prompt
> action necessary to anticipate
> and meet problems as they arise.
> This very seriously affects the
> ability of this Government to
> give decisive leadership in an-
> ticipating and meeting the prob-
> lems affecting the unity of this

Hemisphere, except in those cases
where you, or the Under Secretary,
personally have stepped in to supply
this direction and leadership.[7]

In implementing information objectives, CIAA
was more overtly a propaganda operation than its
two predecessor agencies cited above. CIAA established propaganda priorities according to military
requirements or those of hemispheric solidarity.
Its diverse aims included countering Axis propaganda
and arousing support for the war effort from the
American republics. While this study will not attempt to evaluate the actual content of the CIAA information program, one must share Thomson's conclusion that it failed in reaching broad masses of the
population.[8] None of CIAA's arrangements for cultivating Latin American masses paralleled the care
which it took in keeping up to date a selected
group of more than 378,000 persons on its press and
publications mailing lists. The bulk of the population, it was believed, could be more effectively
reached through motion pictures.

With the deepening world crisis of the early
1940's, the United States turned its attention to
positive action in international information. In
appraising information objectives in this period,
it must be emphasized that the United States, as
Dyer put it, was "starting from scratch."[9] The
purpose in undertaking such an appraisal, however,
is to indicate the slight growth to the present in
the poignancy of information objectives.

While the USIA has operated in the absence of
total military warfare, the record of the American
persuasion program in World War II is highly relevant to the present inquiry. Lerner stresses that
psychological warfare is simply a special version
of the propaganda process. Essentially, it is the
same operation as in peacetime only modified by
certain transitions. During war, the competition
for a larger share of world power is publicly
declared to be unattainable through nonviolent modes
of intercourse, and the techniques of coercion are

invoked as the final arbiter of competing claims.

Psychological warfare, Lerner maintains, adapts
the techniques of symbol selection to the conditions
that its audience is an "enemy," that its purpose
must always include "victory," and that the stakes
of success in this contest are higher than usual.
Thus failures in war include death as a consequence,
whereas failures with nonviolent techniques usually
entail only loss of power and other lesser depriva-
tions.

> These adaptations are illuminating
> and important, but they indicate
> that the variations between prop-
> aganda and psychological warfare
> are mainly technical, whereas the
> function of both relative to the
> total flow of events in the polit-
> ical process (which includes both
> war and peace) remains constant.[10]

In order to consolidate the various information
programs set up in the early 1940's, President
Roosevelt established the Office of War Information
in 1942. Elmer Davis, its Director, acknowledged
that OWI was an auxiliary rather than the master of
American foreign policy. In this sense, he shared
the determination of every USIA Director to avoid
"empire-building" for the role of the information
program in foreign affairs.[11] This phenomenon has
not served in eliminating, however, the controversy
over information objectives.

Despite Davis' disclaimers, the struggle for
control of overseas propaganda between OWI and OSS
(Office of Strategic Services) was an integral part
of the wartime experiences of the United States.
The latter organization, headed by Colonel William
J. Donovan, was designated to take charge of all
functions of military psychological warfare, including propaganda. The basic distinction between
them was that the OWI was to concern itself with
"white" propaganda (that which could be attributed to
the United States Government), while one function of the

OSS was the supervision of unattributable propaganda.
Inasmuch as the USIA does not currently face coordination problems with a cloak-and-dagger operation
such as the OSS, this study will not treat in detail the relationship between the two wartime organizations.

The unsettled atmosphere in Washington during
this period was a factor which handicapped the
operations of the entire information community. For
example, in the early days of OWI, a War Information
Policy Committee was established. It met only three
times. At its first session, either the directors or
assistant secretaries of such agencies as the CIAA,
the War Production Board, the War Department, and
the Navy Department were present. But the Department of State sent only its public relations officer.
At the second meeting, the War and Navy units sent
their opposite numbers of the Department of State's
representative. At the third meeting, the representatives were all information chiefs. The committee was never convened a fourth time.

More serious, however, were the problems
affecting OWI in its relationships with the Presidency and the Executive departments. As previously
suggested, an overseas information program must be
closely attuned to the Chief Executive for policy
direction if the incumbent is a strong leader.
President Roosevelt was such a leader--and an ex-
cellent propagandist to boot--who went out of his
way to avoid identification with OWI. Some of the
most fundamental public opinion doctrines, such as
the Atlantic Charter, were reached without first
consulting OWI as to their possible effects abroad.12
In his account of OWI operations, Carroll relates
Roosevelt's lack of enthusiasm for that organization.

It was a curious fact--and I had con-
firmation of it later--that the President who established the Office of War
Information never knew what it was
doing and sometimes apparently confused
it with the Office of Censorship. He

had been opposed to the creation of
a propaganda service and had established
OWI with considerable reluctance . . .
Once the organization was established,
he did not want to be bothered about
it.[13]

In its arrangements with the Department of
State, OWI shared the main difficulties experienced
by CIAA. To begin with, the Department was suspicious of OWI as a result of its relations with the
FIS (Foreign Information Service), one of OWI's
predecessor organizations. The location of FIS in
New York presented coordination obstacles for the
Department in Washington. Many of FIS' staff held
the private newsman's distrust of government press
functions. They refused to accept the view that the
responsibilities of a government servant in wartime
differed from those of a private citizen. Domesti-
cally trained journalists did not necessarily sense
what material was of high audience appeal, inasmuch
as they projected their domestic standards upon
foreign groups. As a result, individual policy
judgments tended to outweigh willing acceptance of
orders from responsible higher authorities. Although
understanding of the Department's role steadily
mounted under the OWI, there remained, however, this
residue of ill feeling.

Underscoring the Department's attitude to OWI
was the position of Secretary of State Cordell Hull.
According to Carroll, he:

. . . knew even less than the President
about OWI and cared about it as much.
At times, he too, confused OWI with
censorship. "Why doesn't Elmer Davis
stop all this criticism of the State
Department?" he complained to a subordinate one day when the press was
being unkind.[14]

The Department had inadequately developed policy
and intelligence machinery for furnishing material for a fast media operation such as OWI.

In other instances, the needs of OWI were not clearly appreciated or considered of strategic worth by
the Department. While policy liaison was vested in
a special assistant for press relations, actual
questions usually were settled through consultation
with the Department's geographic offices. Coordination between the two organizations was more effective, however, in the field, particularly in the
European theater. As a result of this experience,
many members of the Department developed a favorable
view of information operations. OWI left competent
personnel and tested methods to the Department
following the war, due to the more compatible coordination arrangements overseas.

The absence of full-scale military conflict
in the USIA's fifteen-year existence has not raised
coordination issues for the Agency in this area.
Nonetheless, it must be stressed that during World
War II, OWI's task was complicated by reluctant
cooperation from the military. OWI often was forced
to rely upon its British counterpart for information
concerning military strategy. The British Political
Warfare Executive (PWE) was a recognized member of
the British operation and,as such,was furnished with
detailed knowledge of allied plans.[15] It was for-
tunate for OWI that there existed such an indirect
source of illumination on its own nation's activities.

To most effectively implement strategic objectives,OWI either established or inherited advisory
committees. These committees--much more numerous
than those serving the USIA--included such groups
as the Advisory Committee for Negro Newspaper
Publishers, the Sixteen-Millimeter Advisory Committee
dealing with documentary motion pictures, and the
Book Advisory Committee.[16] The panels were not used
to develop techniques for overseas operations. Their
main contribution was supplying OWI with private
advice on such politically delicate matters as
choosing lists of books for translation or distribution abroad. Similarly, the chief advisory unit
for the USIA today, the U.S. Advisory Commission on
Information, does not directly participate in policy
formation. It was shown in the preceding chapter,

however, that there is a substantial body of Americans engaged in communications media favoring an expansion of this unit's contributions.

Regarding content, OWI engaged in both propaganda and information operations.[17] OWI's problems in determining which of the two approaches was superior are similar to those presently facing the USIA. As defined by OWI, "propaganda" referred to the use of instruments of mass communication in direct or close connection with politico-military campaigns. Such propaganda related to the most controversial war activities. The content of these materials was always closely adapted to specific objectives.

Information activities, by contrast, were not so closely involved with war issues. Although the media were often similar, the content of information materials was selected especially for reinforcing favorable impressions of the United States in allied, neutral or liberated territories. The information approach relied more heavily on indirect devices, such as the exchange of persons, or specialized library services for influential overseas opinion. Information also included a larger percentage of ostensibly unfavorable data about the United States.

In determining OWI tactics, a continuing problem was its effort to manipulate news or truthful material for propaganda objectives. According to Elmer Davis, OWI never overtly misrepresented the truth while disseminating material abroad. Yet OWI exercised discretion in choosing which aspect of the truth to incorporate in its program. He explained:

> Now, while our work overseas is
> frankly propaganda, directed to the
> end of a speedier and more complete
> victory, we stick to the truth abroad
> as well at home. . . But in our over-
> seas propaganda we do not tell the
> truth just for fun . . . We tell a true

> story to every area; but to each one
> we tell the kind of story that will
> best serve our interests.
>
> We do our best to stick to the truth.
> We cannot give all the truth because
> in certain cases, for reasons of
> military security, we have to agree
> to the holding back of a certain
> amount of military information . . .
> We do not consciously add anything
> to the truth.[18]

The decision to limit OWI content to the truth
enabled the Agency to escape certain operating problems. Much strife persisted, however, concerning
which representation of the United States would most
poignantly serve the war effort. In balancing factual material, in both information and propaganda,
OWI faced charges that it had wasted funds on unes-
sential activities. The process of "projecting
America" was more difficult for the Agency than many
questions relating to the actual story of the war.
The organization was forced to persuade outside observers that particular entertainment material was
necessary for a vital overseas operation.

On the domestic front, particularly, OWI was
exposed to this brand of criticism. Congress was
continually suspicious over the possibility that
OWI might alter the structure of domestic politics
and affect election contests. At times, Republican
legislators would accuse OWI of serving as a publicity office of the New Deal. OWI budgetary hearings
served as the main occasion for Congress to express
its displeasure in this regard.[19] According to
Carroll, Elmer Davis and his chief assistants were
forced to spend "half their time" defending the
organization at such hearings. Meanwhile, the Axis
powers were devoting their full energies to perfect-
ing their persuasion instruments.

In short, the OWI policy-maker was not completely free to balance presentation and output
from either an ideological or propagandistic stand-

point. As part of its program, OWI had to assure
influential groups, both within and without government, of fair treatment. The organizational impediments experienced by OWI were much like those currently confronting the USIA--only worse, given the
circumstances of a world war and the lack of confidence of the military in OWI. The USIA's problems
of foreign policy determination and coordination
with other Executive departments, as set forth
earlier in this book, are fundamentally those encountered by the OWI some two decades ago.

POSTWAR DEVELOPMENTS IN INFORMATION OBJECTIVES

The objectives of the information program from
the end of the war through the founding of the USIA
in 1953 were determined by the nation's shifting
prospects in international affairs. If it appeared
that the political climate augured peace, the information program would emphasize long-term dispassionate themes of American life. If the future appeared
tense, especially as it related to the growth of
Communism, the information program would disseminate
material stressing American foreign objectives.
This section will attempt to describe the fluctua-
tions in the information program's objectives during
this period.

Following the war, President Truman acknowledged the worth of the overseas information program
by setting up the Interim International Information
Service (IIIS) in the Department of State in August,
1945. Archibald MacLeish, recently named to the new
post of Assistant Secretary in charge of public and
cultural affairs, headed the operation. IIIS was
conceived as an instrument of international understanding rather than American propaganda. Moreover,
the Executive Order setting up IIIS assumed that it
would be a relatively small-scale operation. According to President Truman:

> This government will not attempt to
> outstrip the extensive and growing
> information programs of other nations.

> Rather it will endeavor to see to it
> that other peoples receive a full and
> fair picture of American life and the
> aims and policies of the United States
> Government.20

As will be argued below, both these provisions were
modified in succeeding years.

In 1946, the information program underwent one
of the many reorganizations which characterized its
career prior to the creation of the USIA. The Office
of International Information and Cultural Affairs
(OIC) assumed many of the functions of IIIS on a
substantially reduced basis. William Benton was
appointed Assistant Secretary of State for the program. Secretary Benton's statement of information
objectives represented a modification of Truman's
view,noted above. The Benton position hardly clar-
ified, however, the ongoing debate as to whether
the United States should stress information or propaganda. According to Secretary Benton, the scope of
an undertaking such as OIC must not be merely one of
good-will activities. It must be designed to support American foreign policy in its long-range sense
and to serve as an instrument of that policy.

> I am against any indiscriminate,
> miscellaneous campaign aimed to
> develop so-called "good-will."
> All programs abroad in the field
> of so-called "cultural relations"
> should be designed to support
> United States foreign policy in
> its long-range sense and to serve
> as an arm of that policy. Many
> of the programs will, I trust, be
> educational and humanitarian in
> the highest sense. But his is
> not a bill to create and legiti-
> matize Uncle Santa Claus. 21

The objectives of the information program were
further compounded at this time due to Secretary
Benton's inept testimony before Congress. He used

broad generalities in describing and justifying his program. He failed (or was not allowed) to explain clearly to the Foreign Relations, Foreign Affairs, or Appropriations Committees of both Houses how concrete operations helped in achieving specific objectives. His testimony did not adequately demonstrate how such potentially embarrassing activities as modern art exhibitions served to advance American foreign policy. 22

In the fall of 1947, following a reorganization as a result of reductions in appropriations, OIC was transferred to the Office of International Information and Educational Exchange (OIE), in the Department of State. 23 This Office was concerned with administering the recently passed Fulbright Act and other educational exchange programs, relationships with binational institutes abroad, and the reduced radio (VOA), press, and motion picture operations.

Congressional hearings on OIE indicated once more the contrasting beliefs regarding the objectives of this undertaking. According to General George C. Marshall, then Secretary of State, the program would do well by avoiding propaganda implications. He argued that it was necessary for people overseas to believe implicitly in American pronouncements. Likewise, Secretary Benton maintained that OIE should present a "mirror" of American life rather than a "showcase" displaying only favorable aspects.

This dispassionate approach was questioned, however, by Congressman John Davis Lodge. He argued that if hostile foreign attitudes were to be combated some selection of facts would be inevitable. Consequently, the American position must be presented with conviction and passion.

These divergent viewpoints were carried over into debate relating to the Smith-Mundt Act (U.S. Public Information and Educational Exchange Act-- Public Law 402). While this measure was designed as a definitive statement of the information program, its passage was marked by intense disagreement. The Act itself is one of the basic measures upon which

the activities of the USIA are rooted. Its objectives were:

> . . . to promote a better understanding of
> the United States in other countries,
> and to increase mutual understanding
> between the people of the United States
> and the people of other countries.[24]

Among the means of achieving these goals was an information service making available to foreign people
knowledge about the United States (Section 501).
The Act also considerably determined the nature of
overseas educational exchanges.

Despite the Soviet Union's heightened attacks
on American policies, the Smith-Mundt Act did not
call for an outright propaganda program. The measure represented, according to Oren M. Stephens,
another of the "roller-coaster ups and downs" of the
information program. Its language reflected the
attitude of previous years,when the emphasis was on
"a full and fair picture" of the United States.
Stephens found it an unsatisfactory attempt to clarify information objectives. The envisaged program was as defensive as it was unrealistic.

> It was a holding action. It was based
> on the assumption, dubious at best,
> that if other people understood us,
> they would like us, and if they do not
> like us, they would do what we wanted
> them to do.[25]

Following enactment of the Smith-Mundt Act,
the information program was again reorganized. OIE
was broken down into two offices: the Office of
International Information (OIE), to administer mass
media functions; and the Office of Educational Exchange (OEX), to administer the exchange-of-persons
operations and the support of libraries and institutions. Both offices were under the Assistant
Secretary of State for Public Affairs, George V.
Allen.

A veteran diplomat, Assistant Secretary Allen also served as Director of the USIA from November, 1957, through December, 1960. In both posts he aimed at clarifying the distinct contributions of the information program to over-all strategy. Emphasizing the value of overseas information as a long-range policy instrument, he criticized its worth in meeting day-to-day problems. The "American Way" of foreign persuasion, Secretary Allen stressed, is through voicing arguments so that they appear in the best interests of the populations concerned. This approach differs from both brainwashing and the forced inculcation of belief.[26]

His two experiences with the information program, however, left Assistant Secretary Allen distressed regarding its performance.

> I am convinced, after twelve years of
> close concern with the question both
> at home and overseas, that our broad-
> casts in foreign languages and our
> programs specifically prepared for a
> particular audience are largely a
> waste of time and effort.[27]

Essentially, Secretary Allen attributed this failure to the persistent notion that the USIA must serve as a propaganda organization. Such a view minimizes the chief responsibility of the Agency--that of achieving a clearer understanding abroad of the American people, their character and institutions. If the functions of the information program were properly conceived, members of Congress, he held, would no more think of calling upon the Agency "to throw the book at Castro," for instance, than it would of asking the Associated Press, the New York Public Library, or the Rockefeller Foundation to do so.

Notwithstanding Assistant Secretary Allen's strictures, colleagues cite his contributions in bringing clarity to the program's objectives.[28] His first administration, in particular, was marked by noteworthy advances in elucidating the relationship between information and foreign policy. The estab-

lishment of a separate office for the education program also indicated evolving opinion concerning
overseas information. Increasingly, educators demanded that such "nonpolitical" projects as OEX be
removed from the area of American propaganda.
Senator Smith spoke in support of the educators.
"Educational exchange, service . . . to be truly
effective, must be objective, nonpolitical, and
above all have no possible propaganda implications."[29]

The death blow to the assumption of the Smith-
Mundt Act--that international understanding would
flourish simply through a long-term dispassionate
American information program--was the launching of
the "Campaign of Truth." Soviet hostility and the
Korean invasion brought the issue of information
objectives to a head for the United States. The
"Campaign of Truth" was to be a psychological offensive against Soviet propaganda. According to Edward
R. Barrett, then Assistant Secretary of State for
Public Affairs, its aims were to establish a healthy
international community, counter foreign misconcep-
tions of the United States, deter the Soviet Union
from further encroachments, and push back existing
Soviet influence by all means short of war.[30]

President Truman stressed that the "Campaign
of Truth" would differ from previous American peacetime programs. It would have definite goals advancing American security.

> We must make ourselves known as we
> really are--not as Communist prop-
> aganda pictures us. We must pool
> our efforts with those of the other
> free peoples in a sustained, inten-
> sified program to promote the cause
> of freedom against the propaganda
> of slavery. We must make ourselves
> heard around the world in a great
> campaign of truth.[31]

It is noteworthy that Congress expressed a more
heightened appreciation of the information program
in circumstances of international crises such as

these than during periods of relative tranquility.
The Communist invasion of Korea motivated Congress
to increase drastically the information program's
appropriations. In addition to the regular appropriation of $32.7 million already approved for the
1951 fiscal year, a supplemental request brought an
additional grant of $79 million plus $19.6 million
in counterpart funds. In all, the dollar support
for the program in the 1951 fiscal year amounted to
two-and-a-half times that of 1950, and four times
that of 1949, the first year of complete operations
under the previously discussed Smith-Mundt Act.

The sharpest increases under the propaganda
offensive were for mass media--radio, press, and
motion pictures. According to Assistant Secretary
Barrett, earlier information programs failed in
reaching the masses, where the "raw material" for
Communism was so often found. Insofar as the
campaign was to be more intensive than predecessor
programs, it was designed to include foreign masses.
Hitherto American postwar information efforts con-
centrated on the elites. Secretary Barrett observed:

> It was not getting out enough beyond
> the major cities. It was still too
> heavily concentrated on the upper
> crust. This was defensible in a few
> nations where an elite group dominated
> everything. Certainly it was under-
> standable, since the world-wide infor-
> mation and exchange-of-persons program,
> including the Voice of America, was
> costing less than General Motors spends
> on its public relations and its adver-
> tising. But the fact remained that the
> program was not penetrating deep enough,
> nor reaching out far enough into the
> provinces of most countries.[32]

Thus, the objectives of the information program took
on new clarity under political crises. While it was
possible to ignore the masses in peace, such an
approach was inexcusable during international tension.

To be sure, the new strategy rested on international events in themselves, rather than upon the
suggestions of such official bodies as the United
States Advisory Commission on Information. Were it
not for the Korean conflict, it appears that the
Congress would have disregarded the Commission's
recommendations for more funds for OII--recommenda-
tions which characterize nearly every Report. At
the war's beginning, the Commission, interestingly
enough, endorsed a rise in appropriations so as to
enable the program to cultivate foreign "understanding" of the United States.

> As you are aware, the Commission since
> its organization has called attention
> to the anomaly which exists by reason
> of the expenditure of fifteen billions
> of dollars a year on defense, five to
> six and a half billions a year on
> economic and foreign aid and, this
> year, a little over thirty million
> dollars on our total information and
> education program designed to make
> the rest of the world understand our
> purposes.[33]

Increasingly ignored or contradicted during
the "Campaign of Truth," however, were pronouncements that the objectives of the information program
were to enhance mutual understanding. Even the educational exchanges and other cultural activities
modified their objectives, involving compromises
with earlier principles. The Advisory Commission on
Educational Exchange was one such unit which brought
its program more into line with the unilateral goals
of the "Campaign of Truth." Previous to the campaign, the Commission maintained that the program
must not represent an effort by the United States
to "Americanize" other nations. The objectives of
exchanges were not to make friends for the United
States. Rather, they advanced American foreign
policy through "bringing about growing understanding
of American life, confidence in this country's
broad objectives, and a desire to be associated
with her in working toward these ends."[34]

Upon the origin of the "Campaign of Truth,"
however, the aims of educational exchanges were
brought more into accord with the new unilateral goal
of the information program. The Commission defined
the objectives of these exchanges as keeping alive
the spirit of cooperation among free nations,
strengthening resistance to Communism in countries
under threat of infiltration or aggression, and
weakening the power of Communism in areas under domination of the U.S.S.R. The purposes of this program
as expressed by the independent Commission and by the
foregoing statement of the "Campaign of Truth" by
Secretary Barrett are therefore remarkably similar.

The U.S. Advisory Commission on Information
also favored the new exposition of information objectives. It conceded that these objectives underwent a "marked" change since the appointment of the
Commission in 1948. Essentially, it represented a
shift from an adequate and fair picture of the
United States to one of "hard-hitting propaganda."

> By mid-1950 it was apparent that the
> United States should take the propa-
> ganda offensive, centering its atten-
> tion on the prevention of the further
> spread of Communism and the weakening
> of Communist organizations wherever
> they exist. The determination to
> fight fire with fire, to immunize
> large groups of people against the
> viruses of Communism gave the infor-
> mation program an entirely new aspect.[35]

While the "Campaign of Truth" clearly contradicted earlier statements of information objectives,
it stimulated a more precise formulation of tactics.
Among its contributions were the classification of
different countries according to the strength of
strategic importance to the United States, the selection of target groups abroad, and the choice of the
most effective materials and media for reaching those
groups. The experience with this campaign was
valuable in the future, for it indicated that information objectives must take account of America's

political responsibilities in the Cold War. Recognition of this need contributed to the eventual
creation of an independent USIA. Citing this future
consideration in his appraisal of the campaign's
success, Secretary Barrett noted:

> The campaign at least has begun to put
> Soviet propagandists on the defensive.
> And the whole operation had attained
> a scale and scope much greater than
> ever before in peace-time--and more
> in keeping with the enormous job yet
> to be done.[36]

The first significant attempt at clarifying
the information program's objectives following the
"Campaign of Truth" was its reorganization in the
Department of State. The reorganizations had become so habitual by then that Oren Stephens, a
veteran of many, observed:

> . . . workers in the program complained
> that they spent the first half of each
> year recovering from the last reorgan-
> ization and the second half planning
> for the next one.[37]

The present reorganization consolidated OII and OEX
under the International Information Administration
(IIA). The Administrator of IIA,who was to report
directly to the Secretary and Under Secretary of
State, possessed greater administrative authority
than any earlier head of the information operation.

According to the Committee on Foreign Relations,
the Assistant Secretary for Public Affairs was reduced to a simple "channel" for coalescing foreign
policy and information policy. These arrangements
were to allow for more participation by the Administrator in the formulation of information policy.
They broadened the Administrator's authority over
the program's overseas resources and such administrative services of the organization as budgeting,
facilities, and manpower.

Notwithstanding these changes, Dr. Wilson Compton reported, one year after assuming the office of Administrator, that "semi-autonomy" in the Department left much to be desired. He found the new approach lacking in its provisions for the selection, assignment, and management of information personnel. It also failed to arrange for satisfactory financing of the information program. To attain the semi-autonomy implied in the creation of the IIA would require the consolidation of responsibilities which previously had been widely dispersed. Dr. Compton blamed the Department for a reluctance to accept these changes and if not a resistance, at least a "formidable inertia" to them.[38]

In addition to the information program's coordination problems within the Department, it experienced difficulties in aligning its activities with other Executive agencies. As a unit of the Department, the information program was a party to its parent body's conflicts with agencies similarly concerned with political communication. The Department of State's chief competitor in this area was the Department of Defense. Basically, the dispute over each organization's role in political communication stemmed from the issue of ultimate responsibility for national security. President Truman established the Psychological Strategy Board (PSB) in June, 1951, in an effort to coordinate these operations at the policy-making level. Significantly, the word "information" never appeared in his directive. Regular members of the Board were the Under Secretary of State, the Deputy Secretary of Defense, and the Director of the Central Intelligence Agency. Other agencies participated as needed. Little that is specific concerning the work of the PSB has been made public. The Foreign Relations Committee's investigation of the overseas information program concluded, however, that the Board failed to effectively discharge its functions. Despite the "loosely drawn" Executive Order, the Committee found that each of the component agencies of the Board continued "to go their separate ways" in matters of psychological policy.[39]

The frequent reorganizations and uncertain status of the information program were becoming a deep source of perplexity to those congressmen concerned with the program's objectives. Senator Pat McCarran, Chairman of the Senate Subcommittee dealing with appropriations for the program, for one, was motivated to address a series of questions to the Secretary of State on "The Objectives of the U.S. Information Program." It may be assumed that Senator McCarran's disconcernment was representative of that of his colleagues.

> During the past several years, the Appropriations Subcommittee of the Department of State, Justice, Commerce and the Judiciary has heard a tremendous amount of testimony about the objectives of the U.S. Information and Cultural Program (now termed the International Information Administration). At the time this matter was before the subcommittee last season, I became most concerned as to what these objectives are. I felt, and still do, that a program of this kind must have clear and concise goals in order to accomplish its assigned mission. Hours of testimony before the subcommittee had failed to bring out exactly what these objectives were.[40]

As a result of the information program's unsettled objectives, a series of studies were carried out in 1953 that appreciably determined the nature of the current USIA. The program had become an issue in the Presidential campaign, and General Eisenhower declared that if elected, he would strengthen its effectiveness. In his State of the Union Message of February 2, 1953, the new President stressed that a dynamic information program was essential to the security of the United States and the free world.

He appointed a committee to study the field
of political communication with the intention of
eliminating much of the confusion regarding its role
in American foreign policy. Officially titled the
"President's Committee on International Information
Activities," it was known as the Jackson Committee,
after its Chairman, William H. Jackson. The direction of its thinking is clearly indicated in a
forceful statement regarding the relationship between
psychological activities and foreign policy. It
noted that these activities are effective insofar
as they tie in with official policies and operations.

> In reality, there is a "psychological"
> aspect or implication to every diplomatic,
> economic, or military policy and action.
> . . . Except for propaganda there are no
> "psychological warfare" instruments
> distinct from traditional instruments
> of policy. Every significant act of
> virtually every department and agency
> of Government has its effect, either
> positively or negatively, in the global
> struggle for freedom.[41]

The Report took a compromise position between
the propagandistic intent of the "Campaign of Truth"
and the "full and fair" picture approach of the
Smith-Mundt Act. On the one hand, it observed that
the primary purpose of the information program is
to submit evidence to peoples of other nations that
their aspirations are supported by the United States.
On the other, it emphasized that the United States
should be objective and factual in carrying out
this purpose.

> American broadcasts and printed
> materials should concentrate on ob-
> jective, factual news reporting,
> with particular selection and
> treatment of news designed to pre-
> sent a full exposition of United
> States actions and policies . . .
> The tone and content should be force-
> ful and direct, but a propagandist

note should be avoided. The information
services should not, however, be pre-
cluded from making forceful and factual
refutations of false Soviet accusations.[42]

Accordingly, such a focus would concentrate on
projects stressing bonds of mutual interest between
the United States and other nations. Secondly, as
Thomson and Laves, students of the United States
foreign cultural program, observe, it would require
a shift of emphasis in information activities, where
primary attention had been devoted to the Communist
countries--two thirds of the radio budget going into
broadcasts directed behind the Iron and Bamboo Cur-
tains--while presentation to friendly and neutral
nations of the United States objectives had taken
second place.[43]

With reference to policy coordination, the
Jackson Committee recommended the program be retained
in the Department of State. Since information policy
did not exist apart from national strategy, the para-
mount need was for a coordinating authority for all
national security programs. Such coordination in
Washington, it argued, would encourage the strengthening of coordination in American missions abroad.

The Committee proposed the creation, within
the structure of the National Security Council, of
an Operations Coordinating Board (OCB), whose
chief function would be coordinating departmental
schemes for national security. The members of the
Board were to be the Under Secretary of State, the
Deputy Secretary of Defense, the Director of the
Foreign Operations Administration, the Director of
the Central Intelligence Agency, and the Special
Assistant to the President for Psychological Warfare. While the Director of the USIA was authorized to attend its meetings in September, 1953,
it was not until 1955 that he was formally appointed
to membership.

The OCB was abolished in the early days of
the Kennedy Administration. Like the PSB, this unit
failed in coordinating information objectives. The
members of OCB served first and foremost as depart-

mental representatives, and only secondarily as part
of a board designed to integrate strategic policies.
Since unanimity was required for OCB decisions, it
was possible for any member to veto proposed action
in the field of political communication.

A more revolutionary solution to the problem
was advanced in the February, 1953, Report of the
U.S. Advisory Commission on Information. Its principal recommendation was that:

> . . . IIA be lifted out of the Department
> of State and placed in a new agency of
> Cabinet level in which there is vested
> authority to formulate psychological
> strategy and to coordinate information
> policies of all Government agencies and
> consolidate all overseas information
> programs.[44]

The Commission placed much of the onus for the information effort's failure on the Department of State.
Information officials, it argued, faced "internal
resistance and misunderstandings" within the Department regarding the program. They were hampered
by the establishment of procedures and traditions
developed for the purpose of political diplomacy
rather than information. Moreover, there had been
a "singular lack of enthusiasm and imagination" in
the Department's management of the program.

The Commission found that the administration
of the information program was handicapped through
its association with the Department. The parent
body had reserved the right to use funds from this
program to build up staff and facilities in its non-
information branches. In this sense, it affirmed
Dr. Compton's observation, cited earlier in this
study. The Commission noted that for a four-year
period, only one of the Department's supergrade
positions was assigned to IIA.

The present arrangement also prevented the
coordination of information policy of government
agencies outside the Department. In this regard,

the Commission took exception to the Department's
claim that control of the information program was
necessary for the prompt and authoritative transmis-
sion of policy decisions. It stressed that many of
the policies specified in Public Law 402 (Smith-Mundt
Act), which the information program is charged with
transmitting overseas, were reached outside the Department.

> The real point of final foreign policy
> determination and reconciliation is the
> White House. Only a voice speaking from
> that level can make an objective, bal-
> anced, nonconflicting exposition of
> American policy. 45

Finally, the Commission proposed an independent
agency as a means of consolidating the overseas information services of all government agencies. At
the time of its investigation, five government agencies were sponsoring information programs abroad.
Notwithstanding the attempts to coordinate the information activities of these agencies, both in
Washington and abroad, the Commission reported that
they failed to function as an all-American team.
It related the lack of unity in the field to the
absence of a coordinating agency at home.

Concurrent with the Advisory Commission's
investigation were the hearings conducted by the
Senate Committee on Foreign Relations on the "Overseas Information Programs of the United States."
The Committee's findings were similarly critical of
the information effort. The Committee's Report
concluded that the principal weaknesses of the
information program were ineffective coordination
of psychological policy, and duplication and competition in information activities of American
agencies abroad. Five major reorganizations and
five administrators in the past five years were
found to have reduced the program's effectiveness
and stability.

The Report emphasized that lack of administrative continuity prevented the sharpening of information objectives. These shifts in direction

were responsible for an absence of common understanding as to its objectives on the part of the Administration, Congress, and the American people. Frequently, public affairs officers appeared to distort
the legislative purpose of the program beyond even
the most liberal interpretation. At some posts, the
objectives stated in Public Law 402 were strained to
cover activities of a kind which appeared remote
from the original intent of the Smith-Mundt Act.

> This diversity of interpretation and
> understanding of purpose leads to
> costly, ineffective and sometimes
> questionable activities at many posts.
> It frequently resolves itself into
> superabundant activity calculated to
> satisfy everyone's concept of what
> overseas information should be but
> which instead confuses. The committee
> is convinced that a prime reason for
> the recurrent outbursts of criticisms
> and consequent instability of this
> program has been the administrative
> failure to develop among partici-
> pating personnel a clear and uniform
> understanding of the aims of the
> program.[46]

The Senate Committee blamed the indifferent administration of the Department for the confusion regarding information objectives. It shared the
Advisory Commission on Information's criticism of
the Department's personnel shortcomings in this
area.

As for strengthening the in formation effort,
however, the Senate Committee failed to propose the
immediate creation of an independent agency, as did
the Advisory Commission. The Senate Committee recommended that the IIA be allowed greater autonomy
in the Department for a one-year trial period.
Should this arrangement prove uneventful, it proposed
the establishment of a separate agency. Significantly, the Report opposed removing the exchange-of-
persons program from the Department. In this re-

124 THE U.S. INFORMATION AGENCY

spect, the Foreign Relations Committee echoed the
traditional American distrust of persuasion programs--
whether they be in the area of information or propaganda. It feared the

> . . . likelihood of the loss of prestige
> and nonpropagandistic reputation which
> now attaches to the program if it is part
> of an independent information agency.
> These are essential attributes if the
> exchange program is to continue to
> attract the type of distinguished
> cooperation both at home and abroad
> which is necessary to its effective
> operation.[47]

While the Foreign Relations Committee and the
Advisory Commission on Information were conducting
their aforesaid appraisals, many Americans were
growing steadily alarmed over the spread of Communism. These alarms came to a climax in the hearings held by Senator Joseph R. McCarthy as Chairman
of the Permanent Subcommittee on Investigations of
the Senate Committee on Government Operations.
Initiated in the early days of the Eisenhower Administration, the hearings were concerned with the
activities of many government agencies. Eventually,
they focused upon the overseas radio program, government libraries or information centers abroad, and
the books they contained.

The McCarthy episode represented an aberration
in the evolution of information objectives. Although
this study has stressed the confusion regarding these
objectives, the hearings do not deserve attention
for this matter alone. The McCarthy experience is
noteworthy, primarily as the most flagrant effort to
apply narrow political criteria to information activities in the program's history.[48]

Several years before the launching of the
McCarthy investigation, serious study had been given
to using material in the official information and
cultural exchange program by alleged members and
sympathizers of the Communist Party. For example,

the Committee on Books Abroad, serving as a subcommittee of the Advisory Commission on Educational
Exchange, weighed the desirability of including in
overseas libraries "controversial publications" by
authors of suspect loyalty. In May, 1952, it stated
that any book whatsoever of U.S. origin deserved to
be made available abroad.49

Dr. Wilson Compton, then Administrator of the
International Information Administration (IIA),
argued, however, that the character and reputation
of the author must at least be viewed as a secondary
factor. A directive issued shortly before the
McCarthy investigation maintained that materials by
authors of questionable ideology should be distributed only in exceptional cases. Thus, the directive
opposed the view that works of controversial authors
be barred irrespective of their content.

Once the McCarthy investigation got under way,
careful study of this issue was rejected for a policy attempting to shut off completely material dealing with Communism. This approach reached its nadir
in directives of March 17 and April 23, 1953. The
first statement stressed the banning of books in
American overseas libraries by authors who were
Communist or who belonged to "Communist fronts."
Single issues of magazines containing "anything
detrimental to this country's objectives" were to
be removed from circulation. The latter directive
required the banning of books by authors refusing
to testify before Congressional committees on alleged
Communist affiliation.

According to Dizard, an information officer
at the time, the investigation had the following
impact on the program:

> During the black days of the spring
> of 1953, the organization sagged and
> groaned to a halt. There was little
> direction to the operations and no
> inclination on the part of the under-
> lings to start anything. The Campaign
> of Truth crusade was stopped short.

> Many of the shiny knights who initiated
> it had fled or been voted out of office
> while the troops left behind were wonder-
> ing what they were doing in this army.[50]

Eventually the tide turned against McCarthy
due to forthright stands by his senatorial colleagues
and independent organizations concerned with educational and library operations. Among the latter was
a manifesto by the American Library Association on
June 25, 1953, entitled "The Freedom to Read."
Asserting that freedom to read is essential to
American democracy, it urged a return to the tradition of the free and open mind. An accompanying
statement declared that overseas libraries do not
belong to a Congressional committee or the Department of State, but to the whole American people,who
are entitled to have them express their highest
ideals of responsible freedom.[51]

From a more practical standpoint, the Advisory
Commission warned of damage to information objectives
through such episodes as the McCarthy investigation.
An agency constantly under attack, it held, turns
cautious, anxious, prosaic, and inefficient. Those
who prepare messages for overseas distribution per-
force become concerned as to how the messages will
appear to the investigator. They lose sight of
whether they will be effective with their intended
audience. This situation is all the more vicious
when each employee fears his fellow workers, as
happened during the investigation. The effect on
foreign populations must also be considered in
assessing such investigations, the Commission warned.

> When these people hear through our
> media of communication, constant re-
> ports of attacks upon the Information
> Agency, challenges directed against
> it for supposed failures, inadequacies,
> poor techniques, poor programming, etc.,
> how can we expect them to have any
> confidence in an Agency which does
> not enjoy the confidence of those
> responsible Government officials who

seem constantly to be attacking it.52

Despite a detrimental impact on information objectives, the McCarthy investigation hastened the program's movement out of the Department of State. The incoming Secretary, John Foster Dulles, favored freeing the Department from the operational responsibility of disseminating information. The McCarthy hearings further cemented the views of Department officials seeking the institutional separation of policy and operating activities. Robert L. Johnson, the new administrator of the information and cultural program joined Secretary Dulles in urging its transfer from the Department. Mr. Johnson argued:

> . . . the creation of a separate agency
> will assure these things: (1) A greater
> flexibility, (2) a singleness of pur-
> pose, (3) a sharper, faster approach,
> and (4) a better chance to attract high-
> ly qualified people.53

President Eisenhower sent to Congress, on June 1, 1953, Reorganization Plan No. 8 which, after Congressional hearings, came into effect on August 1, establishing the present USIA. The hearings reveal, once more, divergent opinions regarding the objectives of an official information program. Operationally, there appeared concern that separation of the two organizations would harm the USIA's ability to interpret current foreign policy. Advocates of the transfer maintained that the benefit of an information organization speaking with an independent voice would outweigh problems of policy coordination.

Significantly, the USIA was to control information and library activities of the Department, as well as the information functions of the Mutual Security Agency. The innovation provided for the Department's retention of educational exchanges. No attempt was made, however, to keep books and libraries, long companions to educational exchanges in the cultural field, in the Department. According to Thomson and Laves, the explanation for this illogical separation may have been that:

> The McCarthy onslaught had made the
> libraries a "hot potato," and some
> partisans of educational exchange
> may not have wished to invite attack
> by a link with that activity.[54]

Accordingly, cultural officers of the Department were
made responsible to the USIA in the field. The
union of the two in the embassies belied the alleged
necessity of separation that had been insisted upon
in Washington. The distinction between information
and cultural activities was not implemented at its
most significant level, that of personal contact
overseas.

In conclusion, information objectives suffered
from haphazard direction, neglect, and inconsistent
application prior to the creation of an independent
USIA. While the organization has shown greater pur-
posefulness than it did in the Department of State,
the problems concerning information objectives remain unchanged. To be sure, Agency objectives today
are more long-range and multilateral than was the
case under the "Campaign of Truth." Likewise, information officers do not encounter the suspicious
scrutiny of the McCarthy era. In contrast to propaganda of the old variety, the educational and
cultural aspects of the USIA have been increasingly
stressed. The People-to-People movement launched
by the USIA in 1956 is one such effort enabling
Americans and foreigners to widen their horizons.
The changing character of Communist competition--
especially that of the Soviet Union, which highlights
"peaceful coexistence"--has also been a factor in
eliminating USIA bombast for programs promoting
international understanding.

Nevertheless, the confusion regarding the Agency
role is no less substanital today than it was at the
Agency's establishment in 1953. The problems of
undefined information objectives, inadequate recognition from the foreign affairs community, and misunderstanding by the Congress have persisted to
the present. Organizational autonomy, of itself,
has not produced an information program commensurate

with the international position of the United States.

NOTES TO CHAPTER 2

1. George Creel, How We Advertised America (New York: Harper & Bros., 1920), p. 5.

2. See Frederick E. Lumley, The Propaganda Menace (New York: The Century Co., 1933), for an indication of this viewpoint.

3. U.S. Congress, House Subcommittee on the Departments of State, Justice, Commerce, the Judiciary, and Related Agencies of the Committee on Appropriations, Hearings, 78th Cong., 2d sess., 1944, p. 203.

4. U.S. Department of State, Division of Cultural Relations, Minutes of General Advisory Committee, February 23-24, 1943 (mimeographed), p. 9.

5. History of the Office of the Coordinator of Inter-American Affairs (Washington, D.C.: Bureau of the Budget, 1947), pp. 280-81. Earlier, the history noted in great understatement that "A certain amount of guidance for the information program came from sources outside the Agency, such as the State Department and the Office of War Information" (p. 83).

6. Thomson, op. cit., p. 144.

7. History of the Office of the Coordinator of Inter-American Affairs, p. 184-86.

8. Thomson, op. cit., p. 150.

9. Dyer, op. cit., p. 98.

10. Daniel Lerner, Sykewar: Psychological Warfare Against Germany, D-Day to VE-Day (New York: George W. Stewart, 1949), p. 6.

11. Elmer Davis, "War Information," in Propaganda in War and Crisis, p. 274.

12. Dyer, op. cit., pp. 103-4.

13. Wallace Carroll, Persuade or Perish
(Boston: Houghton Mifflin Co., 1948), p. 7. By
contrast, he expressed much confidence in the OSS.
"Under President Roosevelt, General Donovan had a
free hand, ample funds and unlimited authority in
the espionage and sabotage field. This was all
basic to success. But he had as well the complete
confidence of the President." Robert Hayden Alcorn,
No Bugle for Spies: Tales of the OSS (New York:
David McKay Co., 1962), p. 192.

14. Ibid.

15. Dyer, op. cit., p. 105. Dyer further
argues that for the United States the relationship between the military and information
program in the Korean conflict was no less confusing than the World War II experience (pp. 113-16).

16. See Thomson, op. cit., p. 35, for the
complete list of these committees.

17. According to Dizard, OWI material was
often bland and innocuous, regardless on which front
it chose to operate. Dizard, op. cit. , p. 34.

18. Thomson, op. cit., pp. 40-41.

19. Thus, the House Committee on Appropriations, in recommending a reduction of $1.99 million
in the figure recommended by the Bureau of the
Budget for OWI operations in fiscal year 1943,
proposed that the bulk of the decrease could be
made in domestic activities, since "the increased
rate . . . in domestic operations has challenged
attention as an enlargement which may not be fully
needed" (quoted in Thomson, op. cit., p. 34).

20. Department of State Bulletin, XIII, No.
323 (September 2, 1945), 306. Likewise,

Macmahon argued that the "role of the Government is important but it is facilitative and supplementary . . . the Government's role is seen as positive but limited and essentially residual." Arthur W. Macmahon, Memorandum on the Postwar International Information Program of the United States (Washington, D.C.: Department of State Publication 2438, 1945).

21. William Benton, "The Role of the International Information Service in the Conduct of Foreign Relations," Department of State Bulletin, XIII, No. 330 (October 21, 1945), 590.

22. Thomson, op. cit., p. 205.

23. The 1948 fiscal year marked the low point for the information program. The Subcommittee of the House Committee on Appropriations slashed Secretary Benton's request for $31 million for operations to zero. As a result of Senate action, however, it was finally voted $12.4 million.

24. Legislation on Foreign Relations with Explantory Notes, op. cit., p. 2-4.

25. Stephens, Facts to a Candid World, p. 38.

26. George V. Allen, "Go Tell it to the People," Think XXIV, No. 10 (October, 1958), p. 32.

27. George V. Allen, "USIA: The Big Problem in Belief," New York Herald Tribune, August 4, 1963.

28. In the judgment of one information officer, "I believe--and I think that most of my colleagues would agree--that our organization became of age during George Allen's three year term as its director." Dizard, op. cit., p. 46.

29. Quoted in Thomson and Laves, op. cit., p. 71.

30. Barrett, op. cit., pp. 78-79.

31. Ibid., pp. 73-74.

32. Ibid., p. 77.

33. U.S. Advisory Commission on Information, Third Semiannual Report (July 14, 1950) (mimeographed).

34. U.S. Advisory Commission on Educational Exchange, Sixth Semiannual Report (1952), p. 1.

35. U.S. Advisory Commission on Information, Sixth Semiannual Report, (H. Doc. 526, 82d Cong., 2d sess., July 1, 1952), p. 8.

36. Barrett, op. cit., p. 98.

37. Stephens, op. cit., p. 41.

38. Quoted in ibid., p. 42.

39. U.S. Congress, Senate, Committee on Foreign Relations, Interim Report: Overseas Information Programs of the United States, 83d Cong., 1st sess., 1953, p. 6.

40. U.S. Congress, Senate, The Objectives of the U.S. Information Program, A Reply to Questions Asked by the Honorable Pat McCarran in His Letter to the Secretary of State, 82d Cong., 2d sess., 1952. Senator McCarran was especially concerned about the information program's activities to counter Communism. The international incidents to which he referred are not relevant to the present discussion.

41. President's Committee on International Information Activities, White House Press Release, July 8, 1953, p. 2.

42. Ibid., p. 3.

43. Charles A. H. Thomson and Walter H. C. Laves, Cultural Relations and U.S. Foreign Policy (Bloomington, Ind.: Indiana University Press, 1963).

44. U.S. Advisory Commission on Information, Seventh Semiannual Report, (H.Doc. 94, 83d Cong.,

1st sess., February 23, 1953), p. 1.

45.   Ibid., pp. 1-9.

46.   Interim Report: Overseas Information
Programs of the United States, p. 13.

47.   Ibid., p. 25.

48.   The investigation of the information program will be found in U.S. Congress, Senate Permanent Subcommittee on Investigation of the Committee
on Government Operations, Hearings: State Department Information Program: Voice of America, 83d
Cong., 1st sess., 1953.

49.   U.S. Advisory Commission on Educational
Exchange, Eighth Semiannual Report (August, 1953),
pp. 5-6.

50.   Dizard, op. cit., pp. 41-42.

51.   American Library Association Bulletin,
No. 47 (1953), pp. 481-83.

52.   U.S. Advisory Commission on Information,
Ninth Semiannual Report (H. Doc. 311, 83d Cong., 2d
sess., February 2, 1954), p. 6.

53.   Interim Report: Overseas Information
Programs of the United States, op. cit., p. 24.

54.   Thomson and Laves, op. cit., p. 108.

CHAPTER **3** THE ORGANIZATION FOR
INFORMATION OBJECTIVES

RELATIONSHIPS WITH THE EXECUTIVE

The problem in defining information objectives,
as discussed in the previous chapter, may be attributed to disagreement on program goals within the
USIA. It may also be attributed to the organizational structure of the Agency. The purpose of this
chapter is to set forth the main issues facing the
USIA in the latter connection. Not only do these
organizational issues affect the size, structure
and technique of the information program, they are
important for the Agency's policy formation as well
as its operating procedures. Indeed, they relate
to the central issue of what kind of an information
program is appropriate for a democratic state.

A government overseas information service can
be set up in any of four ways: (1) as a unit in
the Office of the President; (2) as an independent
Executive establishment; (3) as a component of an
existing Executive establishment; and (4) as a public corporation. Since its inception, the USIA has
been organized as an independent Executive Branch,
thus following the second alternative. Rather than
weigh the advantages and disadvantages of the three
other choices, our analysis will proceed from the
standpoint of the USIA's present structure.

The Agency's position in the Executive Branch
was set forth in Reorganization Plan No. 8. This
plan established the USIA on August 1, 1953, as one
of the independent agencies of the Executive Branch
of the government. While the background of the plan
was discussed in the preceding chapter, tracing
the objectives of the American information program,
we will note here the organizational structure that

134

it specified for the USIA.   The new Agency was directed to operate the information and library activities of the Department of State,as well as the information functions of the Mutual Security Agency.
The educational exchange program was not involved in
the transfer move from the Department of State's International Information Administration to the new
information organization.   This activity was retained
in the Department of State under the Assistant Secretary of State for Public Affairs.

The feature of the 1953 reorganization most
relevant to our evaluation of information objectives
was its provision for the Secretary of State's role
in the USIA's program.   The legislation called for
his direction of the policy and control of the content of the program for use abroad on official
United States positions,including interpretations of
current events.   The Secretary was also asked to
continue to provide the Director of the USIA,on a
current basis,full guidance concerning American
foreign policy.[1]

To be sure, every Executive agency must shape
its foreign policies from the viewpoint of the
President's particular dispositions toward foreign
affairs and his role as a world leader.   The President is the major American spokesman abroad to
governments and to peoples.   If, like Roosevelt or
Kennedy, he takes the initiative in deciding all
significant foreign policy issues (sometimes without
reference to the Department of State), the information service must be closely attuned to the Presidency for policy direction and coordination.   If,
like Eisenhower, he decentralizes such matters to a
large degree, the information service must take policy guidance from the agencies exercising real
influence.   In any event, the USIA cannot assume a
position that may be belied by the President in his
public statements.

Such more recent strong Presidents as Kennedy
and Johnson have shown more regard for the role
of the USIA in both policy and operations than
Eisenhower.   The chief organizational difficulties

that the USIA has encountered, however, have not
been with the Chief Executive, but rather with the
other agencies of the foreign affairs community.
We will therefore concentrate on the USIA's relations
with these agencies. It was argued earlier in this
study that the presence of some two dozen other
agencies and departments in foreign information programs has raised problems of coordination for the
USIA, the principal government information organization. The USIA experiences its foremost difficulties
in this connection with the Department of State,
the unit responsible for defining broad foreign policy objectives for the Agency. These difficulties
have related to foreign policy formation, program
operations, and political intelligence.

As will be argued below,there were impressive
organizational and domestic political considerations
for removing the information program from the Department of State. Despite these factors, however, the
reasoning for separating the foreign policy unit
from the operational information program remained a
point of contention in the Congressional hearings
that established the USIA. The debates in the
committees concerning organization are still perti-
nent in current discussions of USIA's relations
with other foreign policy units in the Executive
Branch. The case for separating the policy from
operational units was presented by Rowland R. Hughes,
Assistant Director of the Bureau of the Budget:

> In other words, the President feels
> positively that there should be a
> positive and definite way of identi-
> fying statements of United States
> policy, and it is for the purpose of
> making clear that when there are cer-
> tain declarations or statements which
> should be made concerning the view-
> points and policies of the United
> States, that they should be labeled
> and not lost in connection with a
> general information program or a
> program of activities of certain phases
> of American industry or something of
> that sort.[2]

According to the projected reorganization, the Assistant Secretary of State for Public Affairs was to serve as the source of policy guidance for the information program. It was envisaged that this organizational arrangement would enable the Assistant Secretary to transmit information both "up and down"--up to the Secretary of State and down to the information agency. In his capacity as adviser to the Secretary, the Assistant Secretary was to be responsible for acquainting him with public attitudes in the United States and throughout the world as they would affect foreign policy. Such information was to be taken into consideration by the Secretary in reaching foreign policy decisions.

Once the necessary decisions were arrived at by the Secretary, the Assistant Secretary had the responsibility for acquainting the administrator of the information program with the decisions so that they could be translated into planning and programing.[3] Policy guidance would then go out daily to the Public Affairs Officers in the field. If questions arose under these arrangements, the PAO would consult the Ambassador, and the Ambassador would consult with the Secretary of State.[4]

This organizational setup has brought numerous problems to the USIA in coordinating and, in special instances, even learning official foreign policy positions. It was shown previously that the Agency's difficulties in coordinating policy with other departments operating foreign information programs is a source of confusion regarding over-all USIA objectives. The fears expressed over the separation between policy and operations at these early hearings have proven to be valid since the information program's independent existence. A staff study of the Subcommittee on the Overseas Information Program of the United States noted in this connection that the notion that policy and operations can be divorced is "largely illusory." "Problems arise daily over policy and must be settled at relatively low levels," it stated. Furthermore, under the arrangement where-

by the International Information Administration was
included in the Department of State, media people
could freely consult the PAO units in the Department's
regional bureaus and obtain "quick answers on almost
any policy question that arises."5 Presently, the
USIA must usually contact the Department's Public
Affairs Office, which serves as an intermediary in
these situations, before dealing directly with the
Department's desk officers.

   According to a 1963 account of the organizational arrangements for coordinating information objectives with the broader foreign affairs responsibilities of the Department of State,it would seem that
the USIA would be guaranteed a continuous stream of
guidance and intelligence, its independent status
notwithstanding. Rather than emphasize the absence
of such coordination, the Department official involved, to the contrary, presented a portrait of
harmony in these areas. Robert Manning, Assistant
Secretary of State for Public Affairs, in testifying
before the subcommittee studying the American ideological offensive, cited numerous channels through
which the Agency might possibly receive policy guidance. The most frequent institutional arrangement
consists of the extensive system of meetings held
at various levels in the Department. The Director
of the USIA is said to regularly attend the Secretary
of State's thrice-weekly meeting with the Under
Secretary, the Deputy Under Secretaries, and Assistant Secretaries.

> In the Secretary's meeting, the
> Director of the Information Agency
> is able to get the views of the De-
> partment's ranking officers on U.S.
> policy, as well as to contribute
> his own thoughts and recommendations
> bearing on the responsibilities of
> his Agency.[6]

   To supplement these arrangements, the USIA
Director is a permanent member of the Senior Interdepartmental Group (SIG),with the Under Secretary
of State as its "Executive Chairman." SIG was set

up in 1966.   Liaison at a senior level is continued
at other meetings between officers of the State
Department and the Agency.   For example, a senior
officer of the USIA's Office of Policy and Research
attends the daily meetings of the State Department's
Bureau of Public Affairs.   At these sessions, officers of the Public Affairs Bureau, as well as public
affairs advisers from the various regional and
functional units of the Department, take up questions
that the Department's spokesman may be called upon
to discuss with newsmen at the daily noon briefing.

Assistant Secretary of State Manning described
the ties between the USIA and the Department of
State as being so close that:

> It is quite true to say that our
> officers are in touch with one an-
> other every hour of the working day,
> and very frequently after hours and
> on holidays as well when the public
> business requires it. [7]

Despite these arrangements--and they have grown considerably from the chaotic situation of the post-
World War II years--the USIA continues to have an
unsettled role in policy formulation.   Even the close
personal ties between two recent Agency Directors,
Murrow and Rowan, with Presidents Kennedy and Johnson,
respectively, have not assured the Agency that its
role in this connection will be adequate for the demands of the "New Diplomacy."   It is to the Department of State's advantage to praise the present
arrangement, and therefore escape the possibility of
being saddled with the information program once again.
The price for such praise, however, is that the
American information program must continue to occupy
an ambiguous role regarding foreign strategy and
national objectives.

Accordingly, the establishment of the USIA as
an independent agency has only partially improved
the foreign policy guidance accorded the information
program.   The divorce of both these foreign affairs
agencies, if for these improvements alone, has been

endorsed by the various governmental units connected
with the information program. The U.S. Advisory
Commission on Information and the Sprague Committee
(President's Committee on Information Activities
Abroad) have favored continuing the separation in
view of this relatively strengthened coordination.

Supporters of the purpose of an official information program, such as the U.S. Advisory Commission,
have argued that at least one more major change in
the USIA's position in the Executive Branch is needed
before unified direction of the American communications effort is achieved. This step is the elevation
of the Agency to Cabinet rank. The U.S. Advisory
Commission recommended that all foreign cultural and
educational programs be included with the information
campaign under such a Cabinet position. The separation of these activities one from another, it noted,
made it difficult, moreover, to evaluate their impact on a country-by-country basis. In combining
the diverse cultural, information, and educational
programs, the nation would merely be giving belated
recognition to the fact that communications techniques
for reaching foreign audiences are essentially alike.
Such a consolidation would enable the United States
to compete more effectively on all fronts of the
communications struggle.[8]

It is noteworthy that the Commission's Report
of the following year recommending Cabinet status
for the information and related programs did so not
only on the basis of operational efficiency but also
for policy considerations. The latter argument is
relevant to the present discussion. It said that:

> Regular attendance at Cabinet meetings
> would ensure greater familiarity with
> and access to other departments which
> deal with foreign affairs and with
> domestic issues that have foreign rami-
> fications. It would also assure to
> the President direct access to the
> Director of USIA who would function
> as his chief counsel and adviser on
> foreign public opinion.[9]

The Report added that high stature of the Director and the Agency in the hierarchy of government
departments should help to avoid many of the "contradictory statements" made by personnel in the many
departments of government that are concerned either
directly or indirectly with foreign affairs. These
contradictory statements are a cause of confusion
and perplexity among foreign governments and peoples.

While other independent observers of the information program have not uniformly proposed Cabinet
status for the Agency in recent official reports,
the fact that such an innovation is seriously weighed
indicates the external organizational problems facing
the USIA.[10] Clearly, the present circumstance is in-
sufficient for the Agency's purpose. The Brookings
Institution Report, The Formulation and Administration of United States Foreign Policy (1960), suggested
the creation of a single Department of Foreign
Affairs, encompassing the activities of the Department of State, the USIA, and the Agency for International Development. In a proposal along similar
lines, the Report of the Committee on Foreign Affairs
Personnel advocated the establishment of an Executive
Under Secretary of State who would assure that:

> . . . policies are supported by action
> programs and by the means and resources
> for their realization;
>
> . . . the processes of policymaking, program
> development, budgeting, and administration
> are brought into an effective union . . .[11]

The tendency in both these reports is to argue
against a sharp distinction between operational and
policy formulation agencies in international affairs.

The inadequate arrangement for the USIA in the
Executive Branch illustrates, in some measure, the
absence of recognition of the Agency as a permanent
and vital instrument of foreign policy. There exist
no precise criteria for determining to what degree
the information program would more effectively ad-

vance American goals, if at all, were it to receive
its desired budgetary requests from Congress. At
the most, we can blame Congress for failing to appropriate the additional funds sought by the Agency.
Yet in the case of the USIA's deprived position in
the Executive Branch we are not simply considering
a hypothetical issue. The implementation of the information program unquestionably suffers under the
Agency's present rank in the federal establishment.
The Agency's influence in the foreign policy process
will grow--as well it should--only to the extent to
which it will acquire a heightened organizational
recognition in the Executive Branch of the government.

                THE USIA AND THE U-2 EPISODE

     The position of the USIA as a member of the
foreign affairs community has never been defined with
finality. A cardinal operating principle for an effective political communication program is that the
information instrument engage in the policy formulation process. Such participation provides the other
Executive agencies with advice as to foreign public
opinion. It also enables the information agency to
gain keener understanding of national policies.
Knowledge of these policies must emanate from the
Executive Branch, and this an agency for political
communication cannot possess without the former's
consent.

     Another basic premise of this study is that the
USIA has suffered because this consent has been
niggardly and uncertain. Despite the stream of reorganizations of the information program, the USIA
remains a neglected instrument in foreign policy
planning--especially in crisis situations. The record of cooperation of other Executive foreign affairs agencies with the USIA has not served to out-
date Thomson's description of the World War II information specialist:

          He was not called to policy councils
          to contribute to policy decisions from
          his special resources. He often was

> not told of important developments
> long enough in advance for him even
> to carry out the mechanical operations
> of "news" efficiently and expeditious-
> ly.[12]

Divorced from knowledge of international political objectives, the activities of the USIA are
futile. Three major diplomatic confrontations since
the founding of the Agency in 1953 revealed that the
information program was divorced from U.S. policy
formulation. These were the 1956 Suez Canal crisis,
the 1960 U-2 incident, and the 1961 Bay of Pigs invasion.

In demonstrating this flaw, it would prove
instructive to trace the absence of the USIA in the
decision-making process at the time of the U-2 incident. Unlike other Cold War crises, the U-2 incident
marked the first time in its 184-year history that
the Government of the United States conceded publicly
that it had deliberately lied, committed espionage,
and violated the territory of another country.[13]
More personally, this event accounted for the most
humiliating experience of President Eisenhower's
public career.

The downing of a U-2 plane engaged in espionage
over the Soviet Union affected the image of the
United States in four areas: vis-à-vis allies,
neutral nations, Communist nations, and U.S.
citizens. Since the USIA is removed from influencing domestic opinion, it cannot be held
responsible for the meager confidence on the part
of U.S. citizens. It is proper, however, to explore
the Agency's role in the first three areas.

The United States launched the U-2 reconnaissance
plane in 1956 for the purpose of securing military
intelligence. These operations were sponsored by
the Central Intelligence Agency. As a cover for its
flights, the CIA used the National Aeronautics and
Space Administration. The ostensible purpose of the
flights, according to NASA, was to gather weather
data for the Air Force. Furthermore, NASA had a

contract with the Lockheed Aviation Corporation to
fly these missions, and U-2 pilots were on the pay-
roll of this private firm.

In the vernacular of intelligence, U-2 over-
flights were so "black" that communication among the
small group of men running the program was mostly by
word of mouth.14 George V. Allen, Director of the
USIA, was excluded from this group. Moreover, the
CIA's prepackaged "cover" stories, which were to be
drawn from the files and issued by Air Force public
information officers if and when a U-2 failed in returning from a secret mission, were strictly hidden
from the information agency. The USIA was not only
ignorant of policy-making decisions responsible for
such flights, but was lacking contingent plans should
the espionage undertakings be uncovered.

Normally, none of the coterie of the CIA, Department of State, or NASA aware of the U-2 would
know of particular flights. None, therefore, could
be charged with responsibility for the one that was
shot down. Decisions of when and how to obtain
specific information would be reached in subordinate
ranks in the field.

While the U-2 had overflown the Soviet Union
intermittently for four years, the advisability of
continuing these flights came into question following
Premier Khrushchev's tour of the United States in
September, 1959, at the invitation of President
Eisenhower. In foreign affairs, the result of this
visit was the "Spirit of Camp David." The meeting
of the leaders of the two most powerful nations on
earth in a weekend retreat represented a turning
point in the Cold War. The USIA gained from this
détente, inasmuch as Voice of America broadcasts were
heard more clearly in the Soviet Union during the
final months of 1959 than they had been in ten years.
Soviet jamming of stations that had for years operated
almost incessantly to drown out the Voice, allowed
VOA programs to be heard freely once Premier
Khrushchev set out on his visit to the United States.15

In keeping with the improved international cli-

mate, a Summit Meeting was arranged for May 16, 1960,
in Paris. The leaders of France, the Soviet Union,
the United States, and the United Kingdom were expected to attend. President Eisenhower announced
plans to visit the Soviet Union following the Summit
Meeting. The USIA Russian-language magazine,
America Illustrated, devoted its May, 1960, issue to
President Eisenhower's sustained efforts on behalf
of peace.

> The American Embassy in Moscow reported
> that this edition aroused even more in-
> terest than any previous issue of the
> magazine, which has enjoyed spectacular
> popularity with its Soviet readers since
> it began publication in October 1956.[16]

It would appear that the USIA found the atmosphere generated by the "Spirit of Camp David" beneficial to United States information objectives. Had
the policy-makers responsible for the U-2 flight of
May 1, 1960, consulted the elaborate polls of the
Agency's Research and Reference Service, they might
have postponed the flight, in view of the detrimental
impact its discovery would have on foreign public
opinion. The polls, as well as any other form of
advice the Agency could supply regarding the desirability of the U-2 intelligence mission, were ignored
by those responsible for the mission.

Thus, from the outset, the USIA was divorced
from the decision to send a U.S. plane over the
Soviet Union only fifteen days before the Summit
Meeting. The absence of the USIA from the U-2 scheme
of May 1 is all the more flagrant if one supports
the conclusion that the timing of the flight and
the scheduling of the Summit Meeting were not coin-
cidental. The CIA officials testifying before the
Committee on Foreign Relations' investigation of
the U-2 incident refused to reveal the reasoning
for the flight on May 1. In the judgment of Wise
and Ross, two United States journalists, however,
there was an uneasy feeling among the U.S. intelligence community as the Summit approached that a
détente might be reached at Paris. If so, the
U-2 flights might be grounded, perhaps perma-

nently. An international rapprochement followed
by President Eisenhower's trip to the Soviet Union
would make further flights practically impossible
for the foreseeable future. There was a strong
desire, therefore, to undertake one final espionage
mission.

> The policy-makers at the top of the
> government were unable to resist this
> desire, since they had already lost
> genuine control of the U-2 program.
> Responsibility had been delegated for
> such a long-time that only the intel-
> ligence technicians were really able
> to make a judgment on the value of
> each flight.17

The coordination arrangements of the Executive
Branch not only resulted in the exclusion of the
Director of the USIA from all preliminary plans relating to the U-2 mission; the error was compounded
by refusing to consult the information unit even
after the craft was shot down. The Agency was left
out of policy-formulating sessions affecting two
issues of integral concern to the information program: aerial espionage, a particularly tender subject for nations leasing military bases to the
United States; and the Summit Conference, an event
that the USIA had vigorously publicized. Inasmuch
as the Agency was overlooked by the decision-makers
in both these episodes, it remained uncertain as to
the answers to the following questions: In the
large sense, did the United States desire a Summit
Conference? Did it wish to negotiate or not? In
the short range, did the United States intend to
continue the U-2 flights or did one not remember to
stop them? Once caught, was the President to be
held responsible and so close the door to all compromise with the other participants of the Summit Conference?

As the U-2 episode developed, the United States
committed a succession of blunders that the USIA
would ultimately be forced to explain. The United
States lied concerning the intent of the flight

when it could have remained silent. Subsequently,
it admitted it had lied in claiming that the plane
was merely engaged in gathering data. Then, the United
States acknowledged that the U-2's purpose was spying
on the Soviet Union. As regarded Presidential involvement, here, too, the pronouncements of the government went full circle. Initially, the public
statements disclaimed Presidential responsibility.
Then, President Eisenhower confessed complicity in
U-2 espionage flights. Finally, by deliberately
permitting the question of whether or not such flights
would continue to remain ambiguous, the United States
did little to restore the traditional moral tone to
its diplomatic activity. On the strength of these
foregoing inconsistencies, the unwillingness of
Premier Khrushchev to negotiate in confidence at
Paris is understandable--assuming he was sincerely
motivated.

For purposes of this study, there is no need
to sift in detail the decisional stages relating to
the U-2 episode. The chief official source dealing
with both the U-2 and the Summit Conference are the
hearings conducted by the Senate Committee on Foreign
Relations.[18] No USIA officials were asked to appear
at the hearings. The published transcript is limited
to the testimony of Christian A. Herter, Secretary
of State; Douglas Dillon, Under Secretary of State;
Allen W. Dulles, Director of the CIA; Charles E.
Bohlen, Special Assistant to the Secretary of State
for Soviet Affairs; Dr. Hugh L. Dryden, Deputy
Administrator of NASA; and Thomas S. Gates, Secretary of Defense.

The inquiry was conducted with extraordinary
Congressional secrecy and restraint. All testimony
was taken in Executive session. It was edited by
Bohlen and by Richard Helms, Deputy Director of the
CIA for Plans. Not a word was made public of Dulles'
five-and-a-half-hour presentation,which included
elaborate maps, charts, and U-2 photographs.

The Committee's main finding, relative to the
USIA, was the absence of direction among the agencies
concerned with espionage and the success of the Sum-

mit Conference. The Report noted:

> . . . there are few, if any, ref-
> erences to direction, and this seems
> to the Committee to be what was
> most lacking in this period. There
> were many interagency meetings to
> coordinate activities, but there
> was apparently no one official
> to direct activities.[19]

The USIA had the unhappy task of persuading foreign
public opinion that there existed an official U.S.
policy in this episode despite the plethora of
contradictory statements and retractions.

The interview of USIA Director Allen on the
television program "College News Conference," on
May 15 (a day before the scheduled Summit Conference),
poignantly indicates the uncertainty characterizing
the Agency's role in this crisis. While official
announcements first lied regarding the nature of the
U-2 mission, Allen was arguing on the program that
the Agency tries to

> . . . present the United States as
> honestly and as fairly as we can.
> Insofar as the recent events are
> concerned, we have played them right
> down the middle just as straight as
> we know how to play them.[20]

How the Agency depicted events "down the middle" at
this time is questionable, inasmuch as Allen went
on to claim that even he was uncertain of policy.
In answering a question on the "unfavorable aspects"
of the U-2 incident, Allen seemed to be as much an
outsider to the decision-making councils as was his
audience. One such shortcoming concerned

> . . . the confusion, shall I say of
> the announcements that came out of
> Washington on the subject and not
> only the original announcement saying
> that the plane was on a weather

> mission, but subsequent announce-
> ments which need some clarification
> here today, I think, concerning our
> right to carry out activities of
> this kind which have caused dismay
> in various foreign cities.[21]

The interview also revealed a series of additional admissions and apologies by Allen concerning
the public opinion impact of the shooting down of
the U-2. Allen acknowledged it was "unfortunate"
that NASA was used as a decoy for the CIA operation.
The USIA was "not consulted with regard to the nuclear testing statement" issued shortly before the
convening of the Summit Conference. He appeared
relieved in agreeing with the judgment of the program moderator that the agencies responsible for
the original statements "should consult with you so
that it doesn't take a whole week for the refutation
to penetrate.[22]

In sum, the interview demonstrated that the
Director of the USIA, the man most responsible for
cultivating favorable foreign opinion for the United
States, was completely divorced from the decision-
making aspect of one of the most momentous international events since World War II.

In the U-2 episode, there was little chance to
measure the quality of the USIA. If the information
agency was not consulted, it could not be judged.
We can only go to the results and guess backward.
This study follows the line of foreign policy ana-
lysts who argue that

> . . . the key of understanding why a state
> behaves as it does lies in understanding
> the way in which its official decision-
> makers define the situations in which
> they are operating.[23]

The USIA has suffered because of the refusal of the
foreign affairs community to acknowledge political
communication as a major policy instrument. If the
USIA had had the full confidence of the Department of

State, CIA, and White House staff, it would have
been brought into the decisional aspects of the U-2
episode. While the information instrument is ideally
auxiliary to political action--and never in a primary
role--it must, at the least, be knowledgeable on
decisions reached and the premises of such decisions.

A second and related conclusion of the U-2
episode is the need for closer coordination between
information policy and foreign policy. Whether the
USIA is located within the Department of State or
set up outside as a wholly autonomous agency, the
central consideration is to assure effective communication between those who formulate foreign policy
and those who communicate it abroad. The U-2 demonstrated that the Agency was harmed by the absence
of liaison with the other components of the foreign
affairs community. Perhaps out of consideration of
the aforesaid weakness, the U.S. Advisory Commission
on Information recommended Cabinet status for the
information program.

> Regular attendance at Cabinet meetings
> by the Director of this Agency would
> ensure greater familiarity with and
> access to other departments which deal
> with foreign affairs and with domestic
> issues. It would also assure to the
> President direct access to the Director
> of USIA who would function as his chief
> counsel and adviser on foreign public
> opinion.[24]

In addition, the Commission observed that the high
stature of the USIA and its Director should help in
avoiding many of the "contradictory statements"
issued by agencies concerned with foreign affairs.

When units are properly arranged, the decisions
to be reached can be made with foresight and accuracy.
The USIA lacked an opportunity for demonstrating its
talent for either quality in the U-2 incident. The
lessons here are that the information instrument
will never realize its potential, lacking knowledge
of foreign policy and recognition from foreign policy decision makers.

INTERNAL ORGANIZATION

The objectives of the American information program are appreciably affected by the USIA's relations
with other members of the foreign affairs community.
There are particular internal problems common to
the USIA,regardless of the Agency's uncertain status
in the Executive Branch of the government. Insofar
as this study is mainly concerned with the USIA as
an instrument of American objectives, it will not
dwell at length on the Agency's programing, budgeting, and other internal issues only indirectly related to such objectives. These operational matters
have been the subject of much study during the annual
hearings of the Congressional Appropriations Committees. The purpose of this section is to evaluate
the ways in which the USIA is internally organized
to fulfill information objectives.

Internal structure must enable the Agency (1)
to participate in formulating and coordinating information policy with over-all government policy; (2)
to adjust media and functional policies and operations to areas and among themselves; and (3) to adjust operating and housekeeping functions.

The USIA is organized to formulate and implement information objectives along the following
lines: policy guidance, area direction, and media
services (see Table 4). These units are supervised
by the Director and the Deputy Director. The third-
ranking officer of the Agency is the Deputy Director
for Policy and Research. According to the USIA's
1967 organizational arrangement, there were four
staff offices associated with the Director's Office:
Office of Policy and Research; Office of Inspector
General; Office of Public Information; and Office
of the Commissioner General for the Canadian World
Exhibition (Expo '67).

The policy guidance aspect of the information
program is designed to reflect and support national
positions. The Office of Policy and Research (IOP)
formulates information policy for all USIA operations. The policy coordinator has been responsible

for keeping all functional and area emphases logi-
cally consistent on a current basis, and to some
degree for future planning. Insofar as the State
Department has had the main responsibility for
initiating policy, coordination in this area has
been maintained through it. Thus, the Deputy Director for Policy and Research meets with the State
Department's public affairs personnel in order to
ascertain the direction of national foreign policy
objectives. In addition, IOP coordinates information
policy with the other agencies and departments, cited
earlier in this study, which are vitally concerned
with international affairs. The USIA has specialists
in such areas as labor matters, commercial trade
fairs and defense programs, who serve as liaisons,
respectively, with the Departments of Labor, Commerce,
and Defense. According to Thomas C. Sorenson, a
past Deputy Director for Policy and Research, the
information agency generally remains informed as to
the activities of these departments in foreign affairs.

> I think that, given the size and complex-
> ity of the Government, we are able to
> keep track of what other agencies are
> doing in the international field that
> has an impact on foreign opinion abroad,
> and therefore is of interest to us in
> the operation of our business.[25]

While the USIA manages to stay abreast of many
of their undertakings, the fact remains that these
arrangements are informal in character. President
Kennedy's definition of the Agency's role stressed
that other departments should seek its counsel in
planning programs affecting foreign opinion. As the
Subcommittee on Foreign Affairs' hearings on the
American ideological offensive demonstrated, however,
instances have arisen when these departments con-
cealed certain of their activities from the USIA.
Under such circumstances, the official American information program is forced to operate in the dark.

The Agency is further organized along lines of
geographic direction. Six Area Assistant Directors,

UNITED STATES INFORMATION AGENCY

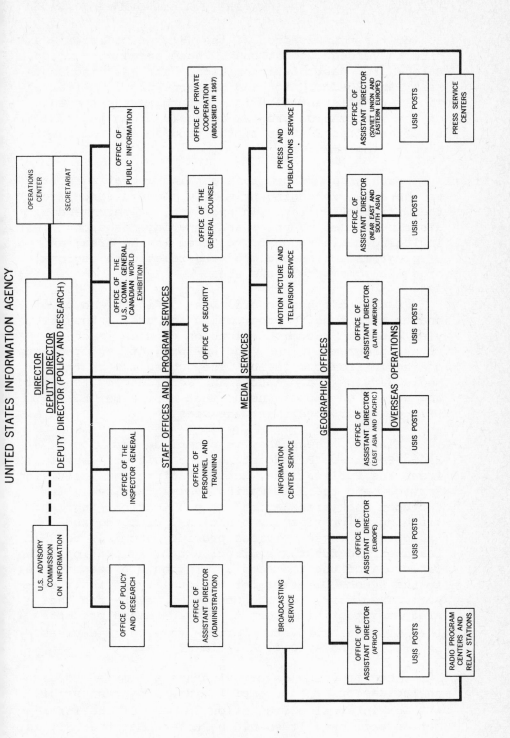

acting for the Director of the USIA, administer and
direct overseas operations. These areas are Africa,
Europe, Far East, Latin America, Near East and South
Asia, and Soviet Union and Eastern European Affairs.
The Area Assistant Directors determine the content
of the information program in their areas and evaluate the effectiveness of the program and the methods
used to implement it.

Each Area Office staff applies operating policy
to the area, depending primarily upon guidance from
the Office of Policy. In addition, it recommends
distribution of manpower and material resources,
including media support, required in the area; and
of programs, plans,and projects related to regional
organizations within the area.

Each staff has several Desk Officers who cover
one or more country programs in the area. They review and make recommendations on changes in objectives, programs, plans, and new projects and requests
coming in from the field. They consult with the
Media Services on products and services for the field
and advise on support needs that can be met by the
USIA or other government agencies.26

Finally, the Agency is organized into four
Media Services: Broadcasting (The Voice of America),
Press and Publications, Motion Picture and Television
Service, and the Information Center Service (which
includes book translation and publication, English
teaching, libraries and binational centers, and
exhibits). These services provide materials to USIS
posts abroad for their direct use or adaptation. The
Directors of the four Media Services are responsible
to the Agency Director for the quality of their output. They work with the Office of Policy and the
Area Assistant Directors to provide media products
that will help promote American foreign objectives
generally, and specifically in each area.

The foregoing description has attempted to give
an indication of the complex mixture of responsibility for internal coordination in each of the information offices. It should be noted that the USIA is

not the only organization plagued by this dilemma.
Area emphasis versus functional emphasis has
also been one of the central organizational difficulties of the Department of State.   In the USIA,
this problem is most evident in the operations of
the media services.   While the scheduling, content,
and language of the media programs are not in the
scope of this study, the strategic requirements of
such activity remain unchanged from what they were
in the post-World War II era.   According to Thomson,
what was needed from the strategic viewpoint was:

> . . . minimum coverage to all areas which
> may come within our range of strategic
> interest; in terms of current world
> strategy, this means an information
> operation in every country where we
> maintain diplomatic missions.   The
> program must have sufficient diversity
> of media and flexibility so that infor-
> mation targets can be reached by one
> means or another. . . There must be
> a balance among media, among home and
> field activities, and between govern-
> ment and private forms of operation.[27]

There is no clear line of demarcation between
the Agency's mass-media and slow-media operations,
although there are certain substantial differences
in operating characteristics and in the time and
distribution of effect.   Mass media, such as radio
and publications, are expected to bring the most up-
to-date materials to bear on large groups.   Slow
media, such as libraries and the exchange-of-persons
program, are, by comparison, not expected to work
quickly or to put the main stress on the latest
available devices.   Yet mass-media operations, as
Thomson notes, constantly use well-ripened materials
that retain broad interest, and the effects of
many mass-media operations are not quickly dissipated.
Likewise, slow-media operations, working in and
through specialized groups for the most part, can
affect the impact of mass-media programs in many
ways, especially through contributing to the background that conditions understanding of mass-media
content.

Combination in one program of mass media and
slow media, large targets and specialized targets,
immediate with long-term impact, appears to be ideal
in such an operation as the USIA. Naturally, this
combined program reflects tight planning and coordination among the different media involved. One
illustration in this regard was the Country Plan
submitted by the PAO of Yugoslavia in 1958. The plan
called for the launching of twelve different campaigns, each of which was scheduled to take effect
in a separate month. During each month, all facilities and media available to the Mission were combined to advance the particular campaign. This
method did not mean, however, that the subject
treated one month was not to be treated again. Nor
did it eliminate the miscellaneous short-range requests that the Mission's information division considered.

The success of this approach motivated the
Advisory Commission on Information to recommend that
missions abroad should agree on the treatment of
identical subjects over a twelve-month period, and
eliminate all marginal ones. Moreover, such an
approach would enable the USIA headquarters staff
to produce material relevant to all Agency posts.

The obstacle to this combination of media
facilities is that internal antipathies might prevent
the creation of a smooth, integrated program. Thus,
the desire of cultural specialists to remain apart
from information specialists, whom they derisively
classify as "propagandists," is one of the long-
standing disputes in the American overseas information effort. Similarly, information specialists
have resented the diversion of staff time, funds
and equipment to activities that do not appear
warranted as parts of a government persuasion program. These internal organizational disagreements
invariably weaken the USIA's capacity to project as
cogent a program of media operations as possible.

The following illustrations indicate the scope
and variety of the Media Services. Between January

and June, 1966, the Voice of America broadcasted 845
hours weekly in 38 languages to a daily audience of
25 million people.

As for the printed word, the Agency's Press and
Publications Service compiles and transmits by radio-
teletype about 12,000 words of material daily to
posts abroad for placement in local newspapers and
periodicals. Collectively, these transmissions are
referred to as the Wireless File. During the period
from January 1 to June 30, 1966, the Service and its
regional centers produced over 10 million leaflets
and pamphlets in 47 languages for use in 115 countries.

The Information Center Service is responsible
for 223 USIA libraries in 84 countries. These centers hold over 2 million volumes, 430,000 of which
are in foreign languages. During the first half of
1966, these libraries and reading rooms were visited
by more than 12 million people and loaned about 3
million books. In this period, the USIA also assisted
in the production of nearly 6 million copies of 799
book titles. Through the Informational Guaranty
Program, the USIA converts foreign curriencies into
dollars for American distributors in the amount of
their sales in some countries that cannot pay dollars.

Between January 1 and June 30, 1966, an estimated
350 million people in 120 countries saw USIA films--
in Agency auditoriums, on television, at private
showings, in commercial theaters, and out in the open.
During the same 6 months, 2,082 television stations
in 94 countries telecasted USIA programs and series.
A total of 9 major film documentaries were produced,
and another 30 were planned or in production on a
broad spectrum of subjects, including the U.S. quest
for peace, the space program, and Vietnam.

At the end of fiscal year 1966, the Agency was
supporting, in varying degrees, 132 binational centers, 112 of which were in Latin America. The teaching of English is perhaps the best-known activity of
these centers, as well as a major source of revenue,
because students pay modest fees. Since 1950, the
USIA has taught English to nearly 2,5000,000 persons

in foreign countries. More than two-thirds of these
students have learned English at binational centers.

The above description has attempted to show how
the USIA is set up to speak to the world. A detailed
content analysis of such material is not within the
scope of this study. Yet it should be emphasized,
in this regard, that dependence of USIA posts upon
these wide-ranging Washington transmissions is,in
itself,inadequate for implementing information ob-
jectives.28 The following section will evaluate the
means by which centrally produced USIA programs are
related to local considerations.

THE COUNTRY PLAN AND COUNTRY TEAM

The most significant aspect of USIA planning
is the concept of the country as the principal unit
of operation. The Country Plan forms the basis of
Agency budgeting as well as field operations. The
existence of individual plans of information strategy is not a new feature of the USIA program. With
the growth of Agency operations, however, Country
Plans have assumed increasing prominence in establishing information objectives. The present discussion will seek to appraise the record of these
plans in advancing American purposes.

Country Plans were used in information programs
even before the creation of the USIA. The International Information Administration (IIA) recognized
that information campaigns must take into account
the differing cultural, regional, and psychological
needs of the countries in which they are conducted.
This realization resulted in a greater decentraliza-
tion of its program. It further allowed for the
Country Public Affairs Officers to reach key decisions
concerning information objectives. According to Dr.
Wilson Compton, Administrator of IIA:

> Country by country we are now setting
> up individual information programs re-
> lated to local conditions and opportu-
> nities. These programs are initiated by

> our own missions in each country sub-
> ject to review by Washington to assure
> that what we do overseas is properly
> within the framework of the United
> States policy. This initiative is
> overseas. The country planning is
> overseas. The tactics and strategy
> are overseas.29

The Agency favored this operational design because it was believed to strengthen field activities
and thereby program effectiveness. More people would
be influenced through a program appealing to particular needs than one standardized in application.
The people best equipped to determine the character
and scope of such an undertaking were the officers
in each country rather than those located in Washington.

The emphasis on field operations in contrast
to home operations is no panacea, however, for an
overseas information program. The chief consideration in distributing the functions between home and
field organizations must be the criteria of foreign
policy objectives. Thomson stressed this consideration in his theoretical analysis of the American
overseas information program as it operated during
the World War II years. It remains equally as relevant in the late 1960's. One must first decide
what groups should be influenced in order to meet
strategic requirements. Then it is possible to
make general decisions regarding the organization of
the total service to carry out these tasks.

In World War II, it was demonstrated that in
some instances a small field staff working closely
with local editors and officials could do what was
needed to see that American policies were accurately
and sympathetically treated in local news channels.
Such a staff required only a minimum of material
from headquarters to carry out its mission. In
addition, attempts to prepare finished material in
New York for use in the South Pacific months later,
for example, ran the risk of going stale or becoming
unsuitable to strategic requirements by the time the

material reached its target.

Perhaps with such illustrations as the above in mind, Congress has increasingly welcomed the change in emphasis from USIA headquarters to the field posts. The Senate Committee on Foreign Relations favored this approach in its 1953 investigation of the American Overseas Information Program. It observed that information posts are the principal focus of the entire program and exercise prime influence in planning the operations for their respective localities.

> The Committee's own observations generally support the views of the many witnesses who found this change of emphasis beneficial. Situations, customs and attitudes differ from post to post throughout the world. By placing the emphasis on the field operations, it has been possible to adjust to these differences and thereby gain greater acceptance for the activities of the program. The absence of such adjustment in the past undoubtedly contributed to general ineffectiveness.[30]

In succeeding years, the importance of field officers vis-à-vis the country program grew to the extent that Edward R. Murrow pictured the Agency in Washington as being merely a "service organization for our field posts." Before the Agency decides to publish a pamphlet, a book in translation, a film, or a television program, it consults the post as to the suitability of the subject and the material.

> . . . once we supply it to the post it is at the discretion of the public affairs officer, generally in consultation with the Ambassador, as to whether that material shall be used because one cannot produce, mass-produce for entire world distribution without touching certain sensitive

centers where it would be counter-
productive to do this thing. [31]

Despite such explanations regarding the role
of Country Plans in Agency operations, it would
appear that these programs do not always fulfill
their intended objectives. The U.S. Advisory Commission on Information has frequently cited the absence of adequate planning of country themes. The
Commission's observations in this connection would
lead one to conclude that an expansion of field
autonomy does not necessarily guarantee more inci-
sive programing of information objectives. Although
it commended this concept for its achievements, the
Commission stressed the responsibilities of Agency
headquarters in directing the information program.
An increase in field autonomy should not detract
from Washington's role in providing over-all creativity and guidance. [32]

According to the Commission, the country program has not eliminated the tendency of many posts
to use all media supplied from Washington,rather
than concentrating their efforts on fewer media and
activities most suited to the particular area.

> The Commission again urges that the
> directors of media and geographic
> areas in Washington, and the public
> affairs officers in the field, re-
> view their programs, country by
> country, in an effort to determine
> and use only those media that are
> effective and applicable, and to
> eliminate all programs that are
> marginal. [33]

The present system of country planning has been
inadequate for an even more fundamental area of information objectives. This relates to its failure
to provide for comprehensive and flexible long-range
program strategy. In this area, too, the Advisory
Commission has been critical of the Agency's performance. According to the Advisory Commission,the
USIA has a commendable record in making the most of
foreign policy guidance from the Department of State

and converting it into daily direction for the fast
media. As for long-range, detailed programs, however, the Advisory Commission maintained that the
Agency has shown weaknesses. In its 1966 Report,
the Advisory Commission noted that the Agency should
consider ten-year plans. This ten-year span (1966-
76), the Commission suggested, would conclude in
the year that our nation marks the bicentennial of
its birth. According to the Report, such a plan
should stress the nature and strength of American
federalism; the growth of its mass educational system;
developments in culture, art, music,and drama; the
progress of its science and technology; the nature
of a society that has accommodated different religions
colors,and nationalities from all over the world;
and the perennially youthful character and optimistic
outlook of American civilization. The Commission
added that all these points must be related to the
"interests, experience and problems" of foreign
audiences.[34]

     In the mid-1960's, the USIA moved toward inte-
grating its country objectives by applying the PPB
(Planning, Programing, and Budgeting) system.
Popularly identified as the "McNamara Management
Revolution," PPB starts with planning about objectives, develops programs on the basis of these objectives, and translates those programs into budgetary requirements. PPB is an analytic technique
attempting to relate policy planning to resource
use and budgets.

     In 1967, the USIA prepared 38 country "Program
Memoranda." They show the total costs of the various media activities in each individual country and
weigh the effectiveness of the total program in
terms of U.S. objectives and target groups. While a
direct relationship between specific media and
specific attitude changes abroad may always be impossible to determine, the USIA has found that much
worthwhile analysis can be undertaken short of this
ideal.

     Although Country Plans are classified documents,
there is sufficient reference to them in Congressional hearings to give us some insight into their

technique. As for content, the Country Plan is
drawn so that it outlines concisely the internal
situation in the country as it affects local USIA
activities. It describes traditional and present
attitudes toward the United States lists the most
significant national issuances; and explains the
problems confronting the American Mission such as the
level of literacy and communications facilities. The
aim of each Country Plan is to interpret the USIA's
over-all mission in terms appropriate to local conditions. The plan also suggests the Agency potential
in each country in the context of the total American
effort there, taking into consideration the inherent
limitations of an information program.

In establishing short-range objectives and programs, the Public Affairs Officer must prepare
specific projects relating to the achievement of
country objectives to resources available or estimated to be available. Projects must be, first,
significant enough to justify advance planning and,
second, capable of accomplishment within local conditions and USIA-anticipated resources. They must
advance at least a single Agency objective,while
reaching one or more of the target audiences of that
country.

Within the policy-making units at USIA headquarters, each Country Plan is reviewed by the Office
of Policy and Research,as well as by the Office of
the Assistant Director for the regional area concerned. This procedure involves problems of internal
coordination described earlier in this chapter's
discussion on the Agency's internal organization.
It would seem, however, that the latter office is
the more important of the two in this regard.
According to an illustration by Thomas C. Sorenson,
former Deputy Director for Policy and Research, the
procedure works briefly as follows:

> For instance, the plan for Egypt
> would be reviewed by my Office and
> the Assistant Director of Near
> Eastern and South Asian Affairs.
> Together we would discuss it, then

approve or disapprove of the plan.
It would then go back to the post
and the post would resubmit it if
changes were desired, and then
when it is approved it becomes our
basic document in that country.[35]

The nature of international relations requires
that these plans avoid rigidity so that they may
react favorably to changing circumstances. Accordingly, specific projects,together with such planned
continuing activities as the operation of libraries
and English instruction,form only the skeleton of each
year's program. Public Affairs Officers are instructed to keep Plans flexible and to accept opportunities for increasing American prestige within
the framework of the defined country objectives and
information guidance supplied from Washington.

In its early years, the Country Plan's basis
was centered upon no more than four or five objectives. Subsequently, it was found that the information program would function more effectively
if these objectives were broken down further into
more specific categories. USIA Director Theodore
Streibert noted that:

. . . we found that although these three
or four or five objectives, such as
anticommunism, developing democratic
processes, helping education or
trying, maybe more specifically to
combat communism in labor organizations, or in education, that we
needed more specific tighter objectives than these. So we are engaging in establishing in each
country, based on their recommendations to us, a short-term objective
or two, which will be worked on in
the nature of six months or a year,
immediate objectives to which we can
apply all our resources.[36]

The Country Plan approach to Agency objectives
has not overcome the organizational problems, de-

scribed elsewhere in this essay, that prevent the
USIA from operating with maximum effectiveness. In
spite of having detailed statements of Country Plans,
the Agency still encounters difficulties because of
the relatively new organizational arrangement and the
use of personnel who are often unfamiliar with the
fine points of administrative technique. There is a
wide variation in the manner in which Agency Public
Affairs Officers view their responsibilities for
planning and budgeting. According to Ben Posner,
USIA Assistant Director of Administration, an examination of various country budgets reveals some
that seem to reflect careful program consideration
with proposed modifications justified in terms of
country objectives.[37] Others appear to be merely
mechanically prepared documents indicating minimum
effort to relate cost data to program objectives.
There are Country Plans that propose no changes for
the future year, or the changes that are recommended
lack adequate justification.

Posner found the Country Plan notion basically
sound but recommended several operational improvements. While this book is not especially concerned
with the budgetary implications of the Country Plan,
his suggestions merit study by students of USIA program objectives. His principal criticism was that
classifications of accounts provide neither for
personnel service costs, nor for direct-media support
costs in the operating reports used by the Agency.
There exists an inadequate system for correlating
fiscal data and performance reports at the country
level. Communications between country missions and
media services concerning the management of direct-
media support resources were in need of clarification. In total, the administration of the Country
Plan suffered due to poor correlation between financial reports and estimates of program performance.

In formulating a Country Plan, the Agency must
coordinate its field program with the broader purposes of American foreign policy. As such, the USIA
is a member of what is known as the United States
Country Team abroad. Each governmental agency must
coordinate its overseas undertakings so that they

will not operate at cross-purposes to or duplicate one
another's efforts. The Country Team approach aims
at avoiding in the field the deep jurisdictional
rivalries evident in Washington. While disputes
still take place under this concept, the Team
acquires a certain solidarity by virtue of common
experiences in dealing with the local government, on
the one hand, and with Washington, on the other.

The USIA, which is newer than most agencies
operating foreign programs, has, perhaps, more of a
stake than the others in securing field conditions free
of interagency strife. Inasmuch as it is the public
relations instrument of the United States abroad,
the USIA also gains when it is able to publicize a
harmonious rather than discordant country effort.
Finally, a coordinated country program benefits the
Agency because it enables Public Affairs Officers
to more readily contribute their expertise to policy
formulation.

Historically, large-scale problems of coordinating American representation abroad appeared roughly
around the same time as the establishment of the
independent information program. The evolution of
the Country Team concept has been in the direction
of strengthening the authority of the Ambassador as
the coordinator of American activities in the country
of his assignment. Essentially, this approach is
designed to return to the Ambassador the position
of leadership as it was exercised before World War
II.

Prior to the "New Diplomacy," the Ambassador's
authority was seldom challenged by other American
representatives abroad. The limited responsibilities
of the few officials from these departments caused
him little hardship. Following World War II this
situation was complicated by the assumption of international leadership by the United States. In addition to an official foreign information program,
a vast network of economic aid missions was introduced into the area of American foreign representation.

The organization of Country Team machinery grew
out of a series of Executive Orders, Presidential
letters and memoranda, official studies, and State
Department instructions. Among the early measures
in this connection were the recommendations of the
Hoover Commission in 1949, the Clay Paper of 1951,
and the Rockefeller Report of that same year. By
July, 1951, the Country Team terminology was in
widespread use in United States Missions in western
and southern Europe. When the Subcommittee on
United States Economic and Military Assistance to
Free Europe of the Senate Committee on Foreign Relations held testimony in Europe in the summer of 1951,
the testimony received was considered to be in the
nature of a Country Team presentation. Whether to
use the Country Team mechanism, however, and the
precise constitution of the Country Team at a specific post was (and still is) a matter for decision
by the individual Ambassador in light of the particular conditions at his post.

Thus, the Country Team concept preceded the
establishment of an independent information program.
Originally, this team included the military and
economic assistance programs, together with the Department of State's representation. When the USIA
was founded, Agency officials argued that it could
best implement its program through the mechanism of
the Country Team. Indeed, the USIA, as well as the
International Cooperation Agency (ICA), recommended
that the Country Team be made mandatory. Such action was opposed, however, by the Department of
State.

The Director of the USIA raised this question
with the State Department in a memorandum of August
2, 1955. After reviewing the problems of coordination in the field, he offered the following recommendation:

> Although there is a marked improvement
> in the integration of foreign activities
> under the direction of Chiefs of Mission
> and the working relationships in the
> United States Missions provide an

168   THE U.S. INFORMATION AGENCY

> effective organizational framework,
> both the day-to-day activities and
> the long-range planning would be
> improved through the establishment
> of a formal organizational arrange-
> ment in every post to insure compliance
> with the directives of the President
> as set forth in Executive Order 10476
> of August 1, 1943.[38]

To achieve this end he suggested that there be established under the chairmanship of the Chief of Mission a "Country Coordinating Committee," which would comprise such officials as the Ambassador, Public Affairs Officer, commanding officer of the Military Assistance Mission, the Economic and Political Counselors of the Embassy, and the Director of the United States Operations Mission. The USIA recognized that the Committee would not serve as a substitute for full staff meetings.

In its reply, the Department of State endorsed the principle of complete and effective coordination of U.S. activities in foreign countries under the Chiefs of Mission. It stated, however, that the policy of full field coordination could best be attained through using varying techniques to meet differing local conditions. The Chiefs of Mission should continue to exercise discretion as to the types of coordinating devices that would prove most adaptable.

The USIA dropped its proposal temporarily. The ICA, however, transmitted to the State Department in December, 1956, a proposed circular message that had been approved in draft by the USIA. The purpose of this message was to stress "the essential nature of Country Team under the leadership and guidance of the Chief of the Diplomatic Mission." The State Department again argued that the Ambassador in each country should determine the type of coordinating machinery best suited to his particular country.[39]

In recent years, the role of the Ambassador as chief administrator of the American program abroad has been increasingly strengthened, thus confirming

the Department of State's position on the foregoing issues. The USIA and the variously titled
economic aid programs did not succeed in encroaching
on the State Department's primary role in Country
Team coordination. Yet the matter of field organization has continued to be of concern to the White
House. The most noteworthy Executive activity in
this area was President Kennedy's message to all U.S.
Ambassadors. It emphasized their role in providing
leadership and coordination for all American activities abroad.[40] The message did not make reference,
however, to such formal machinery for this process
as had been sought in earlier years by the USIA.
After considering the directive at regional confer-
ences with Ambassadors, the Department of State
decided to leave to the individual Ambassador complete control over the form, composition, and
terminology of the coordinating instrument best
suited to accomplish the desired end in his post.[41]

Regardless of the machinery the Ambassador
chooses to implement the Country Team concept, the
USIA has a vital interest in the success of such an
undertaking. A Chief of Mission capable of articu-
lating the American position on a particular issue
facilitates the task of the USIA in this regard.
Donald M. Wilson, former Deputy Director of the
Agency, observed that:

> An interested and articulate ambassador,
> skilled in public affairs, is a prime
> asset for any overseas information pro-
> gram. Close cooperation is not only
> desirable, it is essential; lack of
> it may be disastrous in the public
> affairs field.[42]

Similarly, Edmund A. Gullion, a former Ambassador
to the Republic of the Congo, noted that:

> The Ambassador is personally engaged in
> "public affairs" as much as any member
> of his staff. He may be a gregarious
> type to whom people-to-people diplomacy
> comes naturally, or he may be a sharp-

shooter more effective on certain
groups and individuals . . .
Ideally, the chief of mission should
be the man who is able to sum up in
a seminal phrase, speech, instruction,
or dispatch the position and purpose
of the United States. If he can do
this he will not only infuse the USIA
program with vitality but can polarize
the whole U.S. effort in a given country.[43]

The Ambassador not only affects the USIA as a
practitioner of public relations, but he can also
appreciably determine the nature of the information
program itself. The allocation of resources on a
country-by-country basis rests with the Director of
the USIA. Yet the Ambassador's opinion will have
much weight with respect to the allocation of money
and manpower by media--press versus radio or TV,
for example--and in the selection of target audiences.
The determinations of the Ambassador are, in effect,
decisive for USIA programs.[44]

Accordingly, the Subcommittee on National
Security Staffing and Operations, in its study, "Basic
Issues," observed that the USIA is relatively agree-
able to having its programs coordinated by the
Ambassador.[45] The study distinguished the willingness of the various units of the Country Team to
permit such control. While all members of the Country Team acknowledge the Ambassador's position and
keep him informed on their activities, those involved
in day-to-day operations or possessing their own
reporting lines to Washington are more reluctant to
come under his authority. Most elements of the
Country Team do not regard themselves as parts of
the Ambassador's staff--rather they look outside
the country to intermediate headquarters or Washington for guidance, and their loyalties tend to run in
the same direction.

In the study's classification, the USIA is
perhaps more dependent on the Ambassador than any
of the other major agencies attached to the Country
Team. At one end of the spectrum, it found such
"old-line members" of the diplomatic staff as the

political counselors having the greatest interest in
supporting the Ambassador. These officials had no
line of reporting to Washington except through the
Ambassador--and informal letters to colleagues. At
the other end of the spectrum was the Military Assistance Advisory Group (MAAG). Its work was highly
operational, it had its own lines to the Pentagon,
and it took a limited view of the Ambassador's right
to interpose himself between it and the Pentagon.
The study found CIA closer to the MAAG, and AID
somewhere in the middle of the spectrum. USIA, however, most closely resembled the diplomatic model.

While the mechanics of interagency coordination
under the Country Team approach naturally differ for
each Ambassador, we will conclude our discussion in
this area by citing one illustration. The method
chosen by Lincoln Gordon, former Ambassador to
Brazil, is instructive because he had academic experience with this question before his actual appointment to the post. It would appear, therefore, that
Ambassador Gordon's use of the Country Team reflected
both research and operational considerations.[46]

As a formal entity under Ambassador Gordon, the
Country Team did not have stated meetings at regular
intervals. The basic coordinating group consisted
of a daily staff meeting on Mondays through Thursdays.
Present at these meetings were the Deputy Chief of
Mission, the Economic Minister-AID Mission Director,
the political, economic, and administrative counselors,
the head of the consular section, and finally, the
Director of the USIA Mission. On Friday, there was
a larger meeting, including such officials as the
head of the Peace Corps, the scientific attache, and
the heads of the American military missions.

In view of the many agencies attached to the
Brazilian Mission, it would appear possible that the
USIA would have encountered problems in coordinating
its objectives with theirs. The observation of
Ambassador Gordon that he came upon no "serious
difficulties" in carrying out President Kennedy's
directive on Country Team coordination would indicate, however, that the Agency represented no

obstacle in this connection.

On specific issues involving interagency over-
laps, such as USIA publicity for AID activities,
coordination would be effected through direct col-
laboration in the preparation of reports or negoti-
ating papers. When actual differences of opinion
arose, they were referred to the Deputy Chief of
Mission or the Ambassador for resolution in consultation with the officers concerned. None of these
procedures involved formal voting by Country Team
participants. With reference to policy guidance for
such operating programs as that of the USIA, Ambassador Gordon avoided "interfering" with their daily programs. He tried to serve as the active leader of
the component agencies, however, and not merely the
"passive partner" or resolver of occasional disputes.

In sum, the establishment of an independent information program marked one of the major expansions
of American foreign operations in the postwar years.
Alongside this program grew the concept of the
American Country Team abroad, with the Ambassador
exercising ultimate responsibility. The adjustment
of the USIA to the broad policies and other agencies
of the Country Team is a dynamic and continuous
function. There is no one best method for organizing
the Country Team so as to be most beneficial to the
information program. Yet it is to the Agency's advantage when the Ambassador's authority over the
Country Team members is unambiguous. Simply recog-
nizing his primacy over the Country Team is inadequate;
the extent of his authority must be clearly established. Information objectives are most readily
achieved when the Ambassador's position as manager,
as well as captain of the Country Team process, is
explicit. If the Country Team components do not
respect the Ambassador's authority, how much more
will be their disregard for the USIA, which has been
so severely mistreated by the Congress?

The Country Team is still not always the chief
source of Country Plans. Thus, the confusion in
Washington regarding the position of the USIA in
foreign policy formulation will remain, regardless

of the Ambassador's capacity to coordinate his Country Team. It would seem to be the Agency's hope,
however, that the absence of interdepartmental strife
within the foreign affairs community in the field
would eventually provide the means for eliminating
much of the uncertainty in coordinating policy at
the Washington homes of the foreign affairs agencies.

TRAINING OF USIA PERSONNEL

This study has thus far evaluated the USIA's
capacity to implement information objectives on the
basis of the Agency's internal structure and relationships with other departments engaged in foreign
affairs. It has avoided a content analysis of the
USIA program. What role does the USIA's training
program play in this regard? How well are information officers equipped to influence foreign opinion
about the United States?

It is difficult to demonstrate that the compe-
tency of an information officer is proportionate to
the amount of time devoted toward his instruction.
It may be argued that a successful USIA officer must
possess primarily an inherent understanding of human
motivation. The foremost American information
specialists in World War II represented various professional backgrounds. They were not the products
of any particular career preparation. Yet by the
end of the war, in Thomson's judgment, the Office
of War Information had developed an organization
combining a quality of personnel, procedures, techniques and operations that compared favorably with
the international information programs of American
allies.[47]

Given the dynamic setting of world politics
and the total exposure of the United States, however,
the USIA cannot afford to rely on many of the untried
techniques that characterized the American information effort in earlier years. The professional
nature of a contemporary information program demands
that its practitioners be trained in it through a
rigorous course of instruction.

The requirements of USIA work are formidable.
These include a knowledge of the subtle and complex
problems of gauging foreign attitudes, of media
operations and the processes of communications, of
the structure of foreign societies and international
relations, of American life and culture, and of
methods of managing large staffs and substantial
operating programs. USIA personnel must combine
these talents in a world setting that is growing
increasingly delicate. American private life offers
no counterpart to these various responsibilities,
and fully qualified persons, therefore, do not come
to the Agency already trained.

Accordingly, the instruction that the USIA
provides for Junior Officer Trainees and lateral en-
trants is essential to their capacity for fulfilling
informational goals. The length and intensity of the
Agency's present training programs are inadequate,
however, for the role assigned to the USIA in American foreign policy. This section will attempt to
explain the cause for this shortcoming, as well as
the Agency's plans for producing better-trained
personnel.

Presently, the Agency's training program covers
the role and mission of the USIA and its relationship
to those of other agencies; how USIA field operations
are planned and executed; the media USIA uses to
communicate with foreign peoples; the major efforts
being made in the information field in support of
particular foreign policies; the administration of
USIA posts; and the scale and direction of Communist
efforts in various parts of the world. It also includes aspects of American life that help advance
American policies abroad; the operations of other
agencies in the foreign affairs field; study of the
area to which personnel are assigned; the making and
conduct of foreign policy; and how USIA's capabilities are applied in the special circumstances of the
developing areas of the world.[48]

Junior Officer Trainees receive an eight-week
basic course, with instruction time divided between
the USIA and the Foreign Service Institute of the

State Department. Some USIA officers take part in
an additional four-week program designed to help
them function effectively in either a USIA or State
Department capacity. In the latter course, emphasis
is placed on factors influencing public policy and
foreign affairs, policy coordination,and international Communism.[49] Providing they do not know the
languages already, trainees study for four months if
they are going to a "world" language area, or six
months if assigned to a "hard" language area.

The serious deficit of the Agency's training
program has elicited perhaps more agreement from
parties associated with it in an official capacity
than any other aspect of the USIA's administrative
structure. The U.S. Advisory Commission on Information, official studies such as the President's Committee on Information Activities Abroad (the Sprague
Report) and Personnel for the New Diplomacy, and the
Director of the Agency (in testifying on legislation
proposing a National Academy on Foreign Affairs)
have all emphasized the need for upgrading the training of USIA personnel.[50]

This training suffers in two broad areas: the
quantity of instruction, and the facilities available
for such instruction. The proportion of officer
time dedicated to training in proportion to officer
time in toto suggests the shortcomings of the Agency's
training program. Among the USIA's Reserve Officers,
this proportion is slightly over 2 per cent. The
comparable figure in the military departments is
roughly 12 per cent, exclusive of language instruction. Even Foreign Service Officers and Reserve
Officers in the Department of State spend some 5 per
cent of their total time undergoing training.[51]

The Reports of the U.S. Advisory Commission on
Information have urged the lengthening of the information training program as a means of improving
the quality of Agency personnel. Prior to the establishment of an independent information organization, the Advisory Commission observed that a new
employee assigned to an overseas post should be
intimately acquainted with the policies and opera-

tions of the home office. This familiarity could
not be accomplished through a few weeks of orienta-
tion. All such personnel, it suggested, should have
at least six months of media training before beginning their work abroad. As noted above, however, the
present program is only ten weeks in length.[52]

Inasmuch as the USIA is engaged in fostering
favorable foreign opinion toward the United States,
it would seem that its personnel would have the means
of communicating with these people in their native
languages. This rule should apply not simply to broad-
casters over the Voice of America, but to field personnel as well. The lack of linguistic proficiency on
the part of USIA officers has therefore represented a
major obstacle toward the implementation of American
information objectives. While the proficiency of
Agency officers has risen in recent years, it is still
less than that desirable for a country seeking to
maintain its world leadership.

To be sure, the Agency's problems in this connection are heightened by the absence of university
facilities for instruction in non-Western languages.
It remains for the USIA to train its personnel in
these critical languages. As is the case with the
Agency's entire training effort, intensive language
instruction demands sizable funds. The willingness
of Congress to provide for such a program is no
greater, however, than its willingness to finance a
more extensive information campaign in general.
Nevertheless,the President's Committee on Information
Activities Abroad (Sprague Committee) recommended
that:

> Pending such time as language in-
> struction in our schools and uni-
> versities can take up the slack,
> the language training efforts of
> the Foreign Service and the other
> services should receive greater
> Congressional support. Prior to
> departure for new posts executive
> personnel should, whenever pos-
> sible, be required to undergo an

adequate course of language training.[53]

A further weakness of the Agency's training program is the absence of an institution that would
enable the USIA to deal in depth with specialized
problems in international communications. The Agency
has endorsed legislation for an academy providing
advanced training in foreign affairs. Increasingly,
the Department of State, the Agency for International
Development, and other agencies engaged in foreign
programs have also favored the establishment of
such an institution.

The Report of the Committee on Foreign Affairs
Personnel (Herter Committee) called for the establishment of this institution in the form of a National Foreign Affairs College. The Herter Committee
noted that the parochial training programs of the
leading foreign affairs agencies have prevented them
from considering U.S. policy as a unity. Under the
present organizational division, valuable prospects
were lost for sharing experiences, for exchanging
and challenging points of view, and for learning the
problems not only of one's own job, but of those in
related programs.

> The training structure is a roadblock,
> rather than an avenue, to the realiza-
> tion of a true family of services. And
> the Foreign Service Institute has found
> it difficult to embrace the full dimen-
> sions of the new diplomacy . . . [54]

The institution would provide a recognized center for the planning and coordination of such training programs. It would, moreover, foster a climate
in which officers of the foreign affairs community
could explore common problems and exchange their
knowledge. The Report stressed that the Academy
would not aim at duplicating the offerings of existing educational institutions. Inasmuch as the
Academy would have access to classified research
material, it would be able to draw on sources unavail-
able to university graduate schools. Yet the Report

recommended that visiting professors from outside
universities should supplement the Academy's core
faculty.

> Indeed it may be that not the least
> important consequence of the estab-
> lishment of this National Foreign
> Affairs College would be the creation
> of an effective link between the
> world of scholarship and the world
> of practical experience in foreign
> affairs, to the mutual stimulation
> and benefit of both.[55]

The President's Advisory Panel on a National
Academy of Foreign Affairs likewise favored the creation of such an institution. The panel's head was
James A. Perkins, former Vice President of the
Carnegie Corporation. Its report observed that educational programs for foreign operations personnel
had not kept pace with three basic changes in the
tasks these officials were asked to perform. According to the Report, these changes were:

> (1) . . . the interdepartmental nature
> of foreign policy formation and the
> necessity for closely coordinated team
> operations overseas. In spite of these
> increasingly obvious facts of life, our
> public educational and research programs
> are essentially parochial in character--
> with understanding and vision limited
> by departmental and jurisdictional walls.

> (2) . . . the vast expansion of our
> foreign policy operations in two direc-
> tions from traditional, polite state
> diplomacy: On the one hand, in the
> direction of the U.S. and other inter-
> national public forums . . . on the
> other hand, in the direction of over-
> seas activities projecting our officials
> into local matters . . .

> (3) . . . the need, occasioned by the

> continuous pressure from Communist
> state and ideological interests, for
> carefully prepared strategy and tactics
> focusing equally on preserving societies
> from communism and on building stable,
> democratic, economically progressive
> states.[56]

While both the Perkins and Herter Reports concerned themselves with the entire foreign affairs
community rather than only with the USIA, their conclusions are particularly relevant to the Agency's
mission. Certainly, an official information program
is,in itself,a striking demonstration of the new
setting of contemporary diplomacy referred to above.

Inasmuch as the Agency must come in contact
daily with the changing opinions of foreign popula-
ations, such training at the suggested Academy would
enhance its operating program. The interdepartmental
nature of this institution would serve the USIA from
the policy-making standpoint as well. Information
objectives often have been harmed by the unsettled
status of the USIA in foreign policy formulation.
Through a broadly based educational program stressing the totality of the foreign operations effort,
personnel outside the USIA would more fully
appreciate the role of information objectives. The
USIA therefore has as much to gain from the formation of this Academy as perhaps any other agency.
Indeed, many of the operational and policy problems
discussed in this study would at least receive more
concerted attention, were such an institution set up.

Accordingly, Edward R. Murrow wholeheartedly
endorsed the Administration's bill providing for the
establishment of a National Academy of Foreign Affairs.[57] The Academy would benefit the USIA, he
argued, through its provision for a more intensive
study of foreign opinion formation and its facilities
for interdepartmental coordination among foreign affairs agencies. He did not foresee the Academy replacing the current USIA training course for Junior
Officers. The USIA would still require its own
course for the basic training of these officers.

However, the Academy would fulfill the Agency's need
for advanced training in information technique.
Furthermore, the promise of the Academy lies not in
what it would take over from the present training
program,but in what it would discover for the future.

> Its greatest contribution lies on the
> frontier of the unknown. I trust the
> proposal will be weighed not on what
> it can presently include but on what
> it can potentially create.[58]

It is significant that Mr. Murrow supported
legislation seeking an institution designed exclusively for foreign affairs personnel, rather than one
that would train civilians as well. The latter proposal has been suggested in the writings of some
Americans trained in such communications fields as
broadcasting, public relations, and publishing. David
Sarnoff, of the Radio Corporation of America, and the
late C. D. Jackson, of Time, Inc., are among the
prominent figures who have advocated a broader program than that proposed in legislation for the National Academy of Foreign Affairs. In the mid-1950's, the
Orlando Committee, a body of civic-minded Florida
citizens, campaigned for a potent anti-Communist
training institute.[59]

Legislation for such a program was introduced
in the same Congress considering the National Academy
of Foreign Affairs. The alternative bill called for
the establishment of a Freedom Commission and a
Freedom Academy. According to Senator Karl E. Mundt,
one of the Commission's sponsors:

> We can no longer ignore the capacity
> of the private sector to contribute
> to our total war effort. This group
> should be highly representative, in-
> cluding businessmen, labor officials,
> professional people, educators, agri-
> cultural experts, performing artists
> and scientists. We must begin to
> think of international relations in
> its broadest sense, encompassing both

governmental and private intercourse.[60]

The objection of the foreign affairs community
to the Freedom Commission was on the ground that it
would be impossible to sustain an effective strategy
opposing Communism and promoting freedom unless the
strategy embraced the whole spectrum of foreign affairs. While the legislation for the Freedom Commission correctly assumed the magnitude of the Communist threat, these agencies maintained, it excluded
any consideration of the many problems in other areas
that related to the global struggle.[61]

In addition to the substantive matters associated
with the USIA training course, such discussion is
valuable to the present study for the insight it sheds
into the objectives of the information program. Hearings on the training of American foreign affairs
personnel have raised more fundamental issues than
simply the instruction of Cold War specialists. The
diverse proposals in these hearings raise the issue
whether the USIA would best serve American interests
in the role of an information or propaganda agency.
Can democracy be "sold" more effectively through
multimillion-dollar persuasion programs than through
the comparatively modest USIA budget? Or even more
basically, will a "hard-sell" persuasion campaign
seeking to minimize internal conflicts (such as over
federal-state relations) and concealing short-comings
(such as securing equality for all Americans regardless of race) alienate more foreigners than it would
attract?

As has been shown elsewhere in this study, the
USIA has opposed,in the past, overtly propagandistic
approaches that mirror the worst in American advertising technique. Although it has acknowledged the
need to improve the training arrangement, the Agency
has refused to adopt any of the strident schemes
proposed in this connection. Yet the problem of
producing Agency personnel with a more specialized
and intensive familiarity with communications techniques remains a critical one. Congress has still
not passed legislation upon the various proposals
discussed above.[62] Meanwhile, the dynamic setting

of international politics necessitates a continuous
upgrading of knowledge relating to the communications
process. Or, as Mr. Murrow described it before Congress, changing events require that the USIA must
become increasingly adept in knowing "what to say
and how to say it."[63] Information objectives will
continue to suffer so long as the Agency is incapable
of fulfilling both these criteria.

NOTES TO CHAPTER 3

1. Legislation on Foreign Relations with
Explanatory Notes, p. 217.

2. U.S. Congress, Senate Committee on Government Operations, Hearings: Reorganization Plans
Nos. 7 & 8 (of 1953), 83d Cong., 1st sess., 1954,
p. 27.

3. U.S. Congress, Senate Subcommittee of the
Committee on Foreign Relations, Hearings: Overseas
Information Programs of the United States, 83d Cong.,
1st sess., 1953, p. 103.

4. Hearings: Reorganization Plans Nos. 7 & 8
(of 1953), op. cit., p. 174.

5. U.S. Congress, Senate Subcommittee of the
Committee on Foreign Relations, Organization of U.S.
Overseas Information Functions, Staff Study No. 4,
83d Cong., 1st sess., 1953, p. 8.

6. House, Hearings, p. 813.

7. Ibid.

8. U.S. Advisory Commission on Information,
Fifteenth Report (March, 1960), p. 30. Lay students
of the information program as Walter Joyce, op. cit.,
have also endorsed such an improvement in the Agency's
status.

9. U.S. Advisory Commission on Information,
Sixteenth Report (February, 1961), p. 8.

10. The administrative arrangements for the
American foreign cultural program have similarly come
under criticism. In their thorough study of the
American cultural effort, Thomson and Laves conclude
that the program remains "segmented, poorly coordinated and inadequately financed." However, they do
not recommend a new Cabinet post for the cultural
program as an alternative. Instead, they ask that
the President, the Secretary of State, and the Congress increase their understanding of and support
for this area of foreign policy. Thomson and Laves,
op. cit., pp. 186-87.

11. Report of the Committee on Foreign Affairs
Personnel, Personnel for the New Diplomacy (Washing-
ton, D.C.: Carnegie Endowment for International
Peace, 1962), p. 11.

12. Thomson, op. cit., p. 144.

13. David Wise and Thomas B. Ross, The U-2 Affair (New York: Random House, 1962), p. 108.

14. Ibid., p. 30.

15. Thirteenth Review of Operations, July 1-
December 31, 1959 (Washington, D.C.: USIA, 1959),
p. 5.

16. Fourteenth Review of Operations, January 1-
June 30, 1960 (Washington, D.C.: USIA, 1960), p. 4.

17. Wise and Ross, op. cit., p. 259.

18. U.S. Congress, Senate Committee on Foreign
Relations, Hearings: Events Leading to the Summit
Conference (Report No. 1761), 86th Cong., 2d sess.,
1960.

19. U.S. Congress, Senate Committee on Foreign
Relations, Hearings: Events Leading to the Summit
Conference (Report No. 1761), 86th Cong., 2d sess.,
1960, p. 23.

20. Hearings: Events Leading to the Summit
Conference, op. cit., p. 213.

21. Ibid.

22. Ibid., p. 218.

23. For discussion of this approach, see Richard
C. Snyder, Harold W. Bruck, and Burton Sapin, Foreign
Policy Decision-Making: An Approach to the Study of
International Politics (Glencoe, Ill.: The Free
Press, 1962).

24. U.S. Advisory Commission on Information,
Sixteenth Report (February, 1961), p. 8.

25. House, Hearings, p. 783.

26. USIA: The Agency in Brief (1964), Appendix
C, p. 4.

27. Thomson, op. cit., p. 371.

28. The observation of Edmund A. Gullion,
former U.S. Ambassador to the Republic of the Congo,
is relevant here,

> But much of this activity will be
> beside the point or out of key if the
> Chief of Mission and the USIA yield to
> the temptation of lifting most of their
> material from the whizzing transmission
> belt which runs from USIA Washington.
> It may be that the difference between
> a good information effort and an indif-
> ferent one is the degree to which the
> program is allusive to local conditions,
> produced on the spot, timely, and geared
> to day-to-day advocacy of U.S. interests.
> U.S. Congress, Senate Subcommittee on
> National Security Staffing and Operations
> of the Committee on Government Operations,
> Hearings: Administration of National
> Security, 88th Cong., 2d sess., 1964,
> p. 480.

29. U.S. Advisory Commission on Information,
Seventh Semiannual Report, Feb. 23, 1953, (H. Doc.

94, 83d Cong., 1st sess.), p. 4.

30. U.S. Congress, Report of the Senate Committee on Foreign Relations, Overseas Information
Programs of the United States (Hickenlooper Report),
83d Cong., 1st sess., 1953, p. 10.

31. U.S. Congress, House Subcommittee on Africa
of the Committee on Foreign Affairs, Hearings:
United States Information Agency Operations in Africa,
87th Cong., 2d sess., 1962, p. 10.

32. U.S. Advisory Commission on Information,
Fourteenth Report (March, 1959), p. 17.

33. U.S. Advisory Commission on Information,
Seventeenth Report (February, 1962), pp. 12-13.

34. U.S. Advisory Commission on Information,
Twenty-First Report (February, 1966), p. 22.

35. House, Hearings, p. 776.

36. U.S. Congress, House Committee on Foreign
Affairs, Hearings: U.S. Information Agency, 84th
Cong., 1st sess., 1955, p. 3.

37. See Posner, op. cit., chap. v, "An Evaluation
of the Country as a Principal Unit of Planning,
Programing and Budgeting," for elaboration on this
point.

38. U.S. Congress, Senate Subcommittee on
National Security Staffing and Operations of the
Committee on Government Operations, The Ambassador
and the Problem of Coordination, 88th Cong., 1st
sess., 1963, pp. 24-25.

39. Ibid.

40. Ibid., pp. 155-156.

41. Ibid., p. 35.

42. Senate, Hearings: Administration of
National Security, op. cit., p. 433.

43. Ibid., p. 480.

44. Statement of Donald M. Wilson in ibid.,
p. 433.

45. U.S. Congress, Senate Committee on Government Operations. Administration of National
Security, 88th Cong., 1st sess., 1963, p. 9-16.

46. Ibid., pp. 364-77.

47. Thompson, op. cit., p. 83,

48. Letter from Bryan M. Battey, former Chief
of the USIA Training Division, May 7, 1964.

49. USIA Correspondent, (Washington, D.C.:
Government Printing Office), VIII, No. 8 (August,
1966), 2.

50. For a strong indictment of the management
of the State Department, including its training program, see Smith Simpson, Anatomy of the State Department (Boston: Houghton Mifflin Co., 1967), and my
review, "State and the System," Saturday Review, L,
No. 22 (June 3, 1967), 30-31.

51. Personnel for the New Diplomacy, op. cit.,
p. 105.

52. U.S. Advisory Commission on Information,
Sixth Semiannual Report, July 1, 1952 (H. Doc. 526,
82d Cong., 2d sess.), p. 16.

53. President's Committee on Information
Activities Abroad, White House Press Release, January
8, 1961, p. 5.

54. Personnel for the New Diplomacy, op. cit.,
p. 106.

55. Ibid., p. 108.

56. U.S. Congress, Senate Committee on Foreign
Relations, Hearings: Training of Foreign Affairs
Personnel, 88th Cong., 1st sess., 1963, p. 156.

57. See ibid., pp. 13-16, for the proposed bill dealing with the National Academy of Foreign Affairs.

58. Ibid., p. 109.

59. Arguments for the establishment of such an institution, and its possible effects on foreign policy, are presented in U.S. Congress, Senate Subcommittee to Investigate the Administration of the Internal Security Act and other Internal Security Laws of the Committee on the Judiciary, Hearings: Freedom Commission and Freedom Academy, 86th Cong., 1st sess., 1959, pp. 1-179. For an indication of the sentiments of professional communications specialists, see "The War We're Losing," Printer's Ink, September 14, 1962.

60. Training of Foreign Affairs Personnel, op. cit., p. 173.

61. See ibid., pp. 48-50, for objections of the Department of State, which led the opposition of the foreign affairs agencies to the Freedom Academy.

62. Pending the establishment of an interagency Academy, the Foreign Service Institute is moving in the direction of such an institution. According to the FSI's Director,

> The impact of the Herter and Perkins
> reports, and the insistence on inter-
> agency teamwork in recent years--
> especially country team training--have
> done much to help FSI evolve its spirit
> and practice in the Academy's direction--
> away from State and foreign service pre-
> occupations toward meeting the common
> needs and viewpoints of the Government
> foreign affairs community, including all
> its agencies and services.

George Allen Morgan, "Toward the Academy: A Design for FSIA," Department of State Newsletter, No. 35, (March, 1964), p. 11.

63. Training of Foreign Affairs Personnel, op. cit., p. 113.

CHAPTER **4** THE APPROPRIATIONS
COMMITTEES AND
INFORMATION OBJECTIVES

THE APPROPRIATIONS PROCESS

In an earlier chapter, this study referred to
the causes of Congress' misunderstanding of the information program. It was argued that the Subcommittee on the Department of State, Justice, and
Commerce, the Judiciary, and Related Agencies of the
House Appropriations Committee served as the chief
Congressional critic of the USIA. The present chapter evaluates the organization and politics of both
the House and Senate Committees on Appropriations
as they relate to information objectives.

In theory, such Legislative Committees as the
House Committee on Foreign Affairs and the Senate
Committee on Foreign Relations, are concerned with
the substance or objectives of the USIA. Information objectives are fixed once Congress approves
the bills that these Legislative Committees report
and the President signs them. The Legislative Committees, so the theory continues, set a ceiling on
appropriations in the process. The Appropriations
Committees merely perform a preaudit function to
determine whether all the revenue requested to carry
out what Congress has authorized is really needed.

In fact, the Foreign Affairs Committees in both
Houses of Congress deal with the USIA on an irregular
basis. While the Foreign Affairs Committees in each
chamber are broken down into subcommittees based
upon geographic areas of the world, there are no subcommittees with ongoing interest in the USIA. With
the exception of the obligation of the Committee on
Foreign Relations of the Senate to hold hearings on

confirming new USIA Directors, there is no guarantee
that either body will deal with the Agency during a
Congressional session. Accordingly, the substantive
or policy-making committees of Congress in the area
of foreign relations have abdicated an intimate or
even a regular relationship with the USIA.

Instead, the Appropriations Committees have re-
placed the policy-making committees as the most active overseers of USIA programs. The House Committee
on Appropriations, through its power of the purse, has
had a far deeper impact on the nature of the information program than its Senate counterpart. This development is ironic because the Senate traditionally
is the more important of the two chambers in other
issues of foreign affairs--such as advising and con-
senting to Presidential declarations of war, ratifi-
cations of treaties, and nominations to federal posts.

In foreign affairs appropriations, the Senate
functions most conspicuously as an appellate body.
Tradition dictates that the House must initiate
money bills. Owing to its special prerogatives,
the Senate feels especially duty-bound to keep a
watchful eye upon the lower chamber's involvement in
this area of foreign affairs. The less-harried
atmosphere of the Senate also enables it to more
readily iron out foreign policy inconsistencies.

In serving as a court of appeals on USIA appropriations, Senate hearings run considerably shorter
than those of the House. The Senate tends to concentrate on departures of the lower chamber from official budget estimates. In contrast to the House
Committee, the Senate frequently conducts open hearings and displays less secrecy and mystery.

The chief purpose of USIA officials appearing
before the Senate Committee is to convince it to re-
vise the appropriations bill to approximate more
closely the proposals submitted by the Executive
Branch of the House. The members of the Senate Committee are usually equipped with copies of the hearings and reports of the House group. USIA spokesmen
then submit a detailed statement analyzing the House

measure, answering complaints expressed in the House
Committee's Report, and requesting changes in the
bill. Thus, the Senate's consideration of the Agency's
1959 budget requests began with an "Appeal Letter of
Justifications," addressed to Senator Lyndon B.
Johnson by George V. Allen, USIA Director. The transcript of the occasion read as follows:

> Senator Johnson: We will insert at
> this point in the record the letter
> of May 16, 1958 from George V. Allen,
> Director, United States Information
> Agency, on amendments to the House
> bill . . .

> Dear Senator Johnson: It is respect-
> fully requested that your committee
> make certain amendments to title IV
> of H.R. 12428, 'Departments of State
> and Justice, the Judiciary and Re-
> lated Agencies Appropriation Act,
> 1959.'[1]

Accordingly, the House Committee sets the level
of USIA appropriations while the Senate, at times,
modifies the original estimate. Inasmuch as nearly
all overseas information projects require money for
support, the House Committee wields tremendous influence over USIA objectives. It is not only with
regard to the information program, to be sure, that
the House Committee exercises such power. The House
Committee on Appropriations serves as the leading
agency to control every other area of financing American foreign and domestic undertakings as well. Holbert
Carroll has referred to the Appropriations Committees
as constituting "third Houses" of Congress.[2] Richard
Fenno observes that the Committee, "far from being merely one among many units in a complicated legislative-
executive system, is the most important, most
responsible unit in the whole appropriations process."[3]
Furthermore, when congressmen on this Committee are
interested in learning of USIA policy, they will often
bypass the Agency's Congressional liaison for other
USIA officials.

How has the House Committee on Appropriations come to exercise such decisive influence on the information program, in particular? Its power, to begin with, stems from the fact that its bills are rarely challenged by nonmembers. The Appropriations Committee is a closely-knit body, and a legislator may endanger the likelihood of obtaining approval for domestic projects in his district by setting himself up as too severe a critic of Committee action It is chiefly with this in mind that legislators customarily refrain from taking issues of foreign policy appropriations to the floor, once the Appropriations Committee has stated its verdict.

A further source of the Appropriations Committee's weight is that its operations remain secret to outsiders. The annual hearings concerning the USIA are, in fact, voluminous. Yet these records are heavily edited, leaving only a small, formal part of the Committee in public view. Even the subcommittees of the Appropriations Committee keep their operations secret from each other. It is part of the elaborate esprit de corps of this Committee for each subcommittee to avoid interfering with the work of the others. As a result, Fenno reports, senior committeemen rarely know what is taking place until the subcommittees transmit their reports to the full Committee a few hours (or a few days) before the bills come before the House. Whatever limited public support there exists for adequate financing of the USIA remains stifled until after the Committee has reported.

The full fifty-man Committee usually meets only for an hour or so only on those occasions when its subcommittees have a bill prepared for the floor. Here, too, the hierarchic structure of the Committee on Appropriations works to the detriment of a larger USIA budget. According to tradition, a junior member does not count for much in Committee deliberations. His role is that of an "apprentice" to veteran Committee members. He is expected to acquiesce in an arrangement that gives most influence (except in areas involving him locally) to the senior members. Those who have attained leadership positions in this

body, Fenno noted (on the basis of interviews with
Committee members), have learned that conformity to
Committee norms is the ultimate source of influence
inside the group.[4] Even as ambitious members are
reluctant to criticize Committee action on the floor,
they likewise aim at keeping to a minimum friction
with their colleagues in Committee. Long established
tradition of Committee criticism of the USIA amounts
to a severe obstacle in the way of newcomers wishing
to praise the Agency's performance or defend its
budget requests.

CRITERIA OF CONGRESSIONAL EVALUATION

In evaluating the tactics by which the Committees on Appropriations determine the USIA's budget,
it must be stressed that the essential problem facing
them is how to allocate scarce resources among many
competing national security programs. The mounting
international responsibilities of the United States
require intelligent planning in allocating these
limited funds. As suggested earlier in this study,
the Committees on Appropriations are seriously un-
equipped for making such choices for the information
program. The Committees' views are colored by
domestic and often very local considerations. Agency
requests for wider flexibility in the management of
funds are normally turned down. Long-term projects--
even if they extend barely beyond a single fiscal
year, such as research undertakings--are looked upon
with suspicion. The USIA budget, in short, is not
examined as a whole unit consisting of interrelated
projects designed to strengthen American overseas
objectives.

Nevertheless, these conclusions lack significance unless it can be shown that the Appropriations
Committees' actions harm the USIA. Did their cuts
of the Agency's requests for its research program,
for instance, adversely affect the USIA? This study
has argued earlier that it is virtually impossible
to evaluate precisely the effectiveness of the
foreign information program. Yet it seems that the
USIA's research budget of some $2 million is inade-

quate for assessing the opinion of mankind--however
tentative the Agency's findings may be.

Furthermore, it is safe to argue that the
Appropriations Committees' activities have substantially contributed to public misunderstanding of the
information program. The uncertainty of Agency
officials regarding budgetary requests has also
harmed employee morale. While the Agency could sore-
ly use expert advice from legislators experienced in
public relations, it is forced to content itself
with frequently trivial attacks on its program. Thus,
if Congress is not guilty of adding to existing confusion within the Agency and the foreign policy establishment concerning information objectives, it has
hardly helped in clarifying them.

The Committees on Appropriations employ three
major types of controls over the information program.
First, and most significant, they determine how much
money will be allowed for the USIA. Second, in the
hearings and reports they review policies and their
administration. They wield influence by the language employed in Committee reports and language
inserted in legislative provisions. Third, the Committees exercise year-round surveillance over the
expenditure of funds.

Control Over Funds

The most formidable weapon exercised by the
Committees on Appropriations is determining the amount
of money allocated to the USIA. The approach of the
House Committee to the Agency's budget is a variation of its general attitude toward requests from the
Executive Branch. As an immediate goal, Committee
members maintain that they must strike a highly
criticial, aggressive posture toward budget requests,
and that they should, on principle, reduce them.

Budgetary requests, regardless of the agency or
department, are said to be filled with "fat, padding,
grease, pork, oleaginous substance, water, oil,
waste tissue, and soft spots."[5] Action verbs most

commonly found in transcripts of the Committee are
cut, carve, slice, squeeze, lop off, shave, fry,
whack, and wring. The tools of the trade of the
appropriations unit are referred to as knife, blade,
meat ax, meat cleaver, hatchet, and wringer.[6]

The USIA must therefore make the best of the
traditional hostility of the House Committee on
Appropriations to budgetary increases. The Committee's outlook is evidenced by the observation of an
unidentified subcommittee chairman.

> . . . you see that the bureaus are
> always asking for more money--always
> up never down. They want to build up
> their organization. You reach the
> point--I have--where it sickens you,
> where you rebel against it . . .
> They say, "only $50,000 this year,"
> but you know the pattern. Next year
> they'll be back for $100,000, then
> $200,000.[7]

The level of appropriations for the information
program sharply fluctuated from the year of its
establishment through 1961. Since then, the USIA
budget has been generally raised by several millions
of dollars annually.

Study of the House Committee's action reveals
that it habitually reduced the funds requested by
the President for the Agency. Secondly, the House
of Representatives would normally approve without
change the estimate recommended by its seven-member
Appropriations Subcommittee. Thirdly, the full
Appropriations Committee apparently assumed that its
judgment would be remedied in the Senate. In a
representative four-year period cited below, the
Senate always raised the House-approved sum (see
Table 5). In all cases where the Senate was higher
than the House, the conference agreement reflected
the increase. While the Senate performed its traditional appellate function in this area, it could not
wholly erase the impression of confusion and insta-
bility in information goals created by the House ac-

tion. Furthermore, the tradition of conference
agreement prevented the Senate from restoring substantially the major reductions voted by the House.
(USIA appropriations for 1966, however, it should be
noted, were an exception to the foregoing practice.
The House allowance for the Agency was $140,254,000
and the Senate recommendation was $140,000,000.)

Despite the behavior of both chambers in reducing appropriations sought by the Executive, they
refrained from challenging the basic principles of
the information program. The Committees were bent
on economizing on the USIA budget rather than challenging the need of such an undertaking. According
to Committee Reports, the USIA served a vital function of American foreign policy. The problems of
the Agency stemmed, instead, from faulty program
management. Thus, the more generous Senate noted:

> The Committee again urges the Director
> to reappraise the information program,
> with a view to concentrating its ener-
> gies and funds in areas and activities
> considered to be most productive in
> the accomplishment of the foreign
> policy objectives of the United States.[8]

The House Report of that year also underscored the
need of an effective information operation.

> The Committee is of the opinion that
> a strong and effective program can be
> carried out within the funds allowed.
> It is recognized that in certain fields,
> such as radio and television, some in-
> creases may be justified.[9]

Essentially, the cost criticism of the Appropriations Committees is directed at the internal management procedures of the USIA. The House chamber
normally conducts exhaustive inquiries into this
aspect of the Agency's budget. Representative John
J. Rooney, Chairman of the House Subcommittee, is
the most rigorous prosecutor of the Agency in this
connection.

TABLE 5

USIA APPROPRIATIONS 1954-57

Fiscal Year Bill No.	Estimate of President to Congress	House Appropriations Committee	House Action	Senate Appropriations Committee	Senate Action	Conference Agreement
1954 H.R. 6200 83d Cong.	$ 87,900,000	$ 60,000,000	Same	$ 80,000,000	Same	$ 75,220,000
1955 H.R. 8067 83d Cong.	89,000,000	75,814,000	Same	80,614,000	Same	77,114,000
1956 H.R. 5502 84th Cong.	85,500,000	80,500,000	Same	88,350,000	Same	85,000,000
1957 H.R. 10721 84th Cong.	135,000,000	110,000,000	Same	115,000,000	Same	113,000,000

Thus, the subject of travel allowances for Agency employees en route to an assignment or returning to the United States occupied three pages of the 1965 testimony on the Agency. Painstaking inquiry was made as to the conditions under which USIA officers travel by air in first-class or economy accommodations. Committee members cited varying allowances for flights from Los Angeles, California, to Washington, D.C., of $332 and $188 in an apparent effort to uncover faulty budget procedures. The Committee also examined the Agency's regulations on domestic railroad travel. Representative Rooney noted:

> When I travel on the Congressional Limited to New York from Washington, the Government employees go to the first-class section and I generally go to the day coach.[10]

Another illustration of the Committee's close observation of the Agency's internal management related to its request for a new headquarters in Paris. Representative Rooney commented:

> Here we have the President advocating economy in Government and we are presented with a request for $2 million to buy a parcel of land, not a building, but to buy a parcel of land. . . . I will give you three guesses as to what will happen in connection with this fiscal year 1965 request.[11]

To its credit, the rigorous examination of the House Appropriations Subcommittee often uncovers USIA undertakings of dubious worth. Thus, the hearings revealed that the USIA invested some $44,000 in a film on President Tito's American visit, to be shown only in Yugoslavia. The Agency contracted to produce the film although it lacked any agreement to show films in that country. In effect, the USIA was gambling on the good will of the Yugoslavian Government.[12]

Similarly, Congressman Rooney demonstrated the

rather hollow claim of the Agency regarding the
English-language publication Span, which was said to
be its "best-selling magazine" in all India. It was
shown that the total production expenses of this
publication (exclusive of Washington personnel who
reviewed copy) amounted to over $400,000. Against
this outlay, the Agency's income of $3,000 from sub-
scriptions appeared unimpressive.[13]

By comparison, the Senate's cost criticisms of
the information program reflect more substantive
considerations than those of the House. In keeping
with its role as an appellate body for the USIA, as
suggested earlier, the Senate is content with allow-
ing the House Committee to perform the minute spade-
work regarding Agency appropriations.

                     Hearings and Reports

The uncertainty of the Appropriations Committees
regarding information objectives is revealed more
clearly in the annual hearings and reports than
through the two other methods of policy control. The
pattern of Congressional hearings on the USIA does
not differ considerably from year to year. The same
protagonists conduct their well-worn attacks on the
information program--Congressman Rooney on "giveaways,"
Congressman Frank Bow on unnecessary expenditures,
and Senator Allen J. Ellender on the worth of binational centers. (Binational centers are private,
autonomous organizations governed by democratically
elected Boards of Directors chosen from American
residents and nationals of the host country·) The
fact that similar criticisms are raised year after
year does not mean that the Agency is insensitive
to them. On the contrary, information officials
closely study past hearings and reports in order to
prepare answers for their next appearances before
the Committees. The USIA either acknowledges the
validity of these criticisms or prepares a case
documenting the need for continuing existing programs.

According to the orthodox interpretation of the
responsibilities of Congressional committees, substantive issues relating to the information program

are endorsed before the subcommittees convene to
explore fiscal issues. Yet the annual hearings constitute the chief occasions wherein policy issues
are determined. To this extent, it is instructive
that House inquiries are often designed to catch
Agency witnesses off their guard, rather than to
stimulate high-level discussion over the information
program. To be sure, this attitude marks the Appropriations Committees' over-all dealings with federal
agencies, and is not limited to the USIA. In exploring images and expectations of House Appropriations Committee members, Fenno observes:

> Members do derive some satisfaction
> from the obvious anxiety of agency
> witnesses. They value the chance it
> gives them to manipulate agency un-
> certainty and keep the agency on
> its mettle.[14]

In evaluating the record of the House and Senate
Appropriations Committees, it is worth stressing how
unconvinced the members are that the USIA is actually
succeeding in implementing information objectives.
The fact that each year the most fundamental questions regarding objectives are posed at the hearings
would indicate either the foregoing conclusion or
that the Committee members are almost totally unin-
formed as to USIA objectives. It is possible to cite
numerous illustrations wherein the same basic issues
are raised in the Committees. In the hearings for
1963 appropriations, Senator McClellan, Chairman of
the Subcommittee on Appropriations, told Director
Murrow:

> I agree wholeheartedly with the idea
> that we need to try to influence these
> countries in these areas about which
> you are speaking, to give more coop-
> eration and more favorable action and
> effort in these areas. But I don't
> understand, and I wish you would
> comment on this, how you do that through
> a USIA organization. I thought that
> would be done by our high government

officials . . . That is why I can't
see how this USIA function is calcu-
lated to influence other governments
in that area.[15]

In a similar vein, Representative Rooney, in the hear-
ings for 1965 appropriations, asked the Head of the
Agency's Information Center Service (which sponsors
USIA overseas libraries) the following:

I will now give you a question, and
as a result you might start driving
a brewery truck through your operations. You will then have all the
time you need.
What would happen if all this were
abolished?[16]

Few questions reflect more forcefully the lack
of confidence in the Agency than that posed by Representative Neal Smith in hearings for 1964 appropriations. Following an attack by Representative Rooney
on the USIA's Polish radio broadcasts, Representative
Smith asked:

Is any consideration being given to
the desirability or undesirability
of changing the name of the U.S.
Information Agency so that when
people tune in they don't immediately discount what they hear?[17]

The impatience of the Committees with the USIA
is most cogently expressed in claims that the Agency
lacks inventiveness in program formation. For some
members, the appropriations requests for one year
are, more or less, duplications of the preceding
year's undertakings. Accordingly, if the Agency
failed in overwhelming the world in a given year with
the American cause, why would it be any more successful with the same program in the future? An exchange
between Representative Rooney and Edward V. Roberts,
Assistant Director for Africa, is illustrative.

Mr. Rooney: It looks to me, from your
justifications, like you carry on the
same stuff year after year.

Mr. Roberts: It seems to us, sir,
we are developing a program as we
go along to try to take into ac-
count--

Mr. Rooney: Developing or enlarging,
which would be the proper word?

Mr. Roberts: I think "developing,"
Sir.

Mr. Rooney: What do you have in the
program in this 1965 budget that you
did not have in the 1964 budget program?

Mr. Roberts: We have provision for
making more documentary films than
we did last year. We have provision
for introducing and setting up a
magazine for the young which we do
not have this year . . .

Mr. Rooney: According to your
testimony, year after year, you have
been doing the same thing each year.
I do not consider any of this new.[18]

The foregoing exchange is ironic to the extent
that the House Committee traditionally remains suspicious of, if not hostile to, Agency attempts at
innovating programs. Budget requests are examined
on the merit of previous-year allocations, rather than
through a fresh approach stressing creativity or
newness. Instead of blaming themselves for an unwillingness to approve bold or untried techniques,
the Committee members cite the Agency for alleged
conservative programing. That the Appropriations
Subcommittees fail to face up to the possibility that
they, too, may share responsibility for frustrations
of the information program is an inescapable conclusion in examining hearings in this regard.

A further source of disagreement concerning information objectives relates to the reasoning for
sponsoring programs in nations ostensibly friendly
to the United States. If legislators are convinced
of the need for USIA activities, it is with reference

to either the Communist bloc, the new Afro-Asian
nations, the unsettled Latin American republics, or,
in the mid-1960's,Vietnam. Thus, for fiscal year
1966, 103 Americans were budgeted for the information
program in Vietnam, whereas only 156 Americans are
stationed at USIA posts in all of non-Communist
Europe. Information programs designed for Western
Europe or Australia and New Zealand, where the threat
of Communist penetration is relatively slight, draw
criticism in appropriations hearings.

To be sure, the USIA has been steadily reducing
its European activities in accordance with Congressional sentiment. The information program in France
has, perhaps, drawn the bulk of criticism in these
hearings,in view of that nation's wish for increased
independence from the United States in international
affairs. Since World War II, the USIA sought to
make French intellectuals aware of the great scope
of American artistic, scientific,and educational
achievements. At the peak of its activities about
ten years ago, the Agency operated eight centers
throughout France, in addition to its Paris headquarters. The offices were staffed by about 50 Americans and from 400 to 500 French employees. The USIA
had an annual budget of about $2.5 million in France.

In 1964, however, the only Agency office was in
Paris. It had 25 American and 125 French employees.
The budget for the 1964 fiscal year was about $1
million. The transfer of the Agency's chief in Paris
to Leopoldville may be considered representative of
the shifting emphasis of the information program.

When there are no international incidents to
justify questioning the information program in an
allied country, the Committees take issue from these
undertakings simply on the ground of economy. Accordingly, there were four pages in the House hearings for 1965 appropriations devoted to the need of
the information program in Great Britain. Committee
criticism was directed at the Agency's establishing
a series of chairs and lectureships in English universities. Essentially, the Committee questioned
this proposition on two counts. For one, it was

argued that the Agency had mistakenly assumed the
responsibility for stimulating the British educational
system. Secondly, and of greater importance, was
the contention that such a project would result in
wasting funds on an unnecessary undertaking. Congressman Bow observed:

> It seems to me what we must do is to
> try to save the economy of this country,
> and establishing chairs at Oxford and
> Eton might sound good on paper and
> please some people, but I do not see
> that this is accomplishing much in
> creating peace in the world or in
> creating a U.S. image. If we have not
> done that yet with the time and money
> that has been spent on it, there has
> been something wrong with the program
> from its inception.[19]

In addition to being critical of the raison
d'être of programs in Western Europe, Committee members at one time or another have questioned the need
for the USIA in practically every other country in
the world allied with the United States. Particularly irksome to Senator Ellender are the information
programs in Australia and New Zealand, as mentioned before. In his judgment, these nations did not warrant
the outlay of even a "dime," because there were "no
people in the world more pro-American than the New
Zealanders and the Australians."[20]

In other instances, Committee members have
taken issue with the stationing of information officers in Brasilia, Brazil, and in Puerto Rico.[21] The
Agency's film unit has also been charged with per-
forming the work of the United Nations through producing films publicizing the international organization.[22] Clearly, there exists serious confusion regarding the proper role of the USIA in publicizing
the United States among friends as well as enemies.

The appropriations hearings of both Committees
are rich in examples of personal, political, and
local geographic standards being used to weigh the

strength of the information program. Political scientists have argued that a main difference between
the responsibilities of the President and the Congress concerns the former's devotion to the national
interest (so-called), while individual representatives
are primarily concerned with satisfying local interests. The absence of deep conviction by both Committees regarding the effectiveness of the USIA further
encourages members to assess the USIA from the standpoint of such constituent considerations wherever
possible. Thus, Representative Bow inquired in the
hearings for 1963 appropriations as to the reason
why the Agency distributed abroad more publications
issued by Harvard than by Yale. He then sought information concerning the presentation of newspapers
published in his native state of Ohio. Upon learning
that the Agency sent only one such paper overseas,
he advised: "You would do well to have more papers
from Ohio. There are many fine papers published
throughout the State."23

Although Congress is less suspicious of the USIA
as a partisan political instrument than it was of
the World War II Office of War Information, there
appears in the hearings concern that the USIA may
portray American domestic politics to the disadvan-
tage of either of the two major parties. Accordingly,
Representative Lipscomb, a California Republican,
asked the Director of the Agency's Press and Publications Service to explain the inclusion of a documentary on the era of Franklin Delano Roosevelt in
its 1965 program. The following exchange thereupon
took place in the hearings:

> Mr. Rooney: This is a very fine publica-
> tion, I am sure.
>
> Mr. Lipscomb: I do not understand why
> the USIA programs have to go back and
> spend the kind of money on a pamphlet
> of this type about the Roosevelt years . . .
>
> Mr. Lipscomb: When copy is submitted
> for a book of that kind does USIA's
> Press and Publications Service edit it?
>
> Mr. Mackland (USIA): Yes sir.

Mr. Lipscomb: You followed this copy
on the Roosevelt era closely?[24]

If the hearings of the Appropriations Subcommittees reveal this prejudice of members regarding the
inclusion of certain items in the Agency's program,
they also point up their feelings over the absence
of material. The House hearings are characterized
by rigorous examination of the books and films distributed overseas. Such analysis allows the representatives to express their views concerning the
political content of the Agency's program. For example, in reviewing the Agency's book selections
for the 1965 fiscal year, Representative Rooney expressed surprise over the omission of particular
works on the FBI.

I do not see any of the Director's
books, "The story of the FBI," by
Don Whitehead. Mr. Hoover has
written a number of books which I
think would be just as interesting
on the subject of communism as
some of these things we have been
discussing. Are there any contained
in this list of giveaways?[25]

The hearings also contain illustrations of Committee members referring to their nonpolitical interests as a means for determining the information program's effectiveness. Inasmuch as the USIA acknowledges the absence of precise scientific standards
for measuring the program's impact, Committee members
often rely upon personal experience in sifting the
proposed budget. As an illustration, Senator Lyndon
B. Johnson, the Chairman of the Subcommittee on
Appropriations, devoted considerable energy to prob-
ing the activity of the Agency's "hobby committee on
spaniels." Some three pages of the hearings for
1959 appropriations are devoted to this aspect of
information objectives. Senator Johnson had believed
that the Agency's People-to-People program included
the aforesaid hobby. He was disappointed to learn
that there existed no separate program dealing with
spaniels, but rather it fell under the heading of

the pet subcommittee of the hobby program of the
People-to-People program.

Thus far, this section has examined the approach
of Congress regarding American information objectives
overseas. A recurring theme of the appropriations
hearings, however, concerns the prospect of the USIA
disseminating its material to the American public.
The interest of the Committees in this matter stems
from the traditional American distrust and fear of
propaganda organizations. The Appropriations Subcommittees have performed their functions well in
protecting the public from the possibility that the
Agency would seek to influence American domestic
opinion.

The House hearings for 1965 appropriations indicate the Committee's suspicion that the Agency is
bent on publicizing itself at home through the media
of films, press releases, and personal speaking en-
gagements. In recent years, Representative Lipscomb
has specialized in this aspect of the information
program. During the 1965 hearings, he accused
George Stevens, Jr., Director of the Agency's Motion
Picture Service, of undertaking speaking assignments
in the United States in an effort to gain publicity
for the information program--a procedure forbidden
by the law which originally set up the USIA. He
also charged Mr. Stevens with conducting a campaign
for showing USIA films within the United States.26

The fact that the USIA financed an anti-Communist
book that ultimately became a Book-of-the-Month Club
selection also precipitated a controversy concerning
information objectives. The Agency disclosed that
it had spent some $15,000 to have the book The
Strategy of Deception: A Study in World-Wide Communist Tactics developed and to purchase 2,000 copies
for overseas distribution. The book was edited by
Jean L. Kirkpatrick, a faculty member of Trinity
College.

Neither the copies being distributed overseas
nor several thousand sold in the United States indicated that a government subsidy financed the work's

preparation. The Agency defended this practice on
the ground that it was forced to contract for books
for overseas use that would not otherwise have been
published. To publicize the granting of covert
subsidies for publishing the book, the USIA argued,
would detract from the publication's effectiveness.

According to opponents of this procedure, the
Agency's activities would sow suspicion that the
American Government is secretly propagandizing its
own citizens. Furthermore, if the work in question
was successful enough to merit sales by a national
book club, why was it necessary for the USIA to
finance it initially?[27] While the legal authority
of the Agency to engage in such projects is arguable,
it is noteworthy that the Appropriations Subcommittees
attach some significance to this aspect of foreign
policy operations.

What emerges from the great detail of hearings,
the random flow of questions, and the stress on Agency
witnesses is the conclusion that the Appropriations
Subcommittees exercise immense influence over information objectives. All decisions regarding money
invariably raise policy questions. The real question, therefore, as Holbert Carroll maintains, is
not whether the Committee should wield influence in
foreign affairs, but how it does so and whether it
is a responsible agency of Congress. Although the
Appropriations Subcommittees have been responsible
for some tightening of information objectives, they
have more often failed to relate money decisions to
the policies endorsed by Congress and to the international responsibilities of the United States. The
Agency is blamed in these hearings for the general
failures of American foreign policy. The USIA must
suffer as a result of the antiquated procedures which
the Subcommittees employ for examining the USIA budget. Fortunately, such independent observers of the
information program as the U.S. Advisory Commission
on Information have increasingly called attention to
the shortcomings of the hearings of the Appropriations
Subcommittees. Suggestions for changing the established
procedure of appropriating funds for the USIA will be
examined at the conclusion of this study.

Surveillance Over Expenditures

The final method of control exercised by the
Subcommittees on Appropriations over the information
program is continuing surveillance over the expenditure of funds. The oversight consists of inspections
and investigations by members of the Subcommittees.
The most common means of surveillance is the inspec-
tion--at times also unannounced--of the actual information program overseas. To its credit, it should
be stressed that visits by Subcommittee members have
uncovered such flaws as inaccessibly located information centers, excessive staffing of posts, and ineffective programs. Thus, Representative Rooney, on a
trip to Poland, discovered that the bulk of the population avoided listening to the Voice of America,
inasmuch as its broadcasts were aimed at the intellectual leadership.

The most striking results of the surveillance of
expenditures are the arguments of Subcommittee members on behalf of expanding the Agency's binational
center program. The purpose of these centers is to
foster better understanding between the host country
and the United States. In this connection, the
principal activities of binational centers consist
of an English teaching program and an information
and educational program embracing lectures, movies,
and radio broadcasts designed to explain American
Government and institutions. The centers also provide library and lending services and sponsor semi-
nars and discussion groups for university students.
They are located in the principal and many smaller
cities of Latin America, as well as several Near
Eastern, Far Eastern, and European cities.

The leading champion of the binational center
approach to information objectives is one of the
Senate's most widely traveled members, Allen J.
Ellender of Louisiana. His advocacy of these centers
is worth examining at length, inasmuch as the centers
offer an alternative to traditional USIA operations
abroad. Essentially, Senator Ellender's support of
binational centers is based on the assumption that the
objectivity of the USIA is open to question if it functions as an overt information or propaganda unit.

In operating as an institution chartered by both the
United States and the host country, binational centers,
by contrast, are free of the foregoing suspicion.
In his 1958 Review of American Government Operations
in Latin America, Senator Ellender recommended:

> I particularly urge the Information
> Service to conduct its operations
> with more finesse: the rapier is
> often more effective than the bludgeon.
> In most areas of South and Central
> America, the Information Service
> has become synonymous with propa-
> ganda and, therefore, has either lost
> or is rapidly losing its effectiveness.[28]

According to Senator Ellender's findings, "eager
beavers" in the USIA and the Department of State were
seeking to "take over" these cooperative programs.
So long as binational centers continued under local
control, he argued, they will remain effective ex-
ponents of American purposes. Once an American
agency involves itself in the operation of these centers, their effectiveness becomes "automatically
impaired."[29]

Senator Ellender's 1960 inspection, which took
him to some thirty-five countries, confirmed this
earlier opinion regarding the USIA. On the basis
of its record, he maintained that the information
agency, as presently operated, "has about served
its purpose and that drastic changes as to its operations are in order." He listed seven means for
strengthening the effectiveness of the information
program. The most far-reaching recommendation was
that the United States do away with all the information centers insofar as "they are regarded in most
countries as purely propaganda outlets for spreading
imperialism."[30]

Other suggestions for improving the program include the turning over of existing USIA libraries to
binational centers,with local employees directing
activities. Libraries maintained at American expense
in Western Europe should also be donated to local

organs or operated by joint U.S.-local committees.
USIA movie libraries should be made available through
the binational centers for local use in all countries
where the Agency functions. Finally, the press operation of the USIA should be dispensed with, inasmuch
as this, too, bears the "taint of propaganda" characterizing the information center program. The
latter function would be undertaken by the American
Embassy, making available to the foreign country newspapers, periodicals, and transcripts of important
speeches and messages by American officials.

The arguments on behalf of such centers are instructive, however, inasmuch as they bring to bear
the results of surveillance of Agency operations by
the Appropriations Subcommittees. Binational centers
raise the question of whether the American information program must be discredited merely because it
is labeled as such. The alternative to Agency operations, if binational center enthusiasts have their
way, would be a cultural program of sorts divorcing
the USIA from day-to-day international issues. As
with other aspects of the Appropriations Subcommittees' treatment of the USIA, the case of the binational centers mirrors the deep disagreement between
the Agency and the Legislature over information objectives.

THE REFORMATION OF APPROPRIATIONS CONTROL

The preceding discussion has attempted to demonstrate the techniques of the Appropriations Subcommittees in evaluating information objectives.
These Subcommittees have a confused understanding of
the purpose of the USIA. In many ways, Subcommittee
members would have the Agency perform its task
differently from the present way. The main result of
their over-all dissatisfaction with the information
program has been a capriciousness with its budget.
As suggested earlier, it is questionable to what extent, if any, information objectives have suffered
due to Congress' reluctance to grant larger and more
regular appropriations. By increasing the budget
one year, however, and decreasing it the next--par-

ticularly in the period prior to 1961--Congress has
forced the Agency to spend valuable resources merely
enlarging or retrenching, rather than in conducting
its overseas operations on the basis of long-range,
coherent plans.

The Appropriations Subcommittees have opposed
most serious efforts to reform procedures for han-
dling the USIA's budget in Congress. Their hostility
stems from an inflated notion of their primacy in
money questions. The House unit, more so than the
Senate, has been guilty of this attitude. Because
nearly all proposals for reform in Congressional
budgetary practices require the Committee to share
its prestige, if not its power, with other Congressional Committees specializing in substantive areas,
it has spurned most such proposals. In Carroll's
judgment, the Committees on Appropriations "prefer to
behave irresponsibly in dealing with fiscal matters."[31]
The Appropriations Committees are not especially interested in integrating their control over information
operations with the rest of Congress.

Moreover, it appears that most legislators are
reluctant to lock horns with the powerful Committees
on Appropriations merely for securing larger budgets
for the much-criticized information program. Even
were it not for the USIA, congressmen would continue
to prefer uncoordinated appropriation methods. To
change the budgetary machinery for the USIA would
entail, in effect, a thoroughgoing revision of Congressional technique in this area. Ultimately, such
an innovation could produce an end to the traditional
means used by members of Congress to distribute
federal largess in their districts. In short, the
USIA is not worth such reform.

According to the U.S. Advisory Commission on
Information, a solution to the USIA's problems with
Congress would begin to emerge with the establishing of a joint Congressional committee on international information. In its Eleventh Semiannual
Report, it based its argument for such a committee
not merely on the ground of improved budgeting for
the USIA, but rather on the mounting significance of

international information.

> We would not ask the Congress to add
> another committee to the almost over-
> whelming number that now exist were
> it not for the inescapable fact that
> the importance of information in inter-
> national affairs, and for our own
> national security is rapidly increasing.[32]

Notwithstanding these recommendations, it appears unlikely that Congress will set up a new committee simply to deal with the information program.
A coordinating device of greater probability, however, is that of a joint subcommittee on the USIA.
An arrangement might be instituted whereby the Appropriations and Foreign Affairs Committees of each
chamber would meet cooperatively to assess the information program. Such a procedure would enable
the Committees to coordinate more closely the policy
and budgetary aspects of the information program.
It would also eliminate the duplication of effort
in which the money committee and the legislative
committee exhaust the same witnesses and often similar material.

The joint committee arrangement has been of
value with reference to the Senate's consideration
of military budgets. According to Huzar, participation by senators from the Armed Services Committee
helped the Appropriations Committee "to understand
better the consideration of policy involved in the
military supply bills."[33] The Department of State
has also benefited on occasion from liaison arrangements between the Foreign Relations and Appropriations Committees.

The House, by comparison, is not so organized
as to permit these cooperative arrangements. Insofar as the USIA encounters its main difficulties
with the lower chamber, it would seem that joint
committees do not offer a final solution to the
dilemma. Committees in the House are not so con-
sciously ranked in prestige as in the upper chamber.
Thus, a meeting of the Senate's Armed Services and

Foreign Relations Committees is a meeting of equals.
Should their House counterparts cooperate in such an
enterprise,more than seventy men would comprise the
group,instead of thirty,as in the Senate. Moreover,
the House Armed Services Committee is larger than
the Foreign Affairs Committee and has higher stature.
From the standpoint of size, therefore, joint committee enterprises do not augur much improvement in the
appropriations process for the Agency.

Unless the House Appropriations Committee adopts
the Senate practice in the appropriations area whereby the rules permit three senators from a legislative
committee to participate in the work of the Appropriations Committee in areas of mutual concern, the
USIA must continue to face the same obstacles as in
the past. The most recent illustration of the cost
that Congress and the Agency pay for these faulty
coordination arrangements concerns the hearings held
by the Subcommittee on International Organizations
and Movements of the Committee on Foreign Affairs on
"Winning the Cold War: The U.S. Ideological Offensive." While the hearings, which took place in both
sessions of the Eighty-Eighth Congress, represented
the most intensive examination undertaken by the
legislative committee into the information program
in its decade of operations, the findings were totally ignored in the annual sessions of the House
Appropriations Subcommittee.

As an example, a persistent source of disap-
proval by the House Subcommittee on Appropriations
are the research studies of the USIA. Committee
members argue that research investigations focus on
trivia, and are in effect, divorced from the central
problems facing the United States overseas. They
show little appreciation of the difficulties facing
the USIA--and indeed all students of communication--
in determining audience motivation and behavior.
Committee members are intolerant of the fact that
the Agency still has not conclusively determined the
factors actually influencing foreign opinion. As
Representative Rooney complained:

Of course, you have been asking those

same questions since the year 1 insofar as the birth of this Agency is
concerned.

There is nothing new about this.
This just makes a good scenario.[34]

The hearings on the U.S. ideological offensive
also touched on foreign opinion research studies.
The Foreign Affairs Subcommittee was far less critical of the alleged failure of such research projects.
Questions at these hearings were concerned with
evaluating the potential contributions of research
studies to the Agency's work, rather than opposing
or begrudgingly granting their worth. J. Leonard
Reinsch, Director of the U.S. Advisory Commission
on Information, sought to explain the difficulties
in assessing the impact of any communications media--
not only that of the USIA. Director Edward R.
Murrow explored the possibility of using research
surveys as a means toward more forcefully persuading
foreign students of American values.[35] All of the
foregoing testimony was overlooked in the following
year's appropriations session. Had there been coordination devices between these two Committees, it
is possible that the appropriations body would have
emerged much more knowledgeable in the purposes of
Agency research.

A final solution through which the House could
more effectively coordinate its activity regarding
Agency appropriations is use of the political parties. It has been suggested above that partisan
political debate over USIA program content is a
feature of Congressional appropriations hearings.
Political scientists have debated for decades the
merits of American party discipline. The case for
better-disciplined party procedure with reference
to USIA appropriations is merely a ramification of
the general academic debate in this connection.

The advantage of a political party as a coordinating agency is that it bears some responsibility
for all policies moving through Congress. Inasmuch
as the Congressional Appropriations Committees have

been referred to as "third Houses" of Congress, the
formal leaders of the parties play only a minor role
at this level of policy determination. Furthermore,
the unwillingness of legislative leaders to launch
bitter struggles for an activity as little appreciated
and understood as the USIA--in contrast to some domestic undertaking--cements the control of the
Appropriations Committees.

Leadership groups for each party could be created to assume the functions now scattered throughout each chamber regarding the USIA. Discussion,by
itself,is of great value to rational choice about
complex questions of public policy. According to Robert
Dahl, the decision-making process in the Legislature,
more than in any other significant power institution,
is in actual practice conducted by discussion.[36]
Even if the leadership group took no action, regular-
ized discussion by a broadly representative Congressional group might serve to eliminate some of the
policy-appropriations inconsistencies which plague
the information program.

The traditional impediments to a strong party
leadership role--faction-ridden, loosely organized
parties mirroring local interests--should not prevent
Congress from dealing more responsibly with the USIA.
A weak information program is as unwelcome to a legislator from the urban North as to one from the rural
West--assuming they are equally committed to enhancing
America's international reputation. Opinion varies
concerning the form and composition of such a leadership group. A noted study of the American Political
Science Association proposed that the congressmen of
each party elect and periodically affirm their confidence in a broadly representative legislative group.[37]
As a result of such an innovation, it might be possible for representatives and senators on different
committees with a concern for the USIA to meet and
coordinate policy decisions. Thus, such a setup
would allow for Representatives Rooney and Bow of the
Appropriations Committee to evaluate information objectives with Representatives Fascell and Fraser of
the Committee on Foreign Affairs. Surely, this arrangement could not possibly compound the existing

legislative confusion over information objectives.

Presently, the USIA suffers more than most domestic and foreign operations programs from Congress'
uncoordinated approach to public policies. The
evidence presented in this study supports the conclusion that confusion over information objectives
within Congress is inevitable under existing circumstances. The Agency's difficulties not only stem
from its problems in setting forth and assessing information objectives, they are also traceable to
Congress' haphazard evaluation of the information
program. The case for seriously reconsidering the
means for Congressional treatment of the USIA is
impressive.

NOTES TO CHAPTER 4

1. U.S.Congress, Senate Subcommittee on Departments of State, Justice, Commerce, the Judiciary,
and Related Agencies of the Committee on Appropriations, Hearings, 85th Cong., 2d sess., 1958, p. 372.
Hereafter cited as Senate Appropriations, Hearings.

2. Holbert N. Carroll, The House of Representatives and Foreign Affairs (Pittsburgh, Pa.: University of Pittsburgh Press, 1958).

3. Richard F. Fenno, Jr., "The House Appro-
priations Committee as a Political System: The
Problem of Integration," American Political Science
Review, LVI, No. 2 (June, 1962), 311. Fenno has
also written the definitive study of Congressional
appropriations procedures: The Power of the
Purse: Appropriations Politics in Congress (Boston:
Little, Brown and Co., 1966).

4. Fenno, "The House Appropriations Committee
. . .," p. 322.

5. Ibid., p. 311.

6. Ibid., p. 312.

7. Ibid., p. 320.

8. U.S. Congress, Senate Subcommittee on Departments of State, Justice, Commerce, the Judiciary, and Related Agencies of the Committee on Appropriations, Report No. 424, 86th Cong., 1st sess., 1959.

9. U.S. Congress, House Subcommittee on Departments of State, Justice, Commerce, the Judiciary, and Related Agencies of the Committee on Appropriations, Report No. 376, 86th Cong., 1st sess., 1959.

10. U.S. Congress, House Subcommittee on Departments of State, Justice, Commerce, the Judiciary, and Related Agencies of the Committee on Appropriations, Hearings, 88th Cong., 2d sess., 1964, p. 250. Hereafter cited as House Appropriations, Hearings.

11. Ibid., p. 171.

12. Ibid., p. 430.

13. Ibid., pp. 113-14.

14. Fenno, The Power of the Purse . . ., p. 328.

15. Senate Appropriations, Hearings, 87th Cong., 2d sess., 1962, p. 470.

16. House Appropriations, Hearings, 88th Cong., 2d sess., 1964, p. 453.

17. Ibid., 1st sess., 1963, p. 14.

18. Ibid., 2d sess., 1964, p. 90.

19. Ibid., p. 163.

20. Senate Appropriations, Hearings, 83d Cong., 2d sess., 1954, p. 1453.

21. House Appropriations, Hearings, 87th Cong., 2d sess., 1962, p. 220.

22. Ibid., p. 439.

23. Ibid., p. 474.

24. Ibid., 88th Cong., 2d sess., 1964, p. 384.

25. Ibid., p. 483.

26. Ibid., pp. 434-35.

27. Ibid., pp. 486-87. See The New York Times, May 3, 1964, p. 82, for additional comment on this matter.

28. U.S. Congress, Senate Committee on Appropriations, A Review of the United States Government Operations in Latin America, 1958, 86th Cong., 1st sess., 1959, p. xv.

29. Ibid., pp. xvi-xvii.

30. U.S. Congress, Senate Committee on Appropriations, A Report on United States Operations, 1960, 86th Cong., 2d sess., 1960, pp. x-xi.

31. Holbert Carroll, op. cit., p. 207.

32. U.S. Advisory Commission on Information, Eleventh Semiannual Report (H. Doc. 376, 84th Cong., 2d sess., April 11, 1956), p. 19.

33. Elias Huzar, The Purse and the Sword (Ithaca, N.Y.: Cornell University Press, 1950), p. 29

34. House Appropriations, Hearings, 88th Cong., 2d sess., 1964, p. 565.

35. House, Hearings, pp. 40 and 47.

36. Robert A. Dahl, Congress and Foreign Policy (New York: Harcourt, Brace and Co., 1950), p. 124.

37. American Political Science Association Repor "Toward a More Responsible Two Party System," The American Political Science Review, XLIV, No. 3 (September, 1950), 17-24.

CHAPTER **5** CONCLUSION

The purpose of this chapter is to bring together
the conclusions and recommendations of the entire
study. It has aimed at exploring the controversies
over the objectives of the USIA. No information
policy can be finer than the foreign policy it aims
to support--but clearly it can be worse. This study
has avoided evaluating the actual program content of
the Agency. It has approached the controversy over
Agency objectives from three standpoints: the USIA
itself--including both its organization and its conception of international public persuasion programs;
the Agency's place in the foreign policy establishment; and the Agency's relations with Congress,
especially the appropriations bodies.

This study has not questioned the need for a
government-sponsored program attempting to influence
public attitudes abroad, as well as advising the
President and various departments and agencies on the
implications of foreign opinion. The need for such
an enterprise was well put by Theodore C. Streibert,
the Agency's first Director, shortly following its
creation:

> It is not enough for us to have sound
> policies dedicated to goals of universal
> peace, freedom and progress. These
> policies must be made known to and under-
> stood by all peoples throughout the
> world.[1]

Increasingly, it has been acknowledged by political
leaders of the free world and the Communist nations
that the mutual destruction that would follow an
all-out nuclear conflict makes such a confrontation

prohibitive. Assuming that "total victory"--or even
an international stalemate--is not to be attained by
either side through conventional military means, the
information program takes on strategic meaning as a
Cold War political instrument. While foreign information programs of themselves will not decide the
outcome of this dispute, it cannot be overlooked
that they are integral to the ultimate decision as
to whether the future of mankind will be freedom or
Communism.

The foregoing chapters argued that there exists
much disagreement regarding the general objectives
of the American information program. Intermittently,
there appear pronouncements from the President and the
Directors of the USIA attempting to set forth the
Agency's objectives. Essentially, Agency objectives
are said to aim at the following three goals: encouraging public support abroad for a peaceful world
community of free and independent states, free to
choose their own future and their own system so long
as it does not threaten the freedom of others; iden-
tifying the United States as a strong, democratic,
dynamic nation qualified for its leadership of world
efforts toward this goal; and unmasking and countering hostile attempts to distort or frustrate the objectives of the United States.[2]

Once the principal objectives of the information
program are stated, a series of interrelated obstacles prevent the USIA from fully implementing American foreign policy purposes. We cannot sharply
isolate each of these obstacles from the others.
The only certainty in this regard is that they are
rooted in the organization and attitudes of the Agency
the Executive Branch,and the Congress. By way of
summary, this chapter will review the principal
drawbacks to effective Agency activities and suggest
steps toward their amelioration.

SPECIFIC CONCLUSIONS AND RECOMMENDATIONS

Problems Within the USIA

Conclusion 1. The USIA has failed to determine
conclusively whether its purpose is to serve as an
information- or propaganda disseminating organization,
or both of these simultaneously. This consideration
is perhaps the most fundamental to any prospective
sharpening of the Agency's objectives. Lacking a
policy of insuring effective communication with the
peoples of other nations, all other American foreign
policies may fail. The American information program
has oscillated between a strident preoccupation with
Communism, on one hand, and the casual dissemination
of material about American life, on the other. The
U.S. Advisory Commission on Information has mirrored
the uncertainty regarding this issue as even have
Agency officials in Congressional testimony.[3]

Recommendation 1. That the USIA move further
in the direction of objective reporting. To be sure,
if the USIA moved entirely in this direction, it
would be in the position that the Associated Press
and United Press International now occupy. Nevertheless, the Agency should avoid the vituperative, propagandistic programs marking, for instance, the
"Campaign of Truth" in the early 1950's. In Congressional hearings, the USIA must emphasize its commitment to the broad principle of objective reporting.
This approach is the one best designed to advance
American policies. For the Agency to base its budgetary case on the immediate need of countering Communist activities, as it has argued in the past,
may appease more militant and fearful members of the
Committees on Appropriations. Such an argument,
however, compounds existing confusion within Congress
concerning the USIA and, more important, encourages
legislators to overrule necessary budgetary increases
in times of relative peace.

Conclusion 2. The USIA has failed to determine
conclusively the nature of the public opinion it attempts to influence abroad. Should the American information program concentrate on appealing to foreign
elites or masses? Is it wise investing the Agency's
resources in the comparative few members of the
ruling classes--whose continuance in office is especially uncertain in developing nations--or in a

broader program seeking to reach the largest number
of citizens? While the USIA classified Country
Plans may contain specific information regarding
these questions, the Agency has failed to establish
before Congress precisely who it is that it aims for
abroad. The Agency's deficiency in this matter relates to its limited appropriations from Congress.
With a highly restricted budget, it is unsound for
the Agency to ignore the actual rulers or would-be
rulers for an appeal to mass sentiments.

Recommendation 2. That the USIA stress the
relative importance of the masses as prime targets
for the information program. The growing literacy
and awareness of the masses must be fundamental to
any program of international communication. As
Welles Hangen put it:

> The "people" cannot be defined as a
> handful of English-speaking editors
> in the capital who can dine accept-
> ably in the Public Affairs Officer's
> house and whose views can be congen-
> ially cabled to Washington as evidence
> of "program effectiveness." I know
> some editors and senior reporters in
> New Delhi who rarely face the harsh
> necessity of buying their own lunch
> or dinner, so bounteous is USIS
> generosity.[4]

Such an undertaking implies a marked increase in USIA
appropriations. In reaching the masses, the USIA
must practice balance. Otherwise, the Agency faces
the danger of reaching a point of diminishing returns-
a point at which its operations are so conspicuous
that they tend to defeat the purposes.

Conclusion 3. The concept of country planning
is sound. As an effort to specify Agency objectives,
Country Plans describe traditional and present attitudes toward the United States, and the problems
confronting the American mission. They are drawn up
for flexibility, taking into account possible national upheavals. The quality of Country Plans varies

as well as the skill of information officers implementing them. Insofar as country programs precede
the creation of the present information program
(having been used by the International Information
Administration), they continue to be deficient in
regard to specific themes and long-range schemes.

Recommendation 3. That the country program is
worth retaining and that attention be devoted to
more effective management of these undertakings
through the elements of the Planning, Programing and
Budgeting (PPB) system. Future plans must increasingly incorporate specific projects. They must provide
for distant as well as immediate political eventu-
alities. More than any other operational device,
Country Plans must serve as the chief integrative instrument for the media, regional, and policy units
of the Agency.

Conclusion 4. The length and intensity of the
USIA training program are inadequate for the role assigned to the Agency in its founding legislation.
The proportion of officer time dedicated to instruction in proportion to officer time in toto is seriously deficient. The USIA lacks necessary facilities
for training officers to deal in depth with specialized problems in international communications or for
challenging the Communist commitment in this area.
The absence of requisite instructional facilities
will continue to limit the USIA's effectiveness.

Recommendation 4. That an institution be established for advanced training and research in international communications technique. The purpose
of this institution would be the assembling of a
body of knowledge on all aspects of communications
that persuade men. The Agency would gain this knowledge from the private sector in addition to officials studies. Such an institution may be designed,
at this point, for the limited use of the USIA or may
include other members of the foreign affairs community concerned with ideological and psychological
developments among its student body. However, American businessmen working abroad or students from
other countries should be excluded from enrollment.

Problems Relating to the Executive

Conclusion 5. For most of its history, the
Agency's role in the execution of U.S. foreign policy
has been shaped by the personalities of its Directors
and by their personal estimations of the Agency's
mission. The four men occupying the Presidency since
the founding of the Agency in 1953 have shown no
consistent interpretation of the information program's
objectives,nor its role in the foreign affairs community. As a result, it has been the Directors themselves rather than the Chief Executives who have most
influenced the nature of the USIA and its relations
with other Executive units and Congress.

Recommendation 5. The problem noted in the foregoing conclusion is partially related to Conclusions
and Recommendations 1 and 2 above. In addition, the
White House must demonstrate leadership if the USIA
is to fulfill effectively its persuasion potential.
The White House must regularly affirm the importance
of the information program to U.S. foreign objectives.
The President must establish clear channels of communication enabling the Agency Director to argue his
position in the event of his disagreement with other
members of the foreign affairs community.

Conclusion 6. For reasons noted in 5 above,
the USIA has not always been consulted on crucial
foreign policy strategy. Its role here has vacillated
depending upon the stature of the Director and the
attitude of the Administration. Much progress has
been made in recent years in strengthening coordination between the USIA and other Executive agencies
and departments engaged in foreign affairs. Yet
there still remain areas of conflict between the
Agency and the two dozen other Executive units sponsoring foreign programs. The most serious source
of conflict relates to the willingness and skill of
the Department of State to furnish policy guidance
to the Agency.

Recommendation 6. The information program should
be reorganized as part of a broader reorganization
of the foreign policy establishment. Under the new

arrangement, a senior Secretary of Foreign Affairs
would direct three sub-Secretaries of equal rank--
Secretary of International Public Affairs, Secretary
of International Economic Affairs, and Secretary of
International Political Affairs. This arrangement
would not provide the information program with
Cabinet rank--a status that has become decreasingly
meaningful within the government. However, this
reorganization would assure the information program
of bringing to bear its judgment in matters of foreign policy formation. It would also serve to
eliminate appreciably conflict over the information
program's policy guidance from other Executive agencies.

Conclusion 7. There exists uncertainty over
operational authority for managing information activities in support of U.S. foreign policy. In addition to the policy guidance problem facing the
Agency, noted in Conclusion 6, the information program suffers in the matter of actual program implementation. The Country Team approach has not
thoroughly overcome difficulties arising from the
presence of two dozen Executive agencies abroad.
The program of the United States in any one country
reflects not so much a rational appraisal of actual
needs and opportunities in that country as the adding
together of activities happening to fall within the
budgetary responsibilities of different departments
and agencies.

Recommendation 7. In accord with Recommendation 7, the information program director's presence
at the heart of the policy-making process would help
to clarify the operational authority of the USIA.
Once policy decisions have been reached, it is
necessary for the information program to have a
spokesman among the competing bureaucracies of the
foreign affairs establishment. The authority to
coordinate diverse overseas information and ideological operations must be at a level equivalent to
the diplomatic and political programs.

Problems Relating to Congress

Conclusion 8. The fragmentation of Congressional supervision over the information program prevents it from effectively evaluating the USIA's actual performance and potential. At least six major committees and an even larger number of subcommittees exercise jurisdiction over the information area of foreign policy operations. The absence of a single committee in each legislative chamber--composed of members knowledgeable on international communications--retards the contributions which Congress could possibly make in this area.

Recommendation 8. That the Congress establish a permanent committee on the information aspect of U.S. foreign policy operations. The proposed committee would serve as the chief source of information policy formulation. Its members would devote their main attention to the information dimension of U.S. overseas operations, just as the existing committees on foreign affairs are principally focused on diplomatic activities.

Conclusion 9. Despite the fragmentation of Congressional control over the information program, noted in the above conclusion, the Committees on Appropriations--especially the House unit--function as the leading policy determinants of USIA activities. To their credit, these Committees have uncovered operational shortcomings in the Agency's activities. However, the underlying suspicion and hostility of these Committees toward the USIA weaken the information program. Committee members lack precise notions of an information program's objectives. USIA appropriations fluctuate annually following no consistent criteria. The standards for USIA appropriations are based not so much on exacting analysis of the information program's long-term needs (which a) based on such factors as the Communist commitment) as they are on particular international incidents.

Recommendation 9. The creation of a permanent committee dealing with overseas information operations, noted in Recommendation 8, would help in restoring the Appropriations Committees to their

more limited--and proper--role in policy determination. The Appropriations Committees should ratify
rather than formulate information policy. While
this study hesitates recommending any specific dollar
amount for future appropriations, it proposes increases in the Agency's budgets. The speed with
which developing nations are approaching modern social conditions, as well as mounting Communist propaganda expenditures--especially in spurring "Wars of
National Liberation," as in Vietnam--compels the
United States to raise substantially the level of
current funds. Once the Congressional information
policy committee mapped out future Agency programs,
in accord with over-all U.S. foreign policy objectives,
the appropriations bodies would allocate necessary
funds.

Problems Relating to the U.S. Advisory
Commission on Information

Conclusion 10. In its twenty-two reports to the
Congress, the Advisory Commission has sought to con-
vey confidence in the information program's worth
as well as the expanding potential of the Agency.
The Commission has also aimed at drawing attention
to flaws in the USIA's conception and implementation
of information objectives. Many of the Commission's
suggestions have been adopted by both the Agency and
the Congress. Yet the Commission has unsuccessfully
urged,over a series of years,other reforms that it
considers integral to the information program. Notwithstanding a record of moderate accomplishment,
the size of the Commission is inadequate for the
role it should serve in information operations.
Consisting in 1968 of four members, as well as a
Staff Director, the Commission is unable to investigate closely the far-ranging projects of the USIA.
Thus, in 1966 the Commission met only ten times,
and each of its members independently inspected
Agency facilities in a handful of different countries.

Recommendation 10. That Congress enact legislation expanding the membership of the U.S. Advisory
Commission on Information. Congress should also

consider compensating Commission members, thus encouraging them to devote their main energies to the
information program. Appointment to the Commission
should ultimately bear the same esteem as an ambas-
sadorial assignment. A larger Commission would enable each member to specialize in a specific area of
Agency operations. The USIA would benefit from such
a close advisory relationship with these communications specialists.

Problems Relating to Nongovernmental Activities

Conclusion 11. Business and communications interests, while seeking a more effective information
program, reveal a serious misunderstanding of the
USIA's purpose. These interests are all too willing
to take the Agency to task for alleged failures.
They often overlook the many handicaps it faces--in-
ternal and external--in attempting to sway foreign
public opinion. They have failed to use their resources in persuading legislators and others in
government,as well as the American public,of the
need for an information program of greater influence
in the policy-making process.

Recommendation 11. That business and communications interests vigorously press for an adequate
information program. Within the Agency, these interests should seek a sharpening of information objectives and strengthening of program content. Exter-
nally, they should aim for clarification of the USIA's
status in the foreign policy establishment. They
should also attempt to impress on Congress that an
information effort commensurate with U.S. international goals merits larger appropriations than it
now receives. Conceivably, the aforesaid proposals
might be implemented by business and communications
interests through two means: the formation of pressure groups, such as those which crusade for foreign
aid appropriations; or, in accordance with Recommendation 10, the U.S. Advisory Commission on Information would aim at eliciting the judgment of these
interests on the main issues confronting the USIA
and incorporating them in its annual reports.

The notion that the opinion of mankind is of value and that mankind generally may judge right from wrong goes back to the early Stoic philosophers. The authors of the Declaration of Independence cited the opinion of mankind in declaring the causes for the colonies' separation from England. The Declaration expresses the belief that man and his opinions were worth something, and that a tribunal known as mankind sits in judgment upon the actions of men and states. For much of its history the United States has fulfilled its mission without regard to the opinion of mankind. It has only been in the most recent twenty years that the United States, confronted by international leadership and Communist rivalry, has turned once again to justifying itself before the tribunal of man.

One of the United States' modern pioneers of international persuasion, George Catlin, observed:

> It is one of the oldest observations
> in the history of the world that
> humanity cannot be deceived all the
> time and that it is, in the last re-
> sort, only to be convinced by a
> burning sincerity, a sterling integ-
> rity, and indeed by an almost naïve
> simplicity.[5]

While there is much truth in the foregoing statement, the existence of the USIA indicates that there must be some organized means to convince foreign opinion of the direction of American destiny. The years ahead will see the information program exercising a growing role in foreign policy--not because the USIA desires it, but because U.S. international commitments demand it. In reviewing the USIA's record on its tenth anniversary, Edward R. Murrow argued:

> . . . we are therefore no longer
> mere publicists grinding out our
> appointed quota of press releases.
> This is the superficial function of
> an information effort, and one which,
> without more substance, is doomed

to but slight effect.[6]

The information program now has a contribution to make to policy itself. The future of the United States greatly rests on how this program appeals to the opinion of mankind.

NOTES TO CHAPTER 5

1. Theodore C. Streibert, Department of State Bulletin, XXIX, No. 739 (August 24, 1953), 238.

2. Memorandum for the Director, U.S. Information Agency, from President John F. Kennedy (mimeographed), January 25, 1963.

3. It is noteworthy that the Twelfth Report (January, 1957) of the U.S. Advisory Commission on Information begins with the question, "Why does the U.S. Government need an international information agency?" The Report answers the question primarily on the Communist challenge. In subsequent Reports, however, the Commission generally bases its argument on long-range cultural requirements.

4. Welles Hangen, "USIA in the Next Decade," Foreign Service Journal, XL, No. 7 (July, 1963), 22.

5. George Catlin. "Propaganda and the Cold War," The Yale Review, XLIII, No. 1 (September, 1953), 113.

6. Edward R. Murrow, "USIA Today and Tomorrow," Foreign Service Journal, XL, No. 7 (July, 1963), 21.

BIBLIOGRAPHY

BIBLIOGRAPHY

OFFICIAL SOURCES

Great Britain. Summary of the Report of the Inde-
    pendent Commission of Enquiry into the Overseas
    Information Services (Drogheda Report). Cmd.
    9138. London, 1954.

_____. Overseas Information Services, Cmd.
    225. London, 1957.

_____. Report of the Committee on Represen-
    tational Services Overseas (Plowden Report).
    Cmd. 2276. London, 1964.

U.S. Advisory Commission on Information. Reports
    submitted to Congress pursuant to Sec. 603 of
    U.S. Information and Educational Exchange Act
    of 1948:
    First Semiannual Report, March, 1949; Fourth
        Report, April, 1951; Fifth Report, January,
        1952. Reports prepared for the Commission by
        the Department of State. Washington, D.C.: U.S.
        Government Printing Office, 1949, 1951, and
        1952.
    Second Semiannual Report, September, 1949;
        Third Semiannual Report, July 14, 1950;
        Eighth Semiannual Report, August, 1953.
        Washington, D.C.: U.S. Advisory Commission
        on Information. Processed.
    Sixth Semiannual Report, July 1, 1952 (H. Doc.
        526, 82d Cong., 2d sess.); Seventh Semiannual
        Report, Feb. 23, 1953 (H. Doc. 94, 83d Cong.,
        1st sess.); Ninth Semiannual Report, Feb. 2,
        1954 (H. Doc. 311, 83d Cong., 2d sess.);
        Tenth Semiannual Report (H. Doc. 87, 84th
        Cong., 1st sess.); Eleventh Semiannual Report,
        April 11, 1956 (H. Doc. 376, 84th Cong., 2d
        sess.). Washington, D.C.: U.S. Government Print-

ing Office, 1953, 1954, 1955, and 1956.
Twelfth Report, January, 1957; Thirteenth Report,
January, 1958; Fourteenth Report, March, 1959;
Fifteenth Report, March, 1960; Sixteenth Re-
port, February, 1961; Seventeenth Report,
February, 1962; Eighteenth Report, January,
1963; Nineteenth Report, January, 1964;
Twentieth Report, March, 1965; Twenty-First
Report, February, 1966; Twenty-Second Report,
March, 1967.

U.S. Congress. Congressional Record. Selected
references to proceedings of 80th Congress
through 88th Congress, 2d sess., dealing with
program and appropriations of the USIA and its
predecessor organizations. Washington, D.C.: U.S
Government Printing Office, 1948-67.

_____. House Committee on Appropriations. De-
partments of State, Justice, and Commerce
Appropriations for 1955. Hearings before Subcommittee of the Committee on Appropriations.
USIA hearings held February 1-February 4, 1954,
pp. 366-593. Washington, D.C.: U.S. Government
Printing Office, 1954.

_____. House Committee on Appropriations. De-
partments of State, Justice, Commerce, and the
Judiciary Appropriations. Hearings before Sub-
committee of the Committee on Appropriations.
Washington, D.C.: U.S. Government Printing Office
Dates as indicated below:
F. Y. 1949: Department of State hearings held
   February 4, 1948, pp. 503-618.
F. Y. 1950: Department of State hearings held
   February 21-23, 1949, pp. 712-904.
F. Y. 1952: Department of State hearings held
   March 5-14, 1951, pp. 705-1114.
F. Y. 1953: Department of State hearings held
   February 4-13, 1952, pp. 1-352.

_____. House Committee on Appropriations. De-
partments of State, Justice, the Judiciary,
and Related Agencies Appropriations. Hearings
before Subcommittee of the Committee on Appro-

priations. Washington, D.C.: U.S. Government Print-
ing Office. Dates as indicated below:
F. Y. 1956: USIA hearings held March 3-9, 1955,
     pp. 1-257.
F. Y. 1957: USIA hearings held February 7-20,
     1956, pp. 1-383.
F. Y. 1958: USIA hearings held February 26-
     March 11, 1957, pp. 1-734.
F. Y. 1959: USIA hearings held February 24-
     March 6, 1958, pp. 1-489.
F. Y. 1960: USIA hearings held April 7-30, 1959,
     pp. 1-1183.
F. Y. 1961: USIA hearings held March 1-9, 1960,
     pp. 1-1010.
F. Y. 1962: USIA hearings held March 28-April
     17, 1961, pp. 1-1074.
F. Y. 1963: USIA hearings held March 14-27,
     1962, pp. 1-767.
F. Y. 1964: USIA hearings held April 22-May 1,
     1963, pp. 1-796.
F. Y. 1965: USIA hearings held March 2-9, 1964,
     pp. 1-723.

_____. House Committee on Appropriations. Re-
ports on Departments of State, Justice, Commerce,
and the Judiciary Appropriations Bills. Washington, D.C.: U.S. Government Printing Office. Dates
as indicated below:
F. Y. 1949: H. Rep. 1433 on H.R. 5607, February
     27, 1948, 80th Cong., 2d sess.
F. Y. 1950: H. Rep. 386 on H.R. 4016, April 5,
     1949, 81st Cong., 1st sess.
F. Y. 1952: H. Rep. 685 on H.R. 4740, April 10,
     1951, 82d Cong., 1st sess.
F. Y. 1953: H. Rep. 1665 on H.R. 7289, March
     28, 1952, 82d Cong., 2d sess.

_____. House Committee on Appropriations. Re-
ports on Departments of State, Justice, Commerce,
the Judiciary, and Related Agencies Appropriations Bills. Washington, D.C.: U.S. Government
Printing Office. Dates as indicated below:
F. Y. 1956: H. Rep. 417 on H.R. 5502, April 13,
     1955, 84th Cong., 1st sess.
F. Y. 1957: H. Rep. 2021 on H.R. 10721, April
     20, 1956, 84th Cong., 2d sess.

F. Y. 1958: H. Rep. 351 on H.R. 6871, April
    12, 1957, 85th Cong., 1st sess.
F. Y. 1959: H. Rep. 1708 on H.R. 12428, May 9,
    1958, 85th Cong., 2d sess.
F. Y. 1960: H. Rep. 376 on H.R. 7343, May 21,
    1959, 86th Cong., 1st sess.
F. Y. 1961: H. Rep. 1467 on H.R. 11666, April
    8, 1960, 86th Cong., 2d sess.
F. Y. 1962: H. Rep. 442 on H.R. 7371, May 29,
    1961, 87th Cong., 1st sess.

_____. House Committee on Foreign Affairs.
Report of the Special Study Mission to Africa,
South and East of the Sahara. Report of the
Subcommittee on the Near East and Africa, 84th
Cong., 2d sess. Washington, D.C.: U.S. Governmen
Printing Office, 1956.

_____. House Committee on Foreign Affairs.
Report of the Special Study Mission to the Near
East and Africa, 85th Cong., 2d sess. Washing-
ton, D.C.: U.S. Government Printing Office, 1958.

_____. House Committee on Foreign Affairs.
Report of the Study Mission to Europe. H. Rep.
1683, 84th Cong., 2d sess. Washington, D.C.:
U.S. Government Printing Office, 1956.

_____. House Committee on Foreign Affairs.
Review of United States Information Agency
Operations. Hearings before the Subcommittee
on State Department Organization and Foreign
Operations, 84th Cong., 1st sess., 1955 and
85th Cong., 2d sess., 1958. Washington, D.C.:
U.S. Government Printing Office, 1958.

_____. House Committee on Foreign Affairs.
United States Information Agency Operations in
Africa. Hearings before the Subcommittee on
Africa, 87th Cong., 2d sess. Washington, D.C.:
U.S. Government Printing Office, 1962.

_____. House Committee on Foreign Affairs.
Winning the Cold War: The U.S. Ideological
Offensive. Hearings before the Subcommittee on
International Organizations and Movements, 88th

Cong., 1st and 2d sess., 1963 and 1964; 89th
Cong., 1st and 2d sess., 1965 and 1966; 90th
Cong., 1st sess., 1967.

_____. Senate Committee on Appropriations,
Departments of State, Justice, and Commerce and
the United States Information Agency Appropriations, 1955. Hearings before Subcommittee of
the Committee on Appropriations held April 22-
May 7, 1954, pp. 1085-1592. Washington, D.C.:
U.S. Government Printing Office, 1954.

_____. Senate Committee on Appropriations.
Departments of State, Justice, Commerce, and the
Judiciary Appropriations. Hearings before Sub-
Committee of the Committee on Appropriations.
Washington, D.C.: U.S. Government Printing Office.
Dates as indicated below:
F. Y. 1949: Department of State hearings held
   March 25-29, 1948, pp. 167-216.
F. Y. 1950: Department of State hearings held
   May 9-10, 1949, pp. 174-286.
F. Y. 1952: Department of State hearings held
   June 27-July 11, 1951, pp. 1626-1982.
F. Y. 1953: Department of State hearings held
   May 29-June 11, 1952, pp. 1008-1285.

_____. Senate Committee on Appropriations.
Departments of State, Justice, the Judiciary,
and Related Agencies Appropriations. Hearings
before Subcommittee of the Committee on Appropriations. Washington, D.C.: U.S. Government
Printing Office. Dates as indicated below:
F. Y. 1956: USIA hearings held May 10-17, 1955,
   pp. 859-1235.
F. Y. 1957: USIA hearings held May 14-16, 1956,
   pp. 205-713.
F. Y. 1958: USIA hearings held May 2-9, 1957,
   pp. 449-1068.
F. Y. 1959: USIA hearings held May 27-28, 1958,
   pp. 372-665.
F. Y. 1960: USIA hearings held June 9-11, 1959,
   pp. 309-786.
F. Y. 1961: USIA hearings held June 23, 1960,
   pp. 561-840.
F. Y. 1962: USIA hearings held June 22-July 11,
   1961, pp. 551-1213.

F. Y. 1963: USIA hearings held September 20-21,
     1962, pp. 344-446.
F. Y. 1964: USIA hearings held November 7-11,
     1963, pp. 2119-2332.

_____. Senate Committee on Appropriations. The
Objectives of the United States Information Program. S. Doc. 143, 82d Cong., 2d sess. Washington, D.C.: U.S. Government Printing Office, 1952.

_____. Senate Committee on Appropriations.
Report on Departments of State, Justice, Commerce,
and the United States Information Agency Appro-
priations, 1955. S. Rep. 1541 on H.R. 8067,
June 9, 1954, 83d Cong., 2d sess. Washington,
D. C.: U.S. Government Printing Office, 1954.

_____. Senate Committee on Appropriations,
Reports on Departments of State, Justice, Commerce
and the Judiciary Appropriations Bills. Washing-
ton, D.C.: U.S. Government Printing Office. Dates
as indicated below:
F. Y. 1949: S. Rep. 1166 on H.R. 5607, April
     23, 1948, 80th Cong., 2d sess.
F. Y. 1950: S. Rep. 435 on H.R. 4016, June 1,
     1949, 81st Cong., 1st sess.
F. Y. 1952: S. Rep. 697 on H.R. 4740, August
     21, 1951, 82d Cong., 1st sess.
F. Y. 1953: S. Rep. 1807 on H.R. 7289, June 24,
     1952, 82d Cong., 2d sess.

_____. Senate Committee on Appropriations.
Reports on Departments of State, Justice,
Commerce, the Judiciary, and Related Agencies
Appropriations Bills. Washington, D.C.: U.S. Gov-
ernment Printing Office. Dates as indicated
below:
F. Y. 1956: S. Rep. 378 on H.R. 5502, May 26,
     1955, 84th Cong., 1st sess.
F. Y. 1957: S. Rep. 2034 on H.R. 10721, May
     21, 1956, 84th Cong., 2d sess.
F. Y. 1958: S. Rep. 303 on H.R. 6871, May 14,
     1957, 85th Cong., 1st sess.
F. Y. 1959: S. Rep. 1683 on H.R. 12428, June
     9, 1958, 85th Cong., 2d sess.

F. Y. 1960: S. Rep. 424 on H.R. 7343, June 22,
    1959, 86th Cong., 1st sess.
F. Y. 1961: S. Rep. 1777 on H.R. 11666, June
    29, 1960, 86th Cong., 2d sess.
F. Y. 1962: S. Rep. 731 on H.R. 7371, August
    14, 1961, 87th Cong., 1st sess.

_____. Senate Committee on Appropriations. A
Review of United States Foreign Policy Opera-
tions, 1957. Report prepared by the Honorable
Allen J. Ellender, U.S. Senator from the State
of Louisiana, 85th Cong., 1st sess. Washington,
D.C.: U.S. Government Printing Office, 1958.

_____. Senate Committee on Appropriations. A
Review of United States Government Operations
in Latin America, 1958. Report prepared by
the Honorable Allen J. Ellender, U.S. Senator
from the State of Louisiana, 86th Cong., 1st
sess. Washington, D.C. U.S. Government Printing Office, 1959.

_____. Senate Committee on Foreign Relations.
Events Leading to the Summit Conference. Hearings,
86th Cong., 2d sess. Washington, D.C.: U.S.
Government Printing Office, 1960.

_____. Senate Committee on Foreign Relations.
Overseas Information Programs of the United
States. Parts 1 and 2. Hearings before Sub-
committee of the Committee on Foreign Relations,
83d Cong., 1st sess. Washington, D.C.: U.S.
Government Printing Office, 1953.

_____. Senate Committee on Foreign Relations.
Overseas Information Programs of the United
States. Interim Report, S. Rep. 406, 83d Cong.,
1st sess., June 15, 1953. Final Report, S. Rep.
936, 83d Cong., 2d sess. Washington, D.C.: U.S.
Government Printing Office, 1953 and 1954.

_____. Senate Committee on Foreign Relations.
Staff studies prepared for Subcommittee on Over-
seas Information Programs of the United States:
Staff Study No. 1: United States Overseas In-
    formation Programs. Washington, D.C.: U.S.
    Government Printing Office, 1952.
Staff Study No. 2: The Information Program of
    Great Britain. Washington, D.C.: U.S. Gov-
    ernment Printing Office, 1952.

Staff Study No. 3: Soviet Propaganda Program.
   Washington, D.C: U.S. Government Printing
   Office, 1952.
Staff Study No. 4: Organization of United States
   Overseas Information Functions. Washington,
   D.C. U.S. Government Printing Office, 1953.
Staff Study No. 5: Analysis of Reports from
   United States Mission Chiefs Abroad. Washing-
   ton, D.C.: U.S. Government Printing Office, 195
Staff Study No. 6: Analysis of Reports from
   American Correspondents Overseas. Washington,
   D.C.: U.S. Government Printing Office, 1953.
Staff Study No. 7: Analysis of Communications
   Received from Business and Religious Organiza-
   tions. Washington, D.C.: U.S. Government
   Printing Office, 1953.

_____. Senate Committee on Foreign Relations.
Training of Foreign Affairs Personnel. Hearings,
88th Cong., 1st sess. Washington, D.C.: U.S. Gov
ernment Printing Office, 1963.

_____. Senate Committee on Government Opera-
tions. Administration of National Security.
Hearings before the Subcommittee on National
Security Staffing and Operations of the Committee on Government Operations, 88th Cong., 1st
and 2d sess. Washington, D.C.: U.S. Government
Printing Office, 1963 and 1964.

_____. Senate Committee on Government Opera-
tions. Administration of National Security:
Selected Papers. 87th Cong., 2d sess. Washington, D.C.: U.S. Government Printing Office, 1962.

_____. Senate Committee on Government Opera-
tions. The Ambassador and the Problem of
Coordination. 88th Cong., 1st sess. Washington,
D.C.: U.S. Government Printing Office, 1963.

_____. Senate Committee on Government Opera-
tions. The American Ambassador, 88th Cong.,
2d sess. Washington, D.C.: U.S. Government
Printing Office, 1964.

_____. Senate Committee on Government Opera-
tions. Reorganization Plans Nos. 7 & 8. Hearings, 83d Cong., 1st sess. Washington, D.C.: U.S.
Government Printing Office, 1954.

_____. Senate Committee on Government Opera-
tions. The Secretary of State. 88th Cong.,
2d sess. Washington, D.C.: U.S. Government
Printing Office, 1964.

_____. Senate Committee on Government Opera-
tions. State Department Information Program--
Information Centers. Report of the Permanent
Subcommittee on Investigations of the Committee
on Government Operations, S. Rep. 879, 83d Cong.,
2d sess. Washington, D.C.: U.S. Government
Printing Office, 1954.

_____. Senate Committee on Government Opera-
tions. State Department Information Program:
Voice of America. Hearings before the Permanent
Subcommittee on Investigation of the Committee
on Government Operations, 83d Cong., 1st sess.
Washington, D.C.: U.S. Government Printing Office,
1953.

_____. Senate Committee on the Judiciary.
Freedom Commission and Freedom Academy. Hearings
before the Subcommittee to Investigate the
Administration of the Internal Security Act and
Other Internal Security Laws. 86th Cong., 1st
sess. Washington, D.C.: U.S. Government Printing
Office, 1959.

_____. Senate and House Committee on Foreign
Relations and Committee on Foreign Affairs.
Legislation on Foreign Relations with Explana-
tory Notes. Washington, D.C.: U.S. Government
Printing Office. Prepared annually for use by
both Committees. Citations are to 1964 issuance.

U.S. Department of State. The Biographic Register.
Prepared by Division of Publishing Services,
Office of Operations, Department of State.
Washington, D.C.: U.S. Government Printing Office.
Reissued periodically.

Reissued periodically.

_____. Bulletin. Department of State publica-
tion. Washington, D.C.: U.S. Government Printing
Office, 1945, 1953,and 1954. September 2, 1945,
October 21, 1945, August 24, 1953,and December 20,
1954 issuances.

_____. Memorandum on the Postwar International
Information Program of the United States, by
Arthur W. Macmahon, Department of State
Publication 2438. Washington, D.C.: U.S. Gov-
ernment Printing Office, 1945.

_____. Newsletter. Washington, D.C.: U.S. Govern
ment Printing Office, March, 1964.

_____. Semiannual reports submitted to Congress
pursuant to sec. 1008 of U.S. Information and
Educational Exchange Act of 1948. Washington,
D.C.: Department of State Publications, 1948
through 1953:
First Report, January 1-June 30, 1948.
Second Report, July 1-December 31, 1948.
Third Report, January 1-June 30, 1949.
Fourth Report, July 1-December 31, 1949.
Fifth Report, January 1-June 30, 1950.
Sixth Report, July 1-December 31, 1950.
   Launching the Campaign of Truth: First Phase.
Seventh Report, January 1-June 30, 1951.
   Launching the Campaign of Truth: Second Phase.
Eighth Report, July 1-December 31, 1951.
Ninth Report, January, 1952-June, 1952.
Tenth Report, July, 1952-December, 1952. IIA:
   The International Information Administration.

U.S. Executive Office of the President. Bureau of the
Budget. Federal Budget in Brief. Washington,
D.C.: U.S. Government Printing Office. Issued
annually in January, and reissued periodically.

_____. Bureau of the Budget. History of the
Office of the Coordinator of Inter-American
Affairs. Washington, D.C.: U.S. Government
Printing Office, 1947.

_____. Press release of the President's Com-
mittee on International Information Activities
(Jackson and Sprague Commissions), July 8, 1953,
and January 12, 1961.

U.S. Information Agency. The Agency in Brief.
Publication of USIA brought up to date annually,
for staff training and Congressional use.
Washington, D.C.: USIA, 1966 and 1967.

_____. Binational Center Handbook. Washington,
D.C.: USIA publication, January, 1962.

_____. Correspondent. Selected references to
USIA publications from 1959-64.

_____. The Impact of Hollywood Films Abroad.
Washington, D.C.: USIA Research and Reference
Service, July, 1961.

_____. Mail Survey of Listeners to the Voice
of America World Wide English Service. Washington, D.C.: USIA Research and Reference Service,
June, 1961.

_____. Non-Governmental Activities Affecting
the Image of the United States Abroad. Washington, D.C.: USIA Research and Reference Service,
September, 1959.

_____. Office of Public Information. Selected
references to News Releases, 1953-64.

_____. Review of Operations. First Review, 1954;
Thirteenth Review, 1959; Fourteenth Review, 1960.
Washington, D.C.: U.S. Government Printing Office.

_____. Semiannual reports submitted to Congress
pursuant to Sec. 1008 of U.S. Information and
Educational Exchange Act of 1948 and President's
Reorganization Plan No. 8 of 1953. Reports
issued semiannually beginning with First Semiannual Report, August-December, 1953, through
Twentieth Semiannual Report, January 1-June 30,
1963. Washington, D.C.: U.S. Government Printing Office, 1953-63.

U.S. Public Laws:
Foreign Service Act of 1946, as amended (22

U.S.C. 801 et seq.).

Reorganization Plan No. 8 of 1953 (22 U.S.C. 1461).

United States Information and Educational Exchange Act of 1948, as amended (22 U.S.C. 1431 et seq.).

NONOFFICIAL SOURCES

Books

Alcorn, Robert Hayden, No Bugle for Spies: Tales of the OSS. New York: David McKay Co., 1962.

Almond, Gabriel A. The American People and Foreign Policy. New York: Harcourt, Brace & Co., 1950.

_____, and Coleman, James S. The Politics of the Developing Areas. Princeton, N.J.: Princeton University Press, 1964.

Bailey, Thomas A. The Man in the Street. New York: The Macmillan Co., 1948.

Barghoorn, Frederick C. Soviet Foreign Propaganda. Princeton, N.J.: Princeton University Press, 1964.

Barrett, Edward W. Truth is Our Weapon. New York: Funk & Wagnalls Co., 1953.

Berelson, Bernard, and Janowitz, Morris. Reader in Public Opinion and Communications. Glencoe, Ill.: The Free Press, 1950.

Buchanan, William, and Cantril, Hadley. How Nations See Each Other. Urbana, Ill.: University of Illinois Press, 1953.

Carr, E. H. The Soviet Impact on the Western World. New York: The Macmillan Co., 1954.

Carroll, Holbert N. The House of Representatives and Foreign Affairs. Pittsburgh, Pa.: University of Pittsburgh Press, 1958.

Carroll, Wallace. _Persuade or Perish_. Boston:
    Houghton Mifflin Co., 1948.

Clews, John C. _Communist Propaganda Techniques._
    New York: Frederick A. Praeger, 1964.

Cohen, Bernard C. _The Press and Foreign Policy._
    Princeton, N.J.: Princeton University Press,
    1963.

Coombs, Philip H. _The Fourth Dimension of Foreign
    Policy_. New York: Harper & Row, 1964.

Creel, George. _How We Advertised America_. New York:
    Harper & Bros., 1920.

Dahl, Robert A. _Congress and Foreign Policy_. New
    York: Harcourt, Brace and Co., 1950.

Davison, W. Phillips. _International Political
    Communication_. New York: Frederick A. Praeger,
    1965.

Dizard, Wilson P. _The Strategy of Truth_. Washington,
    D.C.: Public Affairs Press, 1961.

Doob, Leonard W. _Public Opinion and Propaganda_. New
    York: Henry Holt & Co., 1948.

Dyer, Murray. _The Weapon on the Wall_. Baltimore,
    Md.: The John Hopkins Press, 1959.

Elder, Robert E. _The Policy Machine: The Department
    of State and American Foreign Policy_. Syracuse,
    N.Y.: Syracuse University Press, 1959.

Fenno, Richard F., Jr., _The Power of the Purse:
    Appropriations Politics in Congress_. Boston:
    Little, Brown and Co., 1966.

Frankel, Charles. _The Neglected Aspect of Foreign
    Affairs_. Washington, D.C.: The Brookings
    Institution, 1966.

Goodfriend, Arthur. The Twisted Image. New York:
     St. Martin's Press, 1963.

de Grazia, Alfred, et al. Target Analysis and Media
     in Propaganda to Audiences Abroad. Baltimore,
     Md.: The John Hopkins Press, 1953.

Haviland, H. Field (ed.). The Formulation and
     Administration of United States Foreign Policy.
     Washington, D.C.: The Brookings Institution,
     1960.

Hohenberg, John. Between Two Worlds: Policy, Press,
     and Public Opinion in Asian-American Relations.
     New York: Frederick A. Praeger, 1967.

Holt, Robert T. Radio Free Europe. Minneapolis,
     Minn.: University of Minnesota Press, 1958.

_____, and van de Velde, Robert W. Strategic
     Psychological Operations and American Foreign
     Policy. Chicago, Ill.: University of Chicago
     Press, 1960.

Huzar, Elias. The Purse and the Sword. Ithaca, N.Y.:
     Cornell University Press, 1950.

Inkeles, Alex. Public Opinion in Soviet Russia
     (2d ed.). Cambridge, Mass: Harvard University
     Press, 1958.

Joyce, Walter. The Propaganda Gap. New York:
     Harper & Row, 1963.

Kissinger, Henry A. Nuclear Weapons and Foreign
     Policy. New York: Harper & Bros., 1957.

Lerner, Daniel (ed.). Propaganda in War and Crisis.
     New York: George W. Stewart, 1951.

_____. Skyewar: Psychological Warfare Against
     Germany, D-Day to VE-Day. New York: George W.
     Stewart, 1949.

Lockhart, R.H. Bruce. Comes the Reckoning. London:
     Putnam, 1947.

Lumley, Frederick E. The Propaganda Menace. New
     York: The Century Co., 1933.

Markel, Lester. Public Opinion and Foreign Policy.
     New York: Harper & Bros., 1949.

Martin, L. John. International Propaganda: Its
     Legal and Diplomatic Control. Minneapolis, Minn.:
     Univeristy of Minnesota Press, 1958.

Meyerhoff, Arthur E. The Strategy of Persuasion.
     New York: Coward-McCann, 1965.

Morgenthau, Hans J. Politics Among Nations (3d ed.).
     New York: Alfred A. Knopf, 1964.

Nicolson, Harold G. Diplomacy (3d ed.) New York:
     Oxford University Press, 1963.

Qualter, Terence H. Propaganda and Psychological
     Warfare. New York: Random House, 1962.

Robinson, James A. Congress and Foreign Policy-
     Making (Revised Edition). Homewood, Ill.: The
     Dorsey Press, 1967.

Rosenau, James N. Public Opinion and Foreign Policy.
     New York: Random House, 1961.

Rowan, Carl T. Go South to Sorrow. New York:
     Random House, 1957.

Schramm, Wilbur. The Process and Effects of Mass
     Communication. Urbana, Ill.: University of
     Illinois Press, 1954.

Simpson, Smith. Anatomy of the State Department.
     Boston: Houghton Mifflin Co., 1967.

Smith, B.L., Lasswell, Harold D., and Casey, R.D.
     Propaganda, Communication, and Public Opinion.
     Princeton, N.J.: Princeton University Press,
     1946.

Snyder, Richard C., Bruck, Harold W., and Sapin,
    Burton. Foreign Policy Decision-Making: An
    Approach to the Study of International Politics.
    Glencoe, Ill. : The Free Press, 1962.

Stephens, Oren M. Facts to a Candid World. Stanford,
    Calif.: Stanford University Press. 1955.

Summers, Robert E. (ed.). America's Weapons of
    Psychological Warfare. New York: H.W. Wilson
    Co., 1951.

Thomson, Charles A. H. Overseas Information Service
    of the United States Government. Washington,
    D.C.: The Brookings Institution, 1948.

_____, and Laves, Walter H. C. Cultural Re-
    lations and U.S. Foreign Policy. Bloomington,
    Ind.: Indiana University Press, 1963

Westerfield, H. Bradford. Foreign Policy and Party
    Politics. New Haven, Conn.: Yale University
    Press, 1955.

White, William S. Citadel. New York: Harper &
    Bros., 1957.

Whitton, John B., and Larson, Arthur. Propaganda:
    Toward Disarmament in the War of Words. Dobbs
    Ferry, N.Y.: Oceana, 1963.

Wise, David and Ross, Thomas B. The U-2 Affair.
    New York: Random House, 1962.

Wright, Quincy. The Study of International Relations.
    New York: Appleton-Century-Crofts, 1953.

Periodicals and Published Reports

Allen, George V. "Go Tell it to the People," Think,
    XXIV, No. 10 (October, 1958), 29-32.

_____. "The People to People Program:

Let Facts be Submitted to a Candid World," Vital
Speeches of the Day, XXIV, No. 10 (March 1, 1958),
292-95.

American Political Science Association Report.
"Toward a More Responsible Two Party System,"
The American Political Science Review, XLIV,
No. 3 (September, 1950), 17-24.

Bogart, Leo. "A Study of the Operating Assumptions
of the U.S. Information Agency," Public Opinion
Quarterly, XIX, No. 4 (Winter, 1955-56), 369-79.

Catlin, George. "Propaganda and the Cold War," The
Yale Review XLIII, No. 1 (September, 1953),
103-16.

Davison, W. Phillips, and George, Alexander L. "An
Outline for the Study of International Political
Communications," Public Opinion Quarterly, XVI,
No. 4 (Winter, 1952-53).

Fenno, Richard F., Jr. "The House Appropriations
Committee as a Political System: The Problem
of Integration," American Political Science
Review, LVI, No. 2 (June, 1962).

Goss, Bert, and Durbin, William A. "How Effective
Is the United States Overseas Information Program," Challenge, XI, No. 2 (November, 1962),
18-21.

Hangen, Welles, "USIA in the Next Decade," Foreign
Service Journal, XL, No. 7 (July, 1963), 22-23.

Larson, Arthur. "The USIA: How Effective Is It?"
Vital Speeches of the Day, XIII, No. 16 (June 1,
1957), 492.

Lasswell, Harold D. "Psychological Policy Research
and Total Strategy," Public Opinion Quarterly,
XVI, No. 4 (Winter, 1952-53), 491-500.

Murrow, Edward R. "USIA Today and Tomorrow,"
Foreign Service Journal, XL, No. 7 (July, 1963),
21-22.

The New York Times. 1953-67.

Personnel for the New Diplomacy. Committee on Foreign
    Affairs, Personnel, Washington, D.C.: Carnegie
    Endowment for International Peace, 1962.

Public Opinion Quarterly. Special Issue: "Inter-
    national Communications Research," XVI, No. 4
    (Winter, 1952-53).

Rubin, Ronald I. "The Legislative-Executive Relations
    of the United States Information Agency,"
    Parliamentary Affairs, XX, No. 2 (Spring, 1967),
    158-69.

_____. "The UN Correspondent," The
    Western Political Quarterly, XVII, No. 4
    (December, 1964), 615-31.

_____. "USIA: The Muffled Voice,"
    Columbia Journalism Review, VI, No. 2 (Summer,
    1967), 37-39.

de Sola Pool, Ithiel, "Information Goals," Foreign
    Service Journal, XL, No. 7 (July, 1963), 20-21.

Taylor, Edward, "How the Russians Wage Political
    Warfare," The Reporter, XXVI, No. 10 (May 10,
    1962), 16-20.

Unpublished Material

Binkley, Jonathan A. "Congressional Controls and
    Influence Over the United States Information
    Agency." Unpublished M.A. thesis, University
    of Toledo, 1966.

DeVos, Ton Peter. "A Field Study in the Effective-
    ness of the United States Information Service
    in the Netherlands." Unpublished Ph.D.
    dissertation, University of Oklahoma, 1962.

Posner, Ben. "Major Budgetary and Programing Prob-
    lems of the United States Information Agency

in its Operations of Overseas Missions."
Unpublished Ph.D. dissertation, American
University, 1962.

Interviews (Position, 1964)

Edward W. Barrett   Dean, Graduate School of
                         Journalism, Columbia University;
                         Assistant Secretary of State
                         (for Public Affairs),1950-52

Bryan M. Battey   Director of Training, USIA

Martin B. Cox   Congressional Liaison, USIA

Jeanne C. Gildea   Staff Assistant to Director,
                         Office of Private Cooperation,
                         USIA

Richard T. Hamilton   Deputy Director, Office of
                         Private Cooperation, USIA

Ralph Hilton   Executive Secretary, Joint
                         Board of Examiners, USIA

John P. McKnight   Agency Planning Officer, USIA

Louis T. Olom   Staff Director, U.S. Advisory
                         Commission on Information

David Parson   Deputy General Counsel, USIA

Ben Posner   Assistant Director (for Admin-
                         istration), USIA

Edward J. Savage   Director, Office of Public
                         Information, USIA

Oren M. Stephens   Director, Research and Reference
                         Service, USIA

Edward B. Strait   Assistant Chief, International
                         Division, Bureau of the Budget,
                         Executive Office of the Presi-
                         dent.

ABOUT THE AUTHOR

Ronald I. Rubin is Assistant Professor of Social Science at Manhattan Community College of the City University of New York. During the First Session of the 89th Congress (1965), he served as Legislative Assistant to Representative Jonathan B. Bingham of New York.

Dr. Rubin has published widely in the area of political affairs. His articles and reviews have appeared in The Western Political Quarterly, Parliamentary Affairs, Orbis, Columbia Journalism Review, The Annals, and The Pakistan Horizon. He has also contributed to Saturday Review, Commonweal, The Christian Science Monitor, and The Progressive.

Dr. Rubin holds a B.A. and Ph.D. from New York University and an M.A. from Brown University.